NOBODY'S
BUSINESS
BUT YOUR OWN

NOBODY'S BUSINESS
BUT YOUR OWN

**A Business Start-up Guide
with Advice from Today's Most
Successful Young Entrepreneurs**

Carolyn M. Brown

Foreword by Keith Clinkscales
President/CEO of VIBE Ventures

New York

Book design by Nicola Ferguson

Library of Congress Cataloging-in-Publication Data
Brown, Carolyn M.
Nobody's business but your own : a business start-up guide with advice from
today's most successful young entrepreneurs / Carolyn M. Brown. — 1st ed.
p. cm.
Includes bibliographical references (p.).
ISBN 0-7868-8301-4
1. New business enterprises. 2. Small business — Management. I. Title.
HD62.5.B762   1999
658.1'141 — dc21   98-41065
CIP

FIRST EDITION
10 9 8 7 6 5 4 3 2 1

For my niece, Jasmine Janae Parker,
whose loving spirit is my inspiration. You are the future.

FAITH

When you come to the end of all the light you know
and you are about to step off into the darkness,
faith is knowing that there will be something solid
for you to stand on or you will be taught how to fly.

—Iyanla Vanzant

CONTENTS

III   OPPORTUNITY KNOCKS

IV   AS YOU GET BIGGER

I often speak to aspiring entrepreneurs hoping to start their own businesses. Their aspirations are as broad as the businesses they seek to start. Some are looking to launch magazines, others desire to market a line of clothing, while still others seek opportunities in manufacturing or retail. Most recently, the Internet has fueled a great deal of interest in starting cyber businesses. But what all of these would-be entrepreneurs have in common is the desire to be successful in selling a particular product and their need for someone to guide them in that enterprise.

I remember a few years ago reading a quote from an accomplished entrepreneur that stated: "The greatest thing a millionaire could give to someone was the information on how he made his first million dollars." It is from receiving essential information derived from practical experience and examples that a new entrepreneur can launch a business successfully.

There is much speculation on what makes a business successful. Start-up money is high on the list as well as a well-developed business plan. While seed money may be necessary to start your business, knowledge and experience to make that seed money flourish into a growing operation requires the ability to carry out your business plan.

Nobody's Business But Your Own reveals experiences from several individuals who have excelled in many areas of endeavor. Although many endeavors have resulted in success stories, I caution the reader to understand that many entrepreneurs encountered numerous setbacks, and in a few instances, came close to bankruptcy. These hardships, from the launch process, have at times resulted in the laborious process of starting over again. But, in all cases as presented in Carolyn M. Brown's book, these setbacks have been endured by individuals who refused to fail and knew how to persevere.

There is no bottled formula for success, but there are several steps you can take to ensure your business will stay afloat. *Nobody's Business But Your Own* is one of those steps. It is the essential learning guide to entrepreneurship. Carolyn helps the reader discover the entrepreneurial fire that potentially burns in us all.

Carolyn carefully explains how important logic is to your entrepreneurial experience. For it is through the application of sheer logic that you will be kept in the game. Carolyn thoroughly covers all aspects of business management, from identifying key opportunities and potential business acquisitions to selecting management personnel.

I first met Carolyn in 1995, while she was working on a story about magazine publishing. Since that time, we have come together on numerous occasions and we have discussed the VIBE franchise and other entrepreneurial ventures. Carolyn brings to her book the same dedication and diligence that she brought to countless stories as a business journalist. She has garnered knowledge on a wide range of industries and topics from banking to franchising to the business of television.

This book is one that is written from the heart and experience. After completing this compilation of inspirational tales in business I am certain that you will be motivated to embark on your own enterprise.

—*Keith T. Clinkscales*
President and CEO
VIBE Ventures

ACKNOWLEDGMENTS

First and foremost, I have to give thanks to the Father, Son, and The Holy Spirit, for this project truly has been a leap of faith and a labor of love. I especially wish to thank the following people for their guidance and support throughout this project:

Lisa Hudson and Tracey George, there would be no book had it not been for you two. A very, very big Thank You.

My editor, Jennifer Morgan, for picking up this project and keeping me in the race. I appreciate your enthusiasm about this book.

Tania Padgett, my friend, colleague, and number one fan. I am grateful for all of your help on this book, reading rough drafts of the manuscript, editing some of the interviews, and listening to my grumbling when things didn't go my way.

My friend, Lisa Teamer, for serving as my photo editor free of charge. I know it was tedious at times contacting photographers, setting up photo shoots, processing film, and securing pictures. You're number one in my book.

My friend, Nadirah Sabir, for your input and research when this thing was still in its infancy. You were a great help with the proposal. Thank you for lifting my spirits with your chorus of "Food, Glorious Food."

My agent, Marie Brown, for her support before and during this project.

My lawyers, Lisa Davis and Sabrin Padwa, for looking out for my best interests.

My parents, James and Katherine Brown, and my big sister, Evelyn Parker, for their love, ongoing support, and financial contributions.

My cousins Tracy Salmon and Manny (Tony) Brown, you are the "wind beneath my wings." The two of you are great "cheerleaders."

My friend, Rhonda Reynolds, a special thanks to you for coming through when I needed you, whether it was to do research or bail me out of a monetary bind.

Terrie Williams, I greatly appreciate all of the notes of inspiration and encouragement that you have sent me these past two years.

Della Clark, thank you for the career guidance and giving me some real "first-hand" experience when it comes to running a small business.

Ever since I was little girl, I have had some tried and true friends who have always believed in me and my abilities even when I didn't; so my gratitude goes out to Mary Williams, Yolanda Payne, Denise Womack, and Amir (Rodney) and Gilda Salmon.

I would also like to thank the following family members for their ongoing support and encouragement: my aunt and uncle, Ann and Ed Clark, my cousins Mamie and Therese Salmon, and my brother-in-law, Donald Parker.

The last line of the children's book *Charlotte's Web* reads: "It is not often that someone comes along who is a true friend and a good writer." That passage characterizes my friend and mentor, Frank McCoy, who has given me his best and expected nothing less in return from me. Thank you for your support, encouragement, and advice.

My mentor, Sheryl Hilliard-Tucker, your invaluable guidance helped me to grow as a writer. Your faith in me and my abilities gave me the drive I needed to persevere.

Kim Pearson, thank you for critiquing my work as an up-and-coming writer and helping me to believe in myself.

John Rizzo and John Vitale, I am forever grateful to both of you for helping to me discover my life's passion.

There are people who unbeknownst to them have greatly affected my life. For now, this is the best forum for me to show them my appreciation. A very, very special thanks to:

Patti La Belle and Armstead Edwards, for had it not been for you two I may have never become a "real" journalist.

Bill Cosby, thanks to you "I could have gone anywhere, but I chose Temple."

Rosie O'Donnell, thank you for giving me a reason to rise every morning and finish this book.

Ellen DeGeneres, thanks for making me laugh on those days when I felt like crying.

Barbra Streisand, thank you for teaching me the true meaning of "To Thy Own Self Be True."

Last but not least, I want to thank all of the entrepreneurs who took time out of their busy schedules to contribute to this book. And to all young entrepreneurs and wanna-be's throughout the world, thank you for inspiring me to write this book in the first place. Dare to dream and build your own future.

REBELS WITHOUT A CLUE, GENERATION X, SLACKERS, BABY BUSTERS, MALL RATS, AND THE BOOMERANG GENERATION

These are just a smattering of the names reserved for a generation with one thing in common—we happened to have been born between 1965 and 1977. This name-calling made me take notice of my fellow so-called Generation Xers. The July 16, 1990 *Time* magazine cover story read: "Twenty-something: Laid back, late blooming or just lost? Overshadowed by the baby boomers, America's next generation has a hard act to follow." That was the start of it all, a deluge of articles lambasting Generation X. A *Newsweek* essay dubbed us the "whiney generation." *Psychology Today*, "a generation of gripers." *Atlantic Monthly* questioned our existence: "13th Gen: Abort, Retry, Ignore, Fail?"

For me, these and other misguided commentaries were infuriating. Yes, I took it personally. I was a 25-year-old journalist at the time. Were we all a bunch of demanding and dysfunctional loners who were underpaid, unambitious, and unhappy? Maybe many Xers (including myself) were moving back home, changing jobs every two years, and in debt up to our ears from credit cards or college loans. But was the possibility that we were going to be less affluent than our parents really a national crisis?

While a few baby boomers in media and marketing continued to mislabel a group they didn't understand, "twenty-somethings" proved to be anything but slothful. According to the

U.S. Bureau of Labor Statistics, in 1994, 272,000 businesses were started by 20- to 30-year-olds. The following year, Paul Reynolds, professor of entrepreneurial studies at Babson College in Babson Park, Massachusetts, released a study showing that seven out of 10 start-ups are launched by people between the ages of 25 and 34—so-called Generation Xers.

Suddenly, *Forbes* was hailing Generation X as the most entrepreneurial generation in American history. The magazine painted a more accurate picture of Xers stating:

> **A gold watch upon retirement is no longer the goal for a generation wary of climbing the corporate ladder. They don't expect the government or Fortune 500 companies to take care of them the rest of their lives. No, these ambitious self-starters—better equipped to take risks and embrace change than their elders ever were—are living their dreams through entrepreneurship.** —Randall Lane, May 8, 1995

It was at that point that I began to put together an extensive file—articles, contacts, resources, and other information relative to young entrepreneurs. By December of 1996, I was ready to quit my job and write a book on the subject. And why not? I had nearly ten years of business writing under my belt, starting out as an editor at McGraw Hill Inc., one of the nation's largest publishing houses; later as a special assignment writer at Intertec Publishing Corp., a magazine publishing company; and as a senior editor at Earl G. Grave Ltd., a privately owned magazine enterprise.

In addition to profiling business owners and corporate professionals, I had written scores of industry overviews and features on a wide range of topics, including small businesses, sales and marketing, management, franchising, banking, international trade, computers, technology, telecommunications, finance, investments, and career opportunities. All of this seemed to qualify me to write a book on young entrepreneurship. Plus, I had spent two years of hard labor in marketing for a start-up company that eventually went belly up.

But the real impetus behind my writing a "how-to" book on entrepreneurship came about from a series of conversations with friends and colleagues. They wanted to know if they should become their own bosses and how they could go about starting a business. I decided to target the book toward Generation Xers—who were 45 million strong with $125 billion a year in purchasing power—and my younger cohorts—81 million strong born between 1977 and 1997—who are now being labeled the "net" generation, because they are presumably lost in cyberspace.

I remembered when I attended my father's retirement party for 26 years of dedicated service to the *Bergen Record*, the largest newspaper in northern New Jersey. He had worked his way up from overseeing newspaper boys to director of circulation; and, he was actually able to walk away with a pension. It was an impressive affair where former colleagues—and even the paper's owner—toasted him and bestowed fancy gifts.

Would I ever spend nearly half a lifetime working for the same employer? Not likely. At least not in the wake of more than 40 million jobs lost through corporate downsizing, and with more and more companies paying workers less money, offering fewer benefits, and declining to consider merit raises or bonuses.

You're either thinking about starting a business or you've put the wheels in motion, otherwise you wouldn't have bought this book. Like many of our peers, you may not see any tangible results of your efforts in corporate America and you want greater control over your destiny. Or maybe you see owning your own business as a way to become a more productive, creative, and contributing force in your community. Yet, you're tormented by that nagging little voice in your head—which may even sound like that of your parents or friends—telling you you're crazy for trying to go solo.

The good news is, you're in good company should you decide to join the ranks of other youthful corporate refugees. Today, the highest concentration of entrepreneurs are in their twenties and early thirties. A survey by Wells Fargo Bank and the National Federation of Independent Businesses Education Foundation, a Washington, D.C. small-business trade group, revealed that 60 percent of the people who founded a business in the last six months of 1997 were under the age of 40. And a NASDAQ Stock Market Survey found that 19 percent of Generation-X investors planned to use the proceeds from the sale of their stocks to start a business.

Starting a business at age twenty-something is not a new phenomenon. Many of today's top CEOs got their businesses off the ground while still in their twenties, or in some cases, teens. Examples of such entrepreneurs include Bill Gates of Microsoft, Fred Smith of Federal Express, Paul Orfalae of Kinko's, Frank Carney of Pizza Hut, An Wang of Wang Laboratories, and Michael Dell of Dell Computers (the youngest Fortune 500 CEO in history).

The difference is that ten years ago, entrepreneurship was seen as a very risky and even foolish thing to do. These days, starting a multimedia software company out of your bedroom instead of working for IBM is not viewed as a poor career move. It's not meant to be a backlash on corporate America.

In fact, many of today's young CEOs utilized the training, contacts, and experience they gained from their short corporate stints to start a business. The rationale of these youthful entrepreneurs is that they had a better way of doing things or they wanted to do things their way. This is contrary to their over-40 counterparts — managers who start businesses only after a midlife crisis, or as a result of losing their long-held corporate jobs.

In the last couple of years, there have been some high-profile young entrepreneurs. Jerry Yang, 28, and David Filo, 31, created the popular Web-search service dubbed Yahoo!, an anagram for Yet Another Hierarchial Officious Oracle. Today,

Yahoo! Inc., based in Santa Clara, California, has 386 employees and $67.4 million in sales, and averages 95 million pages viewed per day. Marc Andressen, 26, was instrumental in writing the revolutionary Mosaic Web browser. Today, he is executive vice president of products for the $533.9 million Netscape Communications Corp. in Mountain View, California, with over 2,000 employees. His company's product, Netscape Navigator, is among the world's most popular tools for retrieving data on the Internet.

Technology certainly makes the idea of entrepreneurship very tempting: Computers and telecommunications equipment grow ever smaller, cheaper, and better by the minute, making it easier to run a business from home and enabling small fledging enterprises to compete effectively against larger companies.

More than ever before, our generation is looking to achieve financial security and economic independence by owning a business. And yet, there are easier and safer ways to make money. Running a business means giving up a regular paycheck, employee benefits, and set working hours.

Still, you might feel stuck in a dead-end job, that has no bearing whatsoever on who you really are or what matters the most to you. If you're like many of our generation, more than once you've probably said to yourself, "I want freedom from a 9 to 5 routine . . . I hate my present job . . . I'm sick of working for someone else . . . I want to make more money."

But don't be misled into thinking that starting a business is the same thing as creating a dream job. True, we all want to have a meaningful career and to live an exciting and fulfilling life. But a business is much more than just a job. Your success or failure will depend on your ability to provide a quality product or service and satisfy customer demand.

Not only are you held accountable by your customers but also by your employees. How well you meet their needs—from providing pay raises to day-care services—will affect their loyalty to you and the caliber of their work. Furthermore, roughly half of all start-ups go out of business within four years, mostly due to poor management and lack of capital.

The real question becomes, "Do you have what it takes?" You have to get real with yourself about the hows and whys of starting a business. If you're serious about starting your own business, you have to ask, "Am I willing to work from dusk to dawn nearly every day of the week, taking a short rest only on Sunday or the Sabbath, if I'm lucky? Can I get used to eating cereal for dinner? Will I miss hanging out with my family and friends? Am I ready to live cheaply in order to manage my fledging enterprise? Do I have the needed amount of money, contacts, and expertise in a particular industry?" In sum, "Can I run a service or product-oriented operation and still pay the rent?"

By joining the ranks of the self-employed, I experienced the proverbial "shoe being on the other foot." After years of writing about the challenges of entrepreneurs, I was now dealing with issues like managing cash flow (now that I was getting paid in 45 to 60 days versus every two weeks), balancing a budget for personal and business expenses, working with independent contractors, hiring a lawyer and an accountant, and managing debt. There were days when the cupboard was bare and the threat of eviction loomed over my head all in the name of self-rule.

In the end, it comes down to whether or not you have that "entrepreneurial spirit." Having an entrepreneurial spirit knows no geographic, religious, or racial distinction. Entrepreneurs aren't afraid to fail, to take risks, and to make sacrifices to carve out their own niche in the world. They want to make their own choices and decisions, even if they turn out to be lousy ones. But at least they have the courage to make their own mistakes.

Those who thrive relish the rewards of the fruits of their labor, knowing that they worked hard to get where they are. No one gave them anything. There was no free ride, just a long industrious journey on the road to financial freedom.

If you think you're up to the challenge, then, welcome. *Nobody's Business But Your Own* provides step-by-step advice on how to start and run a business, including how to choose a legal structure; how to raise start-up capital from family, banks, or investors; how to sell your wares abroad; and, how to market your products/services over the Internet.

Nobody's Business But Your Own also consists of more than 30 "How I Did It" case studies of noteworthy young entrepreneurs who have distinguished themselves as leaders of the pack through their innovation, creativity, and raw talent. They mark the new breed of young would-be business tycoons.

Take Dineh Mohajer, the 26-year-old CEO of Hard Candy, a cosmetics company in Los Angeles. The $10 million company makes lip liners, lipsticks, and nail polishes in outlandish colors from metallic silver to red-black Porno. And twins Jason and Matt Olim have built one of the hottest online music stores, with over 250,000 CDs, cassettes, T-shirts, movies and music videos. Four years in business, the 27-year-old owners of Jenkintown, Pennsylvania–based CDnow Inc. have sold $17 million worth of product.

For the purposes of this book, the term young applies to those born after 1963. Some hail from Ivy league schools, others don't hold a college degree at all—proving that the one great thing about being an entrepreneur is that there are no laws or rules about the kind of credentials you need to succeed. This diverse group of entrepreneurs share information on their business hits and misses. Their companies run the gamut—in terms of the services and products they provide—from clothing to computers to cosmetics.

I am confident that you will find this book to be a source of inspiration and information. Taking over the helm of an enterprise and becoming captain of your own fate takes courage. It won't be smooth sailing all the way. But I hope that each chapter will help steer you through the troubled waters of entrepreneurship and to set anchor in prosperous coves for years to come.

I

Are You Ready?

DO YOU HAVE WHAT IT TAKES?

> Without effort, a great vision will remain just an unfulfilled dream. No worthwhile goal has ever been attained without strenuous, meaningful labor.
> — *Kazuo Inamori, chairman,*
> *Kyocera Corp. and DDI Corp.*

A common question of would-be business owners is: "Are entrepreneurs born or made?" The answer is, "both." Certain skills and characteristics are intrinsic to who we are, the way we work, and how we relate to others. Then there are those traits we each hope to develop over the years.

Here's an important check list for the would-be entrepreneur:

- Are you a leader?

- Do your friends or colleagues seek out your advice?

- Are you a people person?

- Are you decisive?

- Are you organized?

- Do you plan ahead?

If you answered yes to all of these questions, you have the makings for an entrepreneur.

Chance—being in the right place at the right time—also plays a part in anyone's career, but entrepreneurs are special in that they make their own chances. In his book *How to Start, Finance, and Manage Your Own Small Business*, Joseph Mancuso, small business guru and founder of the Center for Entrepreneurial Management, Inc., in New York, tells the story about a shoe manufacturer who sent two sons to the Mediterranean to scout out new markets: One wired back: "No point in staying on. No one here wears shoes." The other son wired back: "Terrific opportunities. Thousands still without shoes." Who do you think eventually took over the business?

This anecdote, for me, embodies what it takes to be an entrepreneur. You have to be optimistic and perceptive. You have to see opportunities where others see obstacles. The power of positive thinking is the shock absorber of a steady spirit. You'll need it to survive false starts, near failures, and cutting disappointments—something every entrepreneur deals with daily.

A THIRST FOR KNOWLEDGE, A HUNGER FOR SUCCESS

Motivational speaker Les Brown says, "You've got to be hungry for success. Once you're hungry, you'll turn your appetite into victory." Many entrepreneurial success stories started with very little money or education.

Every one of us has probably ordered a Domino's pizza. It's one of America's favorite franchises and one of the first to feature free home delivery of pizza in less than 30 minutes. But very few people know of the struggles of Domino's Pizza founder Tom Monaghan.

Partly reared in orphanages and foster homes, Monaghan graduated last in his high school class, was expelled from a Catholic seminary, and tried six different colleges—never quite making it past freshman status. In 1960, Tom and his brother

Jim (then a mailman) heard that a pizza shop was up for sale. The brothers borrowed $900 from the post office credit union and bought a floundering pizzeria in Ypsilanti, Michigan. Jim later sold his share of the store to Tom, who broke into franchising in 1967.

Over the years, Monaghan suffered two near-bankruptcies and a fire. He survived those afflictions only to be sued in 1979 by Amstar Corp. for infringing upon the Domino Sugar name. Undaunted, Monaghan grew Domino's Pizza from 290 stores in 1980 to more than 5,000 in the United States today, and another 260 abroad. He even went on to buy the Detroit Tigers baseball team for $54 million in 1983, although he later sold the team.

For other entrepreneurs, their success came from addressing a problem with which they strongly identified, as was the case with Paul Orfalea, the founder of Kinko's. The world's largest chain of copy centers hit it big by targeting college students and pioneering round-the-clock service hours.

In September 1970, Orfalea was a student at the University of California at Santa Barbara when he came up with a way to continue to live near the college town. The hippie with the red Afro secured a $5,000 personal loan from Bank of America and rented a little 100 sq. ft. garage. Originally, he was going to name the shop Paul's Copies, but he called it Kinko's after the nickname given to him by his college buddies for his trademark hair.

His tiny place of business at the back of a hamburger stand featured a single copier, offset press, film processing, and a small selection of stationery and school supplies. Space became so crowded with customers at times, Orfalea had to wheel the copy machine out onto the sidewalk. Orfalea later urged his hippie partners to go forth and multiply Kinko shops in other locations.

Today, the average Kinko's store is 7,000 sq. ft. and offers a full range of services, including digital color copying, binding, computer rentals, and videoconferencing. It also specializes in publishing custom materials for the academic market. The company employs some 23,000 people and operates more than 850 business centers in the United States as well as Japan, the Netherlands, and South Korea.

These amazing stories demonstrate how you can turn street smarts and gut instincts into money-making opportunities. Still, the amount of money you have saved, the contacts you have made from school and work, and the expertise you have gained in a particular industry are all critical pieces to the success puzzle.

You need to be brutally honest with yourself if you think you are ready to you run a business. Regardless of the type of business you want to start, it should fit who you are—based on your personal interests, professional experience, skills, financial resources, and your long-term goals.

Make no mistake, you will be spending most of your waking days and sleepless nights working on your enterprise. A new business requires long hours, pays you little or no salary starting out, and offers no guarantee that it will be a success. If you start a business that isn't right for you, you'll regret even quitting that full-time paying job you hated so much.

THE SUCCESSFUL BUSINESS OWNER

As mentioned earlier, some traits will come naturally to you, like being creative, adventurous, or outspoken. Others will require some level of development, such as being disciplined and well-organized. The National Federation of Independent Business, the Washington, D.C.-based trade and advocacy group of some 600,000 small businesses, spells out the more important characteristics that the successful entrepreneur needs in his or her arsenal:

- **Adaptability**—ability to find creative solutions to problems and cope with situations.

- **Competitiveness**—willingness to compete with and test yourself against others.

- **Discipline**—ability to stay focused and stick to a schedule.

- **Drive**—desire to work hard in order to accomplish your goals.

- **Integrity**—commitment to tell the truth and deal with people fairly.

- **Organization**—ability to structure your life and to keep tasks and information in order.

- **Perseverance**—refusal to quit and the willingness to keep your goals in sight as you work through and around obstacles.

- **Persuasiveness**—ability to get people interested in your ideas and goals.

- **Understanding**—ability to listen and empathize with others.

- **Vision**—ability to see the end results of all your hard work as you work toward your goals.

Equally important is risk taking—the courage to expose yourself to possible losses. As captain of your own ship, you have to gamble and take realistic risks. You want to beat 2-to-1 or even 10-to-1 odds though, not 100-to-1. Gamble on your abilities and your ambition. If you are going to survive, you'll need an ironclad will and determination—when failure strikes, hit back.

SENSE AND SENSIBILITY

It's important that you examine how you react to certain situations and how you relate to others. We all have behavioral or personality tendencies, which cause some people to click, while others clash.

This isn't meant to be Psych 101. However, the following survey is designed to help you better understand yourself and others. Your responses to the following questions essentially provide a framework for examining your personal behavioral pattern. There are no wrong or right answers, nor is one behavioral style better than the others.

Answer *yes* to each of the following characteristics that best describe you.

If your total for I is more than five, you have a dominant personality. This means that you are more inclined to take risks. You like to be in control and you are driven to succeed. If something isn't going your way you tend to move on. Your style tends to be very direct.

If your total for II is more than five, you like to persuade others. You are enthusiastic and entertaining. You like being liked. However, you tend to promise more than you can deliver, because you are not realistic about what you can and cannot do. You style tends to be impatient.

If your total for III is more than five, you have a conscientious personality. You are logical and analytical. In fact, you tend to analyze situations to death. You are diligent and take time to plan projects thoroughly. But you tend to be indecisive, because of your need to weigh everything carefully. You have a low tolerance for conflict and are least likely to facilitate discussions. Your style is systematic.

If your total for IV is more than five, you have a steady personality. You like security; you dislike conflict. You take very few risks. It is hard for you to bounce back from failure. You like identifying with a group. You tend to be the caregiver. Your tendencies include developing specialized skills, creating a harmonious environment, and desiring appreciation for your work. Your style is consistent and predictable.

I	II	III	IV
Impatient	Spirited	Good-natured	Respectful
Unrelenting	Balanced	Conventional	Well-disciplined
Bold	Optimistic	Agreeable	Picky
Determined	Extroverted	Middle-of-the-road	Conscientious
Outspoken	Jovial	Gentle	Insightful
Decisive	Impulsive	Modest	Precise
Adventurous	Sociable	Helpful	Diplomatic
Strong-willed	Irresistible	Neighborly	Cautious
Self-reliant	Expressive	Even-tempered	Observant
Competitive	Friendly	Cooperative	Tactful
Steadfast	Talkative	Content	Reserved
Headstrong	Outgoing	Generous	Perceptive
Independent	Persuasive	Easygoing	Private
Aggressive	Inspiring	Sympathetic	Introspective
Assertive	Cheerful	Amiable	Logical
Tenacious	Playful	Patient	Soft-spoken
Direct	Charming	Loyal	Thorough
Pioneering	Confident	Predictable	Careful
Argumentative	Spunky	Considerate	Exact
Demanding	Attractive	Obliging	Systematic
Pushy	Animated	Compliant	Introverted
	Intriguing	Kind	Accommodating

Add up the number of characteristics you answered *yes* to in each column.

Total column I =_____ Total column II =_____ Total column III =_____

Total column IV =_____

Most entrepreneurs fall into categories I, III, or a combination of I and III. Those entrepreneurs who are IIs often are more service-oriented. The least entrepreneurial personality is IV, because these are people who are not normally risk-takers and do not like uncertainty—they want to know exactly where their next paycheck is coming from.

Whatever category you fit into, keep in mind that this exercise is meant to be interpreted; it is a guideline, not an end-all or say-all. The idea is for you to use what you learned about yourself to create an environment that enables you to achieve business success. This exercise can be used as a guide to explore your management style. It will save you a lot of heartache knowing your shortcomings before you go into business.

Note that it takes some people longer than others to start a business. The purpose of self-analysis is to put you on the road to entrepreneurship much faster, because you will have a clearer, more realistic picture of what you can and cannot do, or are unwilling to do.

Ultimately, it comes down to you. What do you want and why do you want it? Who knows, maybe since you were 10 years old, you felt you were born to be an entrepreneur. Just make sure that your business is challenging, stimulating, and meaningful to you. It should suit your personality and lifestyle, and maximize your experiences, resources, and contacts.

Adopt a holistic approach to starting a business by closely examining your physical, mental, spiritual, and financial well-being. Life as an entrepreneur is about having balance. Being your own boss can provide financial security and bring you personal and professional happiness. I believe that success as an entrepreneur is truly about being happy. However, happiness is a craft, weave it like a tapestry.

DINEH MOHAJER, FOUNDER AND CEO OF HARD CANDY, INC.

In the spring of 1995 pastels and metallics had become all the rage in the fashion world. The chic, and even the not-with-it crowd, sported fuchsia, lime green, and tangerine outfits. It was this color phase in the fashion industry, and a quest for the

Hard Candy

DINEH MOHAJER

right-colored nail polish to match a pair of new baby blue sandals, that led 26-year-old Dineh Mohajer to launch Hard Candy, a burgeoning Beverly Hills cosmetics company.

I created baby blue polish by mixing existing white and dark blue polish and a chemical base. I started making other pastel colors. I had some definite colors that I wanted to wear that just weren't available at any of the stores.

While Dineh and her older sister (by seven years), Pooneh, were shopping for shoes, a saleswoman noticed the unusual color of Dineh's toenails and asked her where she could find such pastel shades, which would match her new line of footwear. After the encounter, the sisters went to lunch to discuss the possibility of selling the polish.

It seemed like a good summer gig for the then 22-year-old burnt-out University of Southern California student, after three years of premed courses and MCAT prep classes. Taking $200 to buy materials, Mohajer started Hard Candy (since the polish looked good enough to eat). The biochemistry major took off a semester and put her skills to work by creating four prototype pastel hues: Sunshine (yellow), Sky (blue), Violet (purple), and Lime (green). She attached a plastic jelly ring to each bottle to make the nail polish line stand out.

Mohajer took her polishes to Santa Monica's trendy Fred Segal boutique (where she worked during her summer break). While talking to store owner Sharon Segal, an ecstatic teen begged to buy the four samples at $18 a bottle.

When we told the girl's mother how much they would cost, she thought it was ridiculously too much. But the girl was adamant, because she knew that she couldn't get these same colors anywhere else. She spent $72 just for the samples. I knew then I had created something so original.

Segal ordered 200 bottles on the spot. Mohajer had to charge a high price because she was buying her materials at a retail price point. Mohajer purchased hundreds of bottles of white nail polish and empty bottles from a beauty supply store. She bought dyes from a pigment supplier.

For two days, I was mixing chemicals in kitchen and bathroom basins and filling bottles spread out all over the living-room floor. Within hours of being on display, [Segal] called saying the polishes had sold out.

Mohajer went into full production with high school sweetheart, USC classmate and business partner, Benjamin Einstein.

Their student quarters became a rough-and-tumble nail polish factory. Friends lent a hand with the seven telephone lines that were constantly ringing off the hook with orders. What started out as a two-hour project was a 22-hour operation.

The Bloomfield Hills, Michigan, native quit school altogether and borrowed $50,000 from her Iranian-born parents to run Hard Candy on sheer instinct. She didn't have any market research or a business plan. Initially, Mohajer solicited swank boutiques, but soon major department store chains, namely Nordstrom, Harrods, and London's Harvey Nichols started placing orders (giving Hard Candy international distribution overnight).

Mohajer's nail polishes caught on like wildfire, showing up on fashion models, Hollywood celebrities, and entertainers. The business grew from four to 35 flamboyant hues (at $12 a bottle), such as Vibe (purple), Trailer Trash (silver), Haze (metallic lavender), Vegas (metallic copper), and Luscious (red-wine metallic).

I had no choice but to develop this into a full-fledged business from a manufacturing, shipping, product development, and billing standpoint. I had to evolve into being able to deal with the situation I created. The company grew too fast [sales were increasing 25 percent a month].

By the spring of 1996, Hard Candy had gone from manufacturing 450 bottles of nail polish a month to more than 75,000 bottles. Even though the Beverly Hills start-up moved into a small 1,500-sq.-ft. office, it couldn't keep up with the rapid growth. With no billing or order-taking system in place, money was falling throught the cracks. To make matters worse, Hard Candy polish started popping up at not-so-exclusive drugstores and tattoo parlors. Instead of calling it quits, Mohajer smartened up. She set out to find a CEO (to replace her temporarily) who could put in some cost control and management systems.

At first, I was concerned about giving up my company to someone else. But you have to be careful not to let those feelings over-

power you. I wasn't handing over the company to someone else, I was just bringing in another team player. If you don't have a team player you can delegate to, you'll lose.

Mohajer bypassed executive search firms, and instead, networked her way through an entrepreneurial program at Ernst & Young. She interviewed 15 highly qualified people, but the one who most shared Hard Candy's vision was 61-year-old William Botts. Mohajer liked that he was more of an entrepreneur than corporate stiff. After leaving Rockwell International in 1978, Botts ran a software company, which he later sold before starting a consulting firm. He even had a track record in the cosmetics industry, having worked with Creative Nail Design, a maker of artificial nails.

Botts set up the necessary infrastructure, hiring talented people from production contractors to marketing professionals. By June 1996, Hard Candy moved its 20-employee staff into a 5,000-sq.-ft. office and installed a network computer system that provided inventory, financial, and communications capabilities.

Hard Candy sold $10 million worth of nail polish in 1996. Mohajer is again the CEO. Her sister Pooneh is chief operating officer and runs the day-to-day operations, while beau Benjamin, company vice president, handles creative development.

There are a whole slew of things that go with manufacturing, shipping, and sales. I have learned a lot about negotiating terms with suppliers. I understand better how stores work, what their goals and philosophies are, and how to adapt to their environment. It's all about relationships. It varies from account to account.

In just two years, Mohajer had created over 60 nail colors, lipsticks and liners, mascara, eye shadows and liner, brow powder pencils, and the first glitter pencil. In 1998, she added to the mix lip gloss, blush/highlight compacts, and a concealer-and-blemish-healer in one. New colors were added such as Cosamic, Galaxy, Hick, and Love. The profits from these sales are donated to the AIDS charity AmFar.

Today, Hard Candy has some 25 distributors worldwide and its line is sold in over 1,000 stores domestically, and 21 countries, including England, Japan, Germany, France, and Italy. Mohajer has acquired her own 30,000-sq.-ft. shipping facility.

For the first year of business, we were just a nail polish company. At some point, we would have reached the limits of the nail polish market. Our next priority was to create a full line of cosmetics. We added lipsticks, eye shadows, and mascara. And we introduced Candy Man, nail polish for men.

Hard Candy has had to face copycat products like Krazy Kandy and Urban Decay. Even cosmetic giant Chanel introduced a similar line. But Mohajer views this as a validation of her marketing savvy. In general, cosmetic lines—from Max Factor to Estée Lauder to Bobbi Brown—have been designed by makeup artists. The Independent Cosmetic Manufacturers and Distributors Association represents more than 650 product lines, most of which are formulated by professionals and marketed in small-scale salons. Mohajer says she was able to break into the entrenched beauty business because she understands her market.

I create a product that caters to my demographic. I happen to be a part of that demographic. And I understand what people my age think is cool. [Hard Candy's products] are just whatever I'd want. It's a very simple equation.

Indeed, Hard Candy has a marketing niche. Traditionalists may frown upon Gangsta Booty (gold glitter) and Heist (chartreuse) polishes, but Hard Candy isn't designed for them. Mohajer's target market is ages 17 to 25, although many younger teens and thirtysomethings find these polishes to be hip. Hard Candy has benefited greatly from its 1998 advertising campaign, which was seen in the pages of *Teen, People, Jane, InStyle, Seventeen, Vogue,* and *Glamour.*

Maybelline and Revlon are mostly drugstore brands. The Mac's and the Bobbi Browns differ in that they are very specialized. Yes, all of it is makeup. Chanel is competing with Mac which is competing with Origins. But these are three different lines with distinct philosophies. Although they sell next to each other at the stores, they represent something different [to consumers]. We represent young, hip, cutting-edge, fashion-oriented women and men.

There are some 40 employees on staff now. Hard Candy is shelved in the self-service areas of department stores. But Mohajer is considering recruiting a team of in-store sales reps, much like those hired by Clinique and Lancôme.

Mohajer says Hard Candy's goal is to stay high-end in its distribution in the United States and overseas, and to maintain a product with quality ingredients and packaging. She attributes her success to being a great team player, having learned how to delegate to competent and accountable people.

It's also because of my drive, ambition, and vision of the company years from now. When you run a business you have to stay focused. I've learned to separate my emotions from the company. You can't be afraid to fail.

SHEILA BRIDGES, CEO OF SHEILA BRIDGES DESIGN, INC.

Design and architecture are the cornerstone of every culture from the great pyramids of Egypt to the majestic Taj Mahal in India. It was a fascination with Roman architecture and history that first piqued Sheila Bridges's interest in the decorative arts. In fact, she studied in Italy her junior year at Brown University.

I have always had an interest in art history, architecture, antiques, and furniture. These are things I felt very passionate about and I spent a lot of free time looking at these things on the weekends. For instance, I would go to a lot of flea markets and auctions in order to learn more about the history and pricing of furniture.

Today, Bridges is blending European, African, and American motifs into exciting living quarters as the owner of Sheila

Bridges Design, Inc., a four-year-old, New York–based interior design firm that generated $1.5 million in revenues in 1997. However, the 34-year-old native of Philadelphia didn't enter the design profession right away.

Upon graduating from Brown University in 1986 with a bachelor's degree in sociology, Bridges moved to New York to explore opportunities in the fashion industry as a retail buyer. A year later she ended up working in men's designer clothing at Bloomingdale's department store. That job landed her a gig with world renowned Italian couturier, Giorgio Armani.

But by 1989, Bridges tired of the fashion business and switched careers. She landed a position as an interior design assistant for a prestigious New York architectural firm that provided both commercial and residential services to its clients.

It was a small company of about 10 employees. I was the only nonarchitect. The position was created as we went along. So, I did just about everything, including shopping for furniture and fabric, sitting in on client presentations, and handling billing, invoicing, and client correspondence. We had a lot of big and exciting projects that gave me an incredible amount of experience and exposure to the business. It gave me the tools I eventually needed to start my own business.

Bridges took night courses at New York's Parsons School of Design. She quit her job in 1992 to study decorative arts in Italy by convincing Parsons to let her do an independent project at Polimoda, a design school in Florence. In 1994, 29-year-old Bridges was ready to venture out. She acquired a business license, incorporated, and converted one of her bedrooms into an office.

I was already doing a lot of freelance work on the side. One day, I decided to work for myself. I had two sizable jobs that were enough to live off. Besides, I figured that if it didn't work, I could always go back to work for someone else. I had the proper experience and educational background. What did I have to lose?

Bridges's start-up costs were minimal since she launched the business out of her four-bedroom Harlem apartment. Armed with the laptop her former boss had given her as a going away gift and a fax machine her friends chipped in to buy for her birthday, Bridges was ready to do business.

She relied heavily on word-of-mouth marketing, attending social gatherings hosted by politicians, museum curators, and big business people. Initially, her clients were people who didn't want to spend the kind of money top full-service design firms commanded. But by 1995, the firm was garnering upscale clients, such as Andre Harrell, the former Motown chairman.

Andre was someone I had pursued for a year. I first met him at a cocktail party. He told me he was looking for an apartment and wanted to do some design work. I kept tabs on him and learned that no one in his office could find anything. I presented the idea to him to let me find the apartment and if I did, then he would have to let me decorate and furnish it. I found a place on the Upper West Side and he kept his word. I recently worked on a third project for him (a country home in Westport, Connecticut).

Bridges has gained notoriety with New York's top bankers, entrepreneurs, and other arts and entertainment personalities, including MTV Host Bill Bellamy and Bad Boy Entertainment CEO Sean "Puffy" Combs. Her portfolio boasts such projects as renovating an apartment in the Trump building for Peter Norton, founder of Norton Utilities software.

On average, Bridges Design, Inc. handles three major jobs at a time and several smaller ones (about ten altogether). Any given job may take months or years to complete, ranging from $100,000 to over $1 million in design costs.

I have positioned myself as a high-end residential interior designer. If you were to use the fashion industry as an analogy, I would describe what I do as creating the couture line (i.e., Donna Karan versus DKNY). I want my business to be very exclusive, because of the quality of the pieces we provide, many of which are fairly costly. But as my business grows, I hope to accommodate a more mass-market appeal.

Bridges's design team comprises an office manager, a full-time designer, and one part-timer—a student in design school—as well as an ongoing pool of interns from the New York School of Interior Design, Fashion Institute of Technology, and Parsons. She hires independent contractors, noting that she would rather staff up for larger projects on an as-needed basis than to be forced to lay off people during downtimes.

For this reason, Bridges maintains an extensive database of architects, suppliers, artists, and so forth and she continually updates a library of resources. All of this enables the firm to tackle any job that relates to the interior of the home.

Sometimes we do full-scale renovations which include extensive electrical work and carpentry. We may knock down walls, put in new flooring, and design window treatments and wall coverings. We purchase furniture as well as design furniture depending on a client's specific need. I may buy china and silverware along with the bedding. We choose paint colors for the walls and frame the artwork. Our work has recently expanded to the exterior of the home—including landscaping.

Round-the-clock hours make Bridges's job especially taxing. The phone is constantly ringing off the hook, with bankers calling at 7 A.M. and entertainers at two in the morning, while others call on the weekend. A big part of her work also involves contracts.

If I were to get another degree, it would be in law. I constantly deal with contracts and budgets, plus the liability for the types of work (construction) we do is sizable. This creates a necessity for legal expertise and advice. In addition to speaking to my lawyer every day, fortunately, I have a lot of friends who are lawyers who generously give me advice for free.

While the artisan never wrote a formal business plan, she has a set vision for growing the business, which entails writing a series of books on design/lifestyle and creating a line of furniture. She's already put her mark on various home furnishings from dining chairs to bookcases.

Because I do a lot of custom work for my clients, it seems only natural to do a collection or line of furniture. A lot of interior designers eventually create their own collections or they license their designs. I think most people recognize my work. I like things that are timeless and classic. Things that don't look dated. So, they're still in style 20 years from today.

Bridges describes her creations as cozy, livable, and aesthetic. The business itself can be summed up in one word, personable. Like most people in her field, Bridges derives her unique designs from her clients' personalities and lifestyles. The ideal client is one that brings repeat business and gives plenty of referrals.

You are in someone's personal space on a regular basis, going in and out of the home for meetings and installations. So, you really have to get to know the person and they really have to trust you. Sometimes, I follow my clients. For example, quite a few years ago I designed an apartment for a couple who lived in New York. When they moved to Boston, I did their home there. It is great to get quick jobs that are going to give you fast money, but that's not how you are going to stay in business in the long haul.

2

FINDING YOUR NICHE AND TURNING IT INTO A MONEY-MAKING BUSINESS

> To dream the impossible dream.
> To fight the unbeatable foe.
> To bear with unbearable sorrow.
> To run where the brave dare not go.
> —M. Leigh, J. Darion, "The Impossible Dream"

There is no one industry or given type of business that will render you riches beyond your wildest dreams. However, there are niches to be found throughout any market. You just have to find yours. Of course, this requires strategy and skill. Here's a four-step process to finding that bright business idea or niche and turning it into a money-making venture:

• **One. Self-examination.** What are your interests, abilities, and experience? Most often, the best business ideas come from people who already worked in a certain industry and decided to start a business in their same field or spun off a business in another segment of that market.

• **Two. Identify an unmet market need.** What products and services are in demand? Commit to memory this entrepreneurial mantra: *No matter how great a product or service is, if no one is interested in buying what I have to sell, I don't have a business.*

- **Three. Target your market.** To thrive in any business you need to get to know your customers intimately—their likes, dislikes, and buying patterns. The best way to get to know your target market is to talk to potential customers, competitors, and suppliers.

- **Four. Examine how much money you have to invest.** How much income do you need to make to meet your financial obligations and still live comfortably? (Can you pay the rent on your apartment and office or buy supplies and still afford groceries?) Limited financial resources could delay the kind of business you want to start. There isn't a business idea worth pursuing unless you can earn enough money to satisfy your basic financial needs.

EXAMINING YOURSELF

By taking a close look at your capabilities, you should gain some insight into the kind of business worth starting. Begin by asking yourself: What is the sum total of my experience, knowledge, and skills? What expertise have I gained from my education, from past jobs, from internships? What are the responsibilities of my current job? How does my level of expertise relate to the business I want to start? How much do I know about managing cash flow? How will I be able to determine the skills level of others? How well do I manage people? If I don't have adequate training, can I get some?

Once you figure out your strengths and weaknesses, spend a great deal of time and money—within your reasonable financial reach—mastering the one or two things that will give you the most return. There is an old Asian proverb that states: *By mastering one thing completely, you gain access to all things.* This is to say that you need to be able to position yourself as an expert in whatever business you decide to start. Take a hard look at what you are good at and what you really enjoy doing. Now combine those two things into a business.

Nothing drove this point home for me like MTV's *Real World* in Miami:

This is the story of seven strangers picked to live in a house and have their lives taped to find out what happens when people stop being polite and start getting real.

However, the producers added a different twist to that fifth episode:

As the cast of Real World, *Miami you have been given a unique opportunity—to form a business. Each cast member will be a shareholder of the company. A business advisor will be appointed to help with logistical decisions, but other than that, it's up to you, the Miami cast, to figure out how to make a success story out of a $50,000 donation from* Real World. *There aren't too many rules, except that cash expenditures will be checked by an appointed advisor. The type of business chosen must be on the up-and-up (of course), and if a solid business plan is not developed, and the business incorporated, within twelve weeks, that's just too bad, time's up. If all goes well, though, it's up to you to take the business to the future. It's all yours.*

I remember watching the first show with much excitement and anticipation. At that point I knew I wanted to write a book on the subject and this seemed like an ideal case study if all went well. By the second episode, I knew all's well was not how this show was going to end. This wasn't because the roommates weren't bright, aggressive, or ambitious—although they seemed a bit too wrapped up in each other's love lives. The biggest problem was that they were totally clueless about what type of business to start.

During the course of five months, the roommates came up with a host of ideas—a dog-walking service, bagel shop, juice bar, café, movie theater, fashion line (golf wear), and cake-delivery service. Then of course, the roommates had a lot of misguided notions about running a business, such as writing a business plan in a week's time or making the pet dog a shareholder. I think not.

There was a small glimmer of hope when one of the roommates and her boss (whose existing Miami-based enterprise delivered certain paper goods to hotel chains) came up with the idea of a dessert-delivering business, called Delicious Deliveries. But in the end when it came down to choosing a president—a man with previous business experience or a totally green and impractical roommate—the cake business went up in smoke.

If you don't have a realistic and clear picture of what you can feasibly sell to make money, you may end up operating in a fog for longer than five months. If you want to own a business but are unsure what type to pursue, then follow this simple rule: "Go for what you know." That is to say, sell products that you know something about or provide services in areas in which you have received real-life training. You will save yourself a lot of headaches and heartaches by making the connection between your personal background and your business.

Moreover, decide whether you really want to start a full-time business, putting in a considerable number of hours, or would you rather do something on the side, part-time? Do you want to start a business from scratch or would you be interested in buying a franchise or joining a direct sales and marketing organization (for example, Mary Kay or AMWAY).

Needless to say, your business success isn't limited strictly to your abilities or education. So, you shouldn't feel that you are not good enough, creative enough, or smart enough to run a business. Creativity and intelligence are limitless. The goal is to apply your creativity and intelligence to find a market need, satisfy it, and keep customers coming back.

IDENTIFYING AN UNMET MARKET NEED

Some businesses have cropped up in response to the way people live or work. Henry Ford's vision for the automobile was simply his version of a horseless carriage. To cite a more contemporary example: It was out of frustration that Sky D. Dayton created EarthLink Network, a leader among Internet service providers. The then 23-year-old entrepreneur wanted to make Internet access easier for himself and everyone else. Most people tend to buy a product or service that solves a particular problem.

To tap into an unmet market need, you must be in tune with constantly changing consumer needs. How do you get in tune with change? First, you cannot assume that today's solution is the right one or the only one. Second, don't let all of the details of the question blind you to the simple answer.

Here's a perfect example of what this means: the case of the slow elevator. There was a famous New York City hotel that received several complaints a day from guests about its slow elevators. Several mechanical engineers were called in, but none could make the elevators go any faster. How was the problem solved? One engineer concentrated his thinking on the hotel guests, not the elevators. He suggested installing full length mirrors all around the elevators. Just as he guessed, people didn't mind the slow elevators anymore, because they simply killed time by fixing their ties or adjusting their hair and admiring themselves.

The first step in finding an underserved market is simple: Look around you. What is it that you need? Talk to friends and family members. Tap into business and economic professors at colleges and universities to discuss possible ideas. Second, read newsletters, industry publications, and trade magazines to learn about the latest inventions, products, services, and current events. The objective is to look for industry trends that you can capitalize on as a business.

You can contact trade associations to get information on the latest industry developments. A great reference book, available at any library, is the *Encyclopedia of Business Information Sources* (Gale Research, Inc.), which lists books, periodicals, directories, trade associations, and other resources for more than 1,000 industries and business subjects. There's also the *Encyclopedia of Associations* (Gale Research Inc.), which provides an alphabetical listing of some 14,000 trade and professional associations throughout the United States. Many of these groups provide marketing information and publish their own newsletters.

Moreover, scout for trade shows, which are great sources for business ideas, because you get to preview new products and services. This may help you to identify a product or service that you could offer. Observe how attendees or potential customers respond to certain product features. Check with your local convention facility or chamber of commerce to find out about shows coming to your area.

Also, local chambers of commerce are wonderful resources for statistics on different business sectors. These groups are designed to assist and promote the community business sector by devising educational programs and sponsoring networking events. Attending and participating in their meetings and those of professional organizations or trade groups unique to your business will provide you with great sources of information and contacts. For your review, you can always request a membership kit from any organization you are interested in joining. This package will include information on programs, publications, benefits, and fees. More than likely, there will be a few different trade groups in your field. Join the one(s) that boast an array of support services from workshops to financial assistance to technical support to discounted business services.

Don't overlook government agencies. The Department of Commerce (Office of Business Liaison) provides information on business subjects, including patents and trademarks, imports and exports, industry outlooks, and economic and demographic statistics. Also, the U.S. Small Business Administration (SBA) provides information on a host of business topics for start-ups as well as training and educational programs, counseling services, and financial programs.

In fact, the SBA sponsors the Service Corps of Retired Executives (SCORE), a national network of volunteer, retired executives from all types of businesses. Experts in such areas as law, finance, marketing, manufacturing, and retail act as small business consultants, free of charge, providing counseling, workshops, and seminars to prospective business owners. Volunteer counselors have even worked with large corporations, such as Procter & Gamble, IBM, and General Electric. You can contact SCORE at 800-634-0245 or www.score.org. To reach the SBA, call the Answer Desk at 800-827-5722 or visit www.sbaonline.sba.gov.

While you may find some information that leads you to develop an innovative product or service, don't reinvent the wheel. Face it, most of us would love to create a product or service that *no one* else has ever imagined before. But in truth, many successful entrepreneurs have merely put a new spin on old ideas or repackaged concepts by upgrading them with new technology.

For instance, at a time when computers were used only by universities, science labs, and big corporations, Apple Computer founders Steve Jobs and Stephen Wozniak built a company that would help commercialize desktop units. Similarly, the Internet was a leftover relic from the Cold War used by the U.S. Department of Defense network until 1994, when with the introduction of the Mosaic software package, the Net turned into a commercial enterprise.

Some businesses merely found new markets for an existing

product or service. When Timex lost market share in low-cost watches to digital watches, it made a comeback by targeting young people involved in sports activities, such as running, swimming, jogging, and cycling.

It was a low-cost, direct-sales model that turned Austin, Texas–based Dell Computer from a quaint company in a college dorm room to a driving force in the PC business, which sells 90 percent of its computers, workstations, and servers to businesses. With a personal net worth over $4 billion, 33-year-old founder and CEO Michael Dell is richer than software tycoon Bill Gates was at that age. Then again, Dell has been tinkering with computers since he was in junior high, taking apart the motherboard of his Apple II computer at age 13.

To please his parents who wanted him to become a doctor, Dell enrolled as a premed student at the University of Texas in 1983. That first semester he bought outmoded IBM PCs from local retailers, upgraded them in his dorm room, and then sold them on campus and door-to-door to local small businesses. Much to his parents' dismay, Dell dropped out of college at the end of his freshman year. If summer sales from his new venture fell short, he promised to return to school. But business took off, with Dell selling $180,000 worth of PCs in one month.

Dell's next move was to assemble whole PCs instead of upgrading older ones. It proved cheaper to buy the components and he could sell the machine—imprinted with his name—directly to customers at a 15 percent discount to established brands. At the ripe old age of 23, Dell was able to raise $30 million in an initial public offering—his take was $18 million. By 1991 the company had grown to more than $800 million in sales. Despite some early setbacks, namely a cash shortfall, design flaws, and lack of senior managers, Dell Computer has endured. Today, the company employs some 9,000 workers and total sales have climbed to $12 billion.

TARGETING YOUR MARKET

You have an idea for a product or service, but you're not sure whether it is a viable business. Well, good businesses thrive when an entrepreneur understands his or her market—potential customers, competitors, and suppliers.

- **Talk to Your Customers.** Who are your customers? Are they young or old? Single? Working mothers? Financially well-off or struggling college students? Identify your customers based on three areas:

1. *Demographics.* This refers to age, income, educational level, marital status, and gender. There are some products that are age and gender specific, say for instance, diapers, kids' shoes, or women's clothes. Just the same Kmart and Neiman Marcus cater to a different clientele. Does your product or service appeal to a certain group of people?

2. *Geographics.* This means city, state, region, and neighborhood. People's tastes, usage, and buying patterns differ regionally. Where your customers live could easily dictate what you can or can't sell. You wouldn't market surfboards to people living in Minnesota.

3. *Psychographics.* This entails personality characteristics, values, attitudes, and lifestyle. What do your customers like to do or what is it about their daily routines that affects what you have to offer? If you open a day-care center for working parents, your hours can't be from 9:30 A.M. to 4 P.M., since most people have to be at work by nine and don't get home until after five. Also, some people may react differently to a product based on their religious principles or practices.

Get to know your customers intimately. What turns them on? What causes them to tune out? Are they impulse buyers, or do they like to deliberate over their buying decisions? A great way to get some concrete information on your target market is to conduct market research. You can hire a well-established firm. Given limited financial resources, you're probably more inclined to proceed with the do-it-yourself approach. Market research involves two steps. One, you have to gather information—record and interpret it. Second, you have to apply your findings to your target customer.

Don't fret over it, there are several direct and relatively cheap ways of doing this. You can create your own survey using random telephone samplings or personal written queries. Conducting interviews over the phone is efficient because it's quick and allows you to cover a wide geographical range. In-person interviews are more labor-intensive but the most efficient way to go. Students at colleges that have entrepreneurial or business management programs can be hired to do surveys for reasonable or little cost (see Appendix A).

You want to get some general information, name, address, occupation, and so forth. Ask questions specific to why they would buy or use a product similar to yours. After all, you want your surveys to give accurate results and to be effective, not a wheel grinding, self-fulfilling prophecy. Marketing guru Don Debelak, author of *Marketing Magic* (Adams Media), offers four rules to follow when designing a questionnaire:

Rule One. Make a comparison between products. A comparison is made between two similar products. What do customers look for in a product: price, quality, brand name, service, or performance? List features, product benefits, and services that you could offer that your target customers might want. Develop six to ten different models or variations. Ask people which model or combination of variations they would prefer and why. For instance, if you sold cars you could ask: "Do you prefer luxury or compact cars? A car with a tape deck and CD player or just a tape deck? A car with a sun roof or a convertible? Or a car with automatic locks and air bags or just automatic locks?"

Rule Two. Offer people choices. A choice is made between

two different products that provide the same benefit. For example, Little Caesar's, Domino's Pizza, and Pizza Hut all offer the same benefit, pizza. But they all operate differently. Domino's specializes in delivery. Little Caesar's in carry-out and price. And Pizza Hut in sit-down restaurants.

Rule Three. *Ask people to rank their choices.* When they buy a breakfast cereal, what is most important to them? Taste? Price? Nutritional value? Coupons? Or premiums offered on the back of the box? List product features and benefits, then have customers rate them from highest, middle, to lowest priority. Or more simply put, on a scale from one to ten.

Rule Four. *Find out if people will really buy.* There are a lot of products that people like but don't buy. Give people a choice between your product and two similar ones and ask which one they would buy. Make sure you include prices.

When you are ready to hit the pavement, go to where your target market hangs out—supermarkets, coffee houses, college campuses, barber shops, beauty parlors, gyms, Web-based chat rooms, online bulletin boards, or wherever appropriate. Let survey participants know you are looking to introduce a new product or service and you want to get their opinions. Try to collect somewhere between 50 and 100 surveys over a one- to two-month period. Write down your findings and take a very close look at the results.

While you may have to hire a professional to handle this project, focus groups are valuable in generating marketing ideas and gaining insight into attitudes about a new product. A focus group involves getting feedback from a specially picked group of people using controlled interview techniques. The process allows the participants to provide their opinions, come up with new ideas, and to brainstorm. You will need a skilled interviewer and carefully handpicked participants. In order for focus groups to be effective, you have to elicit how people really feel, and to ensure that they are not tapering their answers in front of the group.

• **Talk to Your Competitors.** Study your competitors by visiting stores or locations where their products are offered. Analyze the site, customers, traffic patterns, hours of operation, prices, quality of goods and services, promotional materials, and other handouts. How well do your competitors satisfy the needs of potential customers in your business. How will you compete against them—better location, price, features, quality, or service?

Get to know your potential competitors by networking with them. That is to say, attend trade shows, conventions, association meetings—anywhere people in your industry gather. Just keep in mind that networking is more than just slapping business cards into your rolodex—the objective is to establish and maintain relationships. Make sure you follow through with phone calls, letters, and notes to solidify relationships.

When you research similar businesses in the industry, review their company literature and marketing materials, read articles on them, talk to the owners. If local competitors won't talk to you, then try those in another state (there, you probably won't be viewed as a direct competitor).

Of course, it's possible that marketing information you get from a competitor may be exaggerated. Don't be taken in by it, instead look for consistency in information. Examine a number of resources and analysts' reports to see if they offer the same commentary, then formulate your own opinion.

You can get demographic and competitive information at your local library. Check out the *Rand McNally Commercial Atlas and Marketing Guide* and the *Thomas Register of Manufacturers* (Thomas Publishing), which let you know who and how many people are selling in your market. Companies are listed by size, assets, and employees. The *Dun and Bradstreet Regional Business Directory* (Dun & Bradstreet, Inc.) also lists companies by description, name, address, telephone, when it was started, sales volume, number of employees, and whether or not it is a public company. D&B also provides state guides and compiles lists of companies' financial status and credit rating. *American Demographics* magazine (www.demographics.com) provides population numbers and studies to determine growth trends.

Again, get hold of trade publications—online or in your mailbox—to stay abreast of who's doing what in the industry. The World Wide Web is another excellent source for information on competitors, both in the United States and around the globe. Any "public" company is required by the Securities and Exchange Commission (SEC) to file a 10-K report, which includes financial statements and management analysis. For corporate filings check out the SEC's Edgar database (www.sec.gov). You can find other company data in Hoovers Online (www. hoovers.com) or browse through company sites via search engines like Excite (www.excite.com), Altavista (www.altavista.com), or InfoSeek (www.infoseek.com). Many companies have a Website listing information on their products, services, key personnel, and latest press releases.

- **Talk to Your Suppliers.** Manufacturers, wholesalers, and retailers who provide everything from food and paper goods to office supplies and desktop computers, may share any market research they have done in your industry. Talking to suppliers can tell you a great deal about how your industry works, which product lines are selling off the shelves, and why some companies are more successful than others. Suppliers can also tell you about pricing techniques and mark-ups. They may even be able to tell you what price potential customers would be willing to pay for the products or services you want to sell. These contacts will become invaluable as your business grows. You can get the names and numbers of industry representatives of vendors and suppliers via the *Directory of Manufacturers' Representatives* (Manufacturers' Agents National Association). Also check out the *Directory of Wholesalers and Distributors* (Gale Research).

Or talk to vendors who service your current employer or where your friends and family work.

SHOW ME THE MONEY: DETERMINING HOW MUCH YOU CAN INVEST

Only by determining how much it will cost you to run your business and how much money you are likely to make can you know whether to pursue your idea. Remember your reason for pursuing a business idea should be to make money at it. Even if it is a nonprofit, you still need to raise money to run it.

Start by taking a personal financial snapshot. How much money do you need and how much money do you have? You will be performing a balancing act between living expenses and start-up costs, so it's critical that you determine from the onset just how much money you are willing and able to set aside to get your business off the ground.

Here are four steps to help you better understand your financial picture:

Step One: Create a start-up expense chart. List each cost—inventory, rent, business equipment, and furniture (i.e., computer, desk, fax machine, copier), office supplies, advertising, telephone services, professional services (accountant, lawyer), licenses, or permit fees. Determine how much of your own money you can invest in the business by setting up a personal balance sheet. List all your assets and their value—cash, savings, checking accounts, securities (bonds, stocks, and mutual funds), car, personal assets, and so forth. Next, list all debts—credit cards, rent, monthly bills, student loans, car loans, and any other loan. If your assets exceed your liabilities, you're in pretty good shape, especially when you need to apply for a bank loan or other business credit. But if you have more liabilities than assets, you should consider paying off as much debt as possible before plunging into business. Too many credit card debts or outstanding loans can put a damper on things. How can you concentrate on building your business if you are overwhelmed with debt and constantly trying to beat away creditors with a stick?

Step Two: Build a cash cushion. The rule of thumb is to set aside about six months' worth of living expenses to fall back on during lean-and-mean times. If you are employed, start saving now. Look for a way to build up savings while reducing debt (refer to Chapter 15). Otherwise you will have to figure out how you can make more money from your venture. Or maybe you should stay at your current job until your finances are in order. Always plan on everything in a start-up business to take twice as long and cost twice as much as you expect. If a client says "I will pay you in 30 days," you should plan for having to wait 60 to 90 days until you get your money. Always think through a contingency plan.

Step Three: Develop a budget. Calculate how much money you need to start your business. Include the cost of your living expenses during the start-up phase. Don't assume you can live on bread and water until the business starts to make a profit. Living too harshly can distort your judgment and dampen your spirits. Determine how much money you need to pay yourself to cover basic living expenses and how much you need to run the business. For example, if it will cost you $50,000 to start the business and $25,000 to cover your living expenses, then the initial investment required is actually $75,000. Don't try to raise money to cover business costs without figuring out how much you need to live on. I'm sure it comes as no surprise that if you make $50,000 a year but spend $75,000, you are living well above your means. You know, champagne taste with a beer budget. When calculating how much money you need to earn to cover all living expenses, don't forget to account for taxes, health insurance, and other additional costs.

Step Four: Do a break-even analysis. An efficient way to determine how many products you need to sell to stay in business—and just how much you need to invest in it before you

make money—is to do a break-even analysis. You break even
when your gross profits equal your fixed costs, meaning you're
neither losing nor making money (see Example A). Look at
your short-term and long-term finances. The former is about 12
months, the latter is between two and five years. You will have
to survive the short-term to make it to the long-term. The average business owner makes somewhere around $30,000 to
$40,000 a year in salary.

EXAMPLE A: THE COSTS OF DOING BUSINESS

To better grasp how you break even, you need to understand
the two types of costs. The first is variable costs—total cost
varies depending on how many products you sell. Let's say you
are a retailer who sells baseball jerseys, which you buy from a
wholesaler for $5. Your variable cost per unit (for one) is $5. If
you charge $20 per jersey, your gross profit is $15. Sales revenue per unit ($20) $—variable cost ($5) = gross profit ($15).

The second is fixed costs (a.k.a. overhead costs)—the
amount of money you have to pay each month regardless of
how many items you sell. When thinking of overhead costs, you
may want to use the acronym USAIIR—for utilities, salaries,
advertising, interest (credit card or loan payments), insurance,
and rent. Say, these costs for your retail business add up to
$3,000.

Break Even Formula (fixed costs ÷ gross profit):	
Total overhead costs	$3,000
Gross profit per unit	$15.00

*You need to sell 200 baseball jerseys each month in order
to break even.*

Entrepreneurs are constantly venturing into new markets, trying to supply those markets efficiently to make a profit.
Statistics show that only 20 percent of all start-ups last long

enough to celebrate their five-year anniversary. Closing a business doesn't necessarily signify failure. Some successful entrepreneurs have been known to start and fail at several businesses before hitting on the one that is profitable.

When you start a business, you will take chances by following your whims and risking failure by testing them. But know that it takes some time for a business to turn a profit. On average, it takes three years just to break even. Most businesses fail because they lack the financial wherewithal or management skills needed to stand the test of time. If you are obsessed with constantly improving yourself and your enterprise, both bodies will get bigger, better, stronger, faster, tougher, smarter and—if you hang with it long enough—financially well-off.

KEVIN SMITH, PRESIDENT OF VIEW ASKEW PRODUCTIONS

Kevin Smith has been crowned by the media as the king of Gen X cinema. While most filmmakers head for the hills of

Miramax Films/Lorenza Bevilaqua

KEVIN SMITH

Hollywood, Smith continues to reside in the small town of Red Bank, New Jersey. The 28-year-old director–screen writer has four films to his credit: *Clerks, Mallrats, Chasing Amy,* and *Dogma.* But Smith is more than just a cutting edge young filmmaker, he is an inventive entrepreneur.

The proprietor of View Askew Productions, Smith took his love of filmmaking, comic books, and the Internet and turned it into one of the fastest growing novelty companies in the country.

The View Askew Website (www.viewaskew.com) is a forum where they can speak their minds about Smith's films and an online catalogue to order merchandise. Taking the profits from his films, Smith started an anciliary business called Jay and Silent Bob's Secret Stash, a retail outlet that sells comics, trading cards, toys, key chains, bumper stickers, posters, T-shirts, and paraphernalia related to Smith's movies.

I have always enjoyed commerce, and I wanted to keep a foot in sales to some degree. Having worked in a retail store for years before I started a film production company, it's something I knew well. After the film Mallrats *tanked, I created an electric bulletin board where (moviegoers) could voice their views. On the board, fans started asking about the availability of merchandise, such as T-shirts and posters. It made sense to give them what they wanted. The opportunity came up to buy this comic book store. I had been a long time patron, and since comic books had been a passion of mine since I was a kid, I thought why not run the store and use it as a place to sell merchandise for my flicks as well. It's a lot like what Spike Lee did when he opened his boutique, Spike's Joint, to sell his own clothing line.*

The indie filmmaker isn't banking on just merchandise associated with his flicks or the comics. It's the synergy of the two, he says, that makes the store a profitable business. Loyal comic book fans regularly patronize the shop, while starstruck movie fans visit the store in hopes of meeting Smith and others, such as Jason Mewes, who starred in *Clerks,* and sometimes lends a hand in the store.

Walter Flannagan (store manager) who does our ordering has his finger on the pulse of the comic book industry. But if this was just a flat-out comic book store it might be lackluster in terms of business. If it were just View Askew merchandise there would be no reason to have a store; we could easily sell the merchandise via the Website. But we're unique in that people travel from states away to shop at the store. People like that I take time to chat with them when they make the trip. It's kind of like a mom-and-pop operation.

After spending a semester at Brookdale Community College and several months at the Vancouver Film School, Smith was back in his hometown working at a convenience store, earning $5 an hour. Then it dawned on him: Why not make a movie based on the life of a convenience store clerk? It took him a little over a month to write the screenplay for *Clerks*. He took $27,000 from twelve credit cards, a FEMA grant, and the sale of his comic book collection to finance the film. He shot the black-and-white film at the store where he worked (after hours). Smith sold his film debut to Miramax for $227,000 at the 1994 Sundance Film Festival. *Clerks* received rave reviews and awards at Sundance and Cannes.

At 24, Smith was a highly touted new filmmaker. It was at this point that he incorporated his production company to protect its name and identity. View Askew has its own logo, a "vulgar" clown.

Smith has a first-look deal with Miramax, meaning the studio gets first crack at any new scripts or projects View Askew develops. In exchange, Miramax pays for the day-to-day operations of the production company. The deal is set up in two-year time periods. The retail store basically pays for itself from the revenues it generates.

Smith's second film was *Mallrats*, which Universal Pictures financed for $6.1 million. The 1995 comedy flopped. But he made a comeback that following year with *Chasing Amy*, a raunchy comedy based on the theme: Boy meets lesbian.

Smith made the film for $250,000. It grossed Miramax $12 million.

Smith was commissioned in 1997 to write the script for Warner Bros.' big-budgeted *Superman Lives*. He got paid $375,000 for six weeks of work (but the script was later canned). *Good Will Hunting*, which Smith co-executive produced, has hit $100 million and won the 1998 Oscar for Best Original Screenplay. He and his producing partner were credited as executive producers on the project. In the meantime, fans eagerly await Smith's fourth film, *Dogma*, an end of the world road movie.

Smith uses his paychecks as a script writer to expand his comic book store. He has some 10 employees, about five to eight people at the production company and two at the retail store. Jay and Silent Bob's Secret Stash averages 10 to 15 orders off the Website a day, ranging in price from $20 to $200 per item. The bulk of the revenue is derived from in-store sales

We're attracting a lot of fans now from all over the country. We want to turn the store into a museum of sorts, where we can feature props from the films and showcase other items. Up until now we have relied mostly on word of mouth, and have done quite well. But we want to reach fans who don't have Internet access. We've advertised the store in a series of Marvel Comics to help us expand our market base.

It was consumer demand that led Smith to launch an Internet site in the first place. He came across a number of *Clerks* home pages. There was one that Smith particularly liked. He contacted the designer to develop View Askew's Website; Smith wrote all of the text. The site attracts cybernauts from across the world, ranging in age from 14 to 52.

We listened to and responded to our market. We never planned this. It all resulted from the movies. If we'd tried to plan this, it wouldn't have happened. Sometimes if an idea is calculated too much it's not going to pan out.

The site has five main content areas: The Films—footage

from *Clerks, Mallrats,* and *Chasing Amy;* Gallery Askew—behind-the-scenes movie photos; Jay and Silent Bob's Secret Stash—scripts, posters, T-shirts, and movie merchandise; Links Askew—links and reviews written on Smith; and, The WWWBoard—a bulletin board for inquiring fans, on which Smith interacts regularly with his audience.

Most View Askew merchandise is sold via mail order. Items are shipped directly from the offices of View Askew. There have been a few quandaries, including a backlog—namely orders for autographed items that Smith wasn't able to sign in a timely manner.

There were a few cases where we came up with items that people just didn't take to. We had a shirt that sold slowly—we made 100 of them and it took a year to sell out of them. The shirt was attractive to us but it wasn't what the fans wanted. The Website is a great way for us to interact with our fans and to find out what they want. They'll tell us they want to buy a Clerks *poster or book, so we're not treading water or working in a vacuum. They keep us informed.*

Smith's experiences in Tinsel Town have taught him some serious lessons about negotiations. He notes his hands are somewhat tied, because he doesn't own all of the merchandising rights to his films. Universal Pictures owns *Mallrats* and Miramax owns *Clerks* and *Chasing Amy.* In other words, if Smith wanted to create *Mallrats* T-shirts, he would have to get permission from Universal.

There was a hat that was in Chasing Amy *that people really wanted—one of the characters in the movie wore it all of the time. In order to make that hat we would have to license it back from Miramax even though I designed it myself. In retrospect, I would have created the hat and allowed the production company to use it but retained ownership. So, when it came time to mass produce it and sell it over the Website, I wouldn't have to get permission from anyone else.*

Smith describes his business style as grassroots-oriented. His main concerns right now are satisfying his customers and maintaining his market niche. He has no intention of growing the three-prong business too quickly.

Our audience is big but it's not large enough to sell our items in, say, Suncoast or Blockbuster stores. But then we wouldn't want to, because it would kill the charm or authenticity of the merchandise. That's the appeal of the items we sell—you can't get them just anywhere. Our merchandise has cult, not mass appeal.

DAVID MAYS, FOUNDER AND PUBLISHER
OF <u>THE SOURCE</u> MAGAZINE

David Mays belongs to a small band of people who are fortunate enough to turn a hobby into a million-dollar enterprise. The 29-year-old Mays is the founder and publisher of *The Source*, a magazine of hip-hop music, culture, and politics, which boasts a circulation of about 450,000 copies per month and annual sales revenues of approximately $20 million ($4 million in profits).

The Source got its start ten years ago at Harvard University, where hardly anyone would associate the "blue blood" college with rap music. Mays was in his freshman year—a government/political science major—when a friend and fellow classmate urged him to join Harvard's radio station. An 18-year-old Mays served as an on-air personality in the urban music department and as an off-air sales rep in the advertising department.

Responding to what he felt was an unfulfilled market need—a growing population of fans who wanted to hear more rap music on the air—in his sophomore year, Mays helped launch a two-hour weekly show that focused on rap music, called *Street Beat*. Despite the show's popularity, he needed something to entice local Boston businesses to financially sponsor it. So, he created *The Source* newsletter.

The Source premiered in the fall of 1988, just two years after *Street Beat* first aired. Mays used $250 and a mailing list of

1,000 radio listeners—which he had compiled to learn about their listening and buying habits—to send out copies of the newsletter. *The Source* included a chart of top songs, news columns, and a listing of upcoming concerts and album releases. The newsletter became such a big hit with Boston teens, that Mays thought about expanding it as a magazine— one that would be national and could serve the rising multitude of rap fans.

During my senior year, I did research on magazine publishing. I used Rolling Stone *as my model. It had started out as a newspaper for what was then an underground culture for rock and roll fans. It evolved into what is today—the Bible of popular music and culture.*

Mays hooked up with his roommate Jon Shecter to put out the second issue of the newsletter. When it became a magazine, two fellow grads joined the crew, James Bernard and Edward Young (the only other founder who is still on board, serving as *The Source's* associate publisher). Taking a year off from school, Young, who is 29, had worked at *The New Republic* magazine where he learned the ins and outs of magazine publishing from editorial to production.

The founders went to work on a business plan and a prototype of the publication (content and photos). Initially, they operated out of Mays's dorm room, then a small apartment off campus. *The Source* was self-funded from prepaid ad space sold mostly to record companies that were seeking venues to promote their rap artists. By the fourth issue the partners were printing 80 pages with a four-color glossy cover and charging $1.25 retail.

I targeted independent record stores where their dominant sales were rap. I knew that my market shopped at those places. the challenge was that most of these were mom-and-pop stores that didn't sell magazines. We convinced them to sell ours on a consignment basis (payment was due only after all the copies were sold). Distribution was key to our success.

For a couple of dollars each, Mays purchased little metal typing stands from a local stationery store and used them as magazine racks. He gave each store a stand and about 30 copies of the magazine. They were in business—the magazines sold out.

The stores realize this was a great way to draw repeat customers. Kids would come in every month and ask for the latest copy of The Source. *They were buying a lot of the music that we were reviewing. The record company ads were also influencing their buying habits. We started selling out 200 copies in certain locations. By the fourth issue we were doing about 15,000 copies total.*

For the first several years, Mays handled the editorial, art, and production. On the distribution end of the magazine he maintained a database of readers, printed out mailing lists, coded the magazines, boxed and delivered them to the stores, sent out invoices, tracked payments, and picked up returns. On the advertising sales side, Mays continued to solicit major record companies, but he avoided other large corporate accounts like sneaker companies and automakers; in part, because of the negative stereotypes associated with rap music.

After graduation, the Washington, D.C. native took up permanent residence in New York. With $80,000 in prepaid ads from six major record labels, the group could run *The Source.* Mays looked to more traditional routes of distribution to get the magazine on the newsstands. Even though each region and city has a different set of outlets to sell magazines, every publisher has to go through the same handful of national distributors. *The Source* got rejected by every single one.

After that, we went to wholesalers, the next level down from distributors. We worked out arrangements with them to get the magazine on the stands in certain markets—New York, L.A., and the Bay Area (San Francisco/Oakland). The Source *got a track record this way. In spring of 1991, we landed our first national distributor with a printing of 80,000 copies.*

Mays and his partners used creative strategies to market the magazine. For example, they gave free subscriptions to every radio DJ in the country who played rap, whether it was a station in Iowa or New York. They sent out faxes, labeled *The Weekly Word*, which was a sheet of hip-hop facts that could be read over the air.

By 1997, *The Source* was a top-selling music magazine on the newsstands—next to *Spin*, *Vibe*, *Rolling Stone*, and *Details*. Newsstand sales account for 88 percent of *The Source*'s circulation, or about 375,000. In other words, most of the magazine's sales were single copies; subscriptions accounted for about 50,000. In comparison, notes Mays, *Rolling Stone* had a total paid circulation of 1.2 million, but their newsstand sales accounted for 200,000 copies.

There will come a time where we will max out on what we can do on the newsstand. We have started to examine creative ways to get people to subscribe. Our demographics are 15- to 25-year-old males. There are a lot of challenges involved in getting this demographic group to subscribe. Many of them are still in high school or college, which means they move around a lot. So, they don't really have a permanent address. They may not be able to charge or write a check for subscriptions. It's often easier for them to pay cash and buy a copy of the magazine off the newsstands each month.

Most magazines solicit subscribers through direct mail and insert cards offering discounts, which can be a costly business expense. Mays believes if he can get circulation up to 500,000, he can command more advertising dollars. Advertising has been a formidable task for Mays, who continues to push the idea that his readers are powerful and influential consumers. While rap has become more accepted within mainstream culture, the violent deaths of rappers Tupac Shakur and Biggie Smalls have intensified some advertisers' reluctance to be associated with rap and hip-hop.

In some ways rap is similar to rock and roll, which was consid-

ered a rebellious and corruptive force in the late '50s and '60s. People were afraid that it was destroying America's youth. Rolling Stone has the challenge of dealing with that perception. But the big difference between us and them is that we are dealing with the race element. We still have to combat ingrained stereotypes and prejudices. (Mays is white and so is half of *The Source's* readership.)

The biggest break for *The Source* came in 1993 when it snared advertising from major sneaker companies: Fila, Nike, and Converse. By 1996, the magazine was pulling in beverage ads from Pepsi-Cola, Mountain Dew, and Coca-Cola, and in 1997 it inked deals with VISA USA, DKNY, Gillette, and Nautica. Advertising pages had grown from 550 to 1,076.

In addition, Mountain Dew sponsors *Source* vans (customized Sierra crew cubs equipped with a 500-watt Pioneer mega stereo system, a Sony Playstation and color video monitor, and a 50-case cooler). For the past five years, *Source* vans have traveled from city to city blasting the latest beats and handing out promotional materials, free cassettes, posters, and copies of the magazine. Mays describes it as "the ice cream truck of hip-hop."

The Source is going through a transitional period as Mays and Young (the other two partners bailed out in 1994) try to recoup from negative events—namely, fleeing key editorial members have launched a competitive magazine called *XXL*—and attempt to build up their sales and marketing force. Mays recently added a controller to the 44-person staff. The magazine moved into a new 15,000-sq.-ft office.

Mays and company recently opened an office in Los Angeles to head up Source Entertainment. The company division already has three television programs in development and a screenplay for a feature film. In addition, the company has released two CD compilations (available at any record store): "*The Source* Presents Hip Hop Hits, Volume One," which sold over 800,000 copies, and "*The Source* Presents Hits From The

Vault, Volume One" (a collection of old-school classics). The success of the CDs comes off the growing popularity of May's new magazine.

Last year, we added an offshoot publication, called The Source Sports, *which looks at sports from a hip-hop perspective. If you look at today's athletes, many of the "big" or emerging stars are people who come out of the hip-hop generation.* Source Sports *is a way to give readers more insight into their lives. The long-term goal is to build* The Source *brand name by adding ancillary products, including television and radio programs, merchandising, and retail books.*

Getting Started

3

THE ROAD MAP TO SUCCESS
The Business Plan

Sometimes you need a map, sometimes you need a globe,
sometimes you need a map and a globe—but not very often.
—Ellen DeGeneres, comedian and author of
My Point ... and I Do Have One. . .

You wouldn't take off on a road trip across the country without a set of directions from one city to the next, would you? Well, if you start a company without a business plan, that's exactly what you would be doing—driving along without any real sense of where you are headed. Even though you know your final destination you still could get lost along the way. How would you find your way back without any means of correcting your course?

Any business idea will sound great in your head. It's not until you put it down on paper that you can tell how real it is. Your business plan illustrates your entrepreneurial concept. A business plan forces you and other key managers to clarify the strategic plans for business growth by putting "feelings" and "thoughts" to paper.

There are three resources that must be maximized to ensure your business success—money, strategy, and people. A business plan provides a detailed description of the best way to optimize these resources.

A business plan will help you to recognize risks and weaknesses as well as opportunities and strengths. Solid ideas will be validated by sound calculations. For this reason alone, you should create a business plan. You'll save a lot of time and money if you can work out any kinks in the planning stage rather than sinking thousands of dollars in a venture beset with shortcomings.

Writing a business plan enables you to think your business through—everything you need to do to get the business up and running and to keep it afloat. If your business does veer off course, you can compare actual performance against your written plan.

Just as well, the business plan provides direction for you and your employees, investors, suppliers, and everyone else involved with the business. These people won't want to blindly follow your short-term directions; they will want to know exactly where the company is heading.

The business plan requires enormous time and effort. It should be somewhere between 20 to 50 pages in length and could take up to six months to write. The number one reason would-be business owners fail to have a concrete business plan is because they don't want to take the time to write one—especially when it entails cumbersome financial statements. Don't kid yourself and assume the day-to-day running of the business is more important than putting together some lengthy document.

Any company that is not able to recognize the value of a business plan or unwilling to make such a commitment should not expect outside investors to commit their time and money to its business. A business plan is a sales document for raising capital. The business plan is the first thing investors and bankers ask to see.

While enthusiasm alone may convince your family and friends that your business is destined for greatness, investors and bankers want the facts. They want an objective, in-depth analysis of the business opportunity with all the attendant risks and obstacles laid out in your plan.

In the end, a business plan is a work-in-progress. It's a living document—not a last will and testament. In other words, it should be adjusted once a year based on actual results and changes in the marketplace.

WRITING A WINNING BUSINESS PLAN

A business plan serves several purposes: as a development tool for the company's founders, a planning and evaluation tool for managers and key personnel, and a mission statement for customers. Some business owners write different versions of plans, tailoring them to a specific audience—such as bankers, investors, distributors, suppliers, or customers.

Regardless of a particular target audience, the basic format for the business plan can be broken down into four sections:

Executive summary: An entire description of the business in an easily digestible format.

Strategic overview: What are we doing, and why have we decided to do this?

Tactical overview: How are we going to do this, and what happens if something goes wrong?

Financial overview: How much money do we need and where will it come from?

Executive Summary:

- Description of the business
- Overview of the intended market
- Location of the business
- Brief summary of key management
- Capital requirements
- Collateral/capital sources
- Key success factors
- Achievements to date

Even though every business plan begins with an executive summary, you should write this part last. Think through and fill out the other components first, then write the summary. This concise one-page opening is exactly what its name implies—a summary that tells investors or other interested parties what your business is about. It begins by describing the nature of your business—retail, manufacturing, or service; your product(s) and target market. Second, it notes key officers and their qualifications. Finally, it indicates how much money you're requesting and for what purpose, as well as the potential return on the investment and the payback period.

Strategic Overview: This area explains what type of business you are in, why the market and time is right for your product or service, who's your target audience, and how you plan to go after that market. This section entails:

- *Mission Statement*—This provides a precise definition of the business and answers to the questions: What products or services will it provide? Who's your target market? What customer need does your product or service satisfy? How will the product be produced and distributed? The mission statement also includes a visionary paragraph—your long-term goals.

- *Strategic Plan*—Once you have stated the mission of your business, you need to provide a statement that describes your plan or strategy for success. Your business strategy should be built around two or more key talents or abilities that give your company a competitive edge.

- *Market Audience*—Identify your customer and provide a customer profile. It adds credibility to your plan, showing that you have done your homework in establishing why people are willing to buy what you are selling. You should provide a demographic profile—i.e., age, sex, income, and size of your overall target market—as well as a psychographic profile—values, lifestyle interests, buying habits, and affinities of your target audience.

- *Competition*—What makes your company more attractive and effective than your competitors? Obviously, coming up with new quality products or services appeals to customers. Some characteristics must set your business apart from competitors. This may mean you have a patent for a new product, proprietary technology, access to a scarce resource, greater distribution outlets, or a signature product/service. No matter what the type of business, certain key elements should not be forgotten. For example, good food and courteous service is a must in the restaurant business. Prompt and reliable service is key in the mail/package delivery business. Put down those key factors that will make a difference between success and failure.

Tactical Overview: This component will show how you intend to get your product or service to customers or your target market. Discuss the product, market, and revenues as well as methods of distribution, pricing structure, business operations, and industry trends. A major part of the tactical overview is the sales and marketing plan, which should be both strategic and operational. What are major challenges and opportunities in the market? The main components are:

- *Product Description*—Provide a detailed outline of the product or service offered. Product/service elements include price, features and benefits, services, functions and uses, delivery, look, feel, touch, or any other characteristic associated with the purchase. What market changes are likely to occur? How does your product or service differ from competitors? Is it better, faster, cheaper, or superior in some way?

- *Market Description*—Discuss the history, recent growth trends, expected future growth, and geography of your target market. What are the barriers of entry to this market? How will you time your entry into the marketplace—some products are affected by seasons or the weather. What are the significant economies of scale? The market description should be supported by reputable market research. Back up data and statistics about your customers with census reports, surveys, and test-market results.

- *Competitive Analysis*—This section examines both direct and indirect competitors. Discuss their market share; number, types, and location of customers; profitability; revenues; product strengths and weaknesses, and recent and expected growth. Also, include a brief history on their businesses. Describe the basis on which you will compete (i.e., price, quality, technology, service, and convenience). What is your current and projected market share? How do you stack up against the competition? Are you a leader or follower, innovator or copier?

- *Methods of Distribution*—This segment should describe how your product is physically transported to customers or how services will be made available to customers. Discuss how you will sell your product (i.e., mail-order catalogs, in-store purchases, etc.) and who will sell it (i.e., sales staff, independent sales representatives, telemarketers, etc.). If you have a service business, discuss whether customers will come to you or will you go to them. If you plan to import or export products, describe trade regulations, licensing requirements, tariffs, quotas, and other government-imposed trade restrictions. You should also include backup plans for delivering your product or service and retaining customers—what happens if machinery or delivery vehicles break down or employees don't show up to work?

- *Promotion*—This section describes how you will inform customers about the benefits of your product or service. Will you use direct mail or paid advertising through radio, television, newspapers, or magazines? How much will your advertising campaign cost? Will you promote your business in the telephone Yellow Pages or trade and professional directories? How cost-effective are these directory listings? You should also discuss "free" advertising, such as word of mouth, public service announcements, and interviews or publicity as a result of press releases sent to media outlets. Moreover, will you promote your business by participating in trade shows, community events, or business organizations of which you are a member?

- *Pricing*—New entrepreneurs often give little attention to pricing decisions. They tend to concentrate on volume and fail to examine the complexities of pricing and costs that are linked to sales and profit. Your pricing structure should take into account the material, labor, and overhead costs of producing a product or service. Moreover, determine what is the highest price a customer will pay for your product or service? What is the lowest price you can offer and still meet your costs and make a profit?

- *Packaging*—This section describes the design of your product and package, which should be competitive in terms of size, color, shape, material, labeling, and appearance. It should also address concerns with quality, safety, and technical standards. The Federal Trade Commission (FTC), whose headquarters is in Washington, D.C., but has regional offices throughout the United States, regulates advertising, pricing, packaging, and merchandising. Check with the FTC for any information they can supply to help your business. In particular, ask about the Fair Packaging and Labeling Act. In addition, include information on trademarks, patents, and copyrights.

- *Sales Forecast*—The sales and marketing plan should include a detailed sales forecast for the first year of operation.

This refers to the actual sales you predict your company will attain. You can arrive at this figure from primary sources, including market research, surveys, and tests. Or you can turn to secondary sources such as U.S. Census Bureau Reports, Chamber of Commerce data, *Statistical Abstract of the U.S.*, and the *Sales and Marketing Management Survey of Buying Power* (available at the library).

- *Ancillary Product Opportunities*—This area examines future product and service extensions (i.e., licensing, merchandising, and franchising). Demonstrate the potential for spin-off opportunities. Describe additional costs to execute such opportunities. Ancillary products should contribute to net income.

- *Industry Trends*—An analysis of possible changes in your industry will help you maintain a healthy business through good and bad times. New technology may affect your market, product, or service. Examine economic forces. How much time and money will you need to keep up with new developments in your industry and remain competitive?

The tactical overview also includes a section on operations. How specific you get depends on the type of business you're trying to describe. Operations describes how that product or service is acquired or produced and made ready for sale. Key factors are:

- *Materials*—What supplies do you require and from whom will you purchase them?

- *Labor*—Does your business require specialized skilled labor? Can you attract and afford the kind of people needed to run your business?

- *Facilities*—How much space do you have now and how much will you need in the long run. What's the impact of your location on customers? What are the operating costs (heat, light, phone, water, and general upkeep)? Are you leasing or purchasing the property? Are renovations necessary? Will you need specific types of equipment to operate (i.e., machines, computers, delivery vehicles)? Provide a list of what you will need.

• *Processes*—What's required in the preparation of the product or service being offered? For instance, is your product made to order or stocked as warehousing inventory. With a restaurant, the processes are food preparation and table service. In addition, discuss any business milestones, proprietary items, research, development, service, and external influences (i.e., government regulation or technological change).

Management Team: Smart money invests in people. Your plan should include a section on management, which consists of biographies of yourself and other managers, noting relevant skills, degrees, and experience. Provide a half-page (no more than one-page) narrative on those individuals relative to business operations. While a resume tells a great deal about someone's background, you should include them as appendices. The management section entails:

• *Personal Background*—Provide a brief glimpse into the lives of key members on your team. It doesn't hurt to mention activities relative to the community, especially civic groups. You want to note anything that shows you and your colleagues are levelheaded and serious about the business. Your financial stability will also be called into question. In a sentence or two explain why that individual is eagerly and earnestly partaking in this business venture.

• *Employment History and Industry Experience*—Again, a resume will list previous jobs and titles, but you should pull out and amplify relevant experience. Having worked for a small business is a plus in substantiating that you understand the inner workings of a small enterprise. Another good indicator is previous management experience—supervising and training people is an important part of entrepreneurship. Include the number of years you spent in management, number of people supervised, size of the budget, and the department or division that was your responsibility. It makes perfect sense that you should have had previous experience in the field in which you intend to start a business. If not, you might consider working for someone else to get some experience in that area. You want to demonstrate that you understand this business firsthand. Even if you tried it before and failed, this wouldn't necessarily work against you, because you could show that you learned something from your mistakes and now know what it takes to succeed.

• *Education*—State your educational credentials in a simple, straightforward way. Expand on areas relevant to your business. For instance, a certificate in culinary arts is significant if you're opening a restaurant.

• *Organizational Chart*—Unless your business is very simplistic, you should include an organizational chart that breaks down the company into individuals or groups assigned to certain business functions, such as finance, marketing, management, production, design, personnel, and manufacturing. If you are starting out with only a few people, you should include an organizational chart depicting what the company will look like three years from now. In other words, your name may be filled in several spots for the first year, but by the third year of operation—as the company grows—you intend to bring more employees into the company to take on some of those responsibilities. You can make a list of the job titles you plan to fill and when over the next few years. Ideally, you want to show that you have every base covered in the *people* department. Note that this can be accomplished through advisors, consultants, or independent contractors—as long as someone has the necessary experience.

- *Duties*—Spell out the responsibilities of each person. Who does what? Who reports to whom? Who has final say on decisions?

- *Salaries*—It's vital that your plan clearly examines how much and the manner in which key employees will be paid.

Financial Statements and Requirements: Financial data and calculations are the make-or-break component of any business plan. After all, the goal is to be profitable. Moreover, financial statements are numerical representations of what your company is physically doing. Whether you are a start-up or an existing business, provide projections for three to five years out. The first year's data should be forecast monthly, and later years should be projected quarterly. Indicate expected highs and lows of the business. This section will show how much you'll need to run the business and where the money will come from. You'll need to include the following documents:

- *Pro-forma (Projected) Cash Flow Statement*—This charts the movement of funds coming in (receipts) and flowing out of (disbursements) the company. By monitoring the sources and uses of cash, you will have an idea of how much money or credit you'll need to carry out planned operations. More important, you will be alerted when cash runs short. Forecast three to five years out. (see Example A on page 64)

- *Three-Year Income Projection (or Profit-and-Loss Statement)* —This section compares total revenues against all operating costs and expenses (i.e., salaries, supplies, insurance, marketing, overhead). Organized by fiscal year, these tables are used to determine net income and are updated annually. (see Example B on page 64)

• *Balance Sheet*—This lists current assets (cash, inventory, supplies, equipment, and fixtures). It shows the status of the company's assets, liabilities, and equity ownership. You should have a current financial snapshot of the business as well as a projected balance sheet showing how these figures are likely to change over time. (see Example C on page 65)

• *Break-Even Analysis*—This section shows how long it will take to make a profit. This figure is arrived at by measuring your fixed costs (bills you have to pay every month regardless of sales) and variable costs (the amount it costs you to make or buy each product you plan to sell) against projected revenue. How many products do you need to sell so that your gross profits (revenues minus variable costs) equal your fixed costs each month? Simply put: You're neither making nor losing money.

• *Financial Needs and Uses of Funds*—If you're looking for money from lenders or investors you will have to provide two statements up front. The first is a summary of your financial needs in terms of working capital, expansion capital, and equity capital. Spell out why you are applying for a loan or investment capital, and how much you need. The second is a loan fund dispersal statement, which describes in detail how you intend to utilize the funds, backed up with supporting data.

COURTING FINANCIERS

While a good business plan is one that raises money, it is important that you tailor your plan to the type of financing you need. There are two major categories of financing: debt (loan) and equity (ownership interest).

Bankers are primarily interested in the company's fixed assets (building, equipment, inventory, etc.) and the collateral the business can offer. The bank's main concern is how and if you are going to pay back the loan at the going interest rate.

However, venture capitalists and other investment groups will want a chunk of your company and its profits. Usually, they want to earn at least a 45 percent compounded annual return on their investment. In other words, they want to get back six times their money in three to five years.

Make sure you address the return on the investment (ROI) in your proposal. This figure is arrived at by dividing the business income by the investment amount and multiplying that number by 100 percent. Say, someone invests $20,000 in your business. In a year, you pay that person back $25,000. Your investor will receive a $5,000 income (profit), or an ROI of 25 percent.

Another difference between bankers and venture capitalists is the way they gain control of the business's operations via their loan or investment. Bankers build covenants into the loan arrangement. For instance, if you don't pay, they can fine you for every day the payment is late or call the loan or sell the collateral. Venture capitalists may want seats on your board of directors to exercise control. (You'll find more on bankers and venture capitalists in Chapter 5.)

Most venture capitalists and bankers can analyze your plan in 10 minutes and decide if they are interested. They can tell how realistic your business concept is from your financial statements. In your plan, you should emphasize the figures that are important to a venture capitalist or banker, as well as your personal history, product information, and potential market share. In general, venture capitalists like to provide funds to existing businesses looking to expand, and commercial banks scowl at lending to small fledging businesses.

One success secret of seasoned entrepreneurs is to constantly update the business plan—some revise their plans quarterly.

EXAMPLE A: MONTHLY CASH FLOW

	Month	(January thru December)	Total (Year)
1. CASH ON HAND (Beginning of the month)		$_____	$_____
2. REVENUES (Inflow) (Cash sales)		$_____	$_____
3. TOTAL CASH AVAILABLE (1+2)		$_____	$_____
4. CASH PAID OUT (Outflow) (Expenses)			
(a) Utilities		$_____	$_____
(b) Salaries		$_____	$_____
(c) Supplies		$_____	$_____
(d) Advertising		$_____	$_____
(e) Insurance		$_____	$_____
(f) Interest		$_____	$_____
(g) Rent		$_____	$_____
(h) Taxes		$_____	$_____
(i) Miscellaneous		$_____	$_____
5. TOTAL CASH PAID OUT (Total of 4a thru 4i)		$_____	$_____
6. CASH POSITION (2–5) (End of the month)		$_____	$_____

EXAMPLE B: INCOME STATEMENT

1. Sales Revenue (Selling price x each item sold)		$_____
2. Variable Cost (Unit cost of goods/services sold)		$_____
3. Gross Profit (Revenue–Variable Cost)		$_____
4. Fixed Costs (Monthly overhead costs)		$_____
(a) Utilities	$_____	
(b) Salaries	$_____	
(c) Supplies	$_____	
(d) Advertising	$_____	
(e) Insurance	$_____	
(f) Interest	$_____	
(g) Rent	$_____	
5. Total Fixed Costs (Total of 4a thru 4g)		$_____
6. Profit Before Taxes (Gross Profit–Total Fixed Costs)		$_____
7. Income Taxes		$_____
8. Net Profit (Profit–Income Taxes)		$_____

EXAMPLE C: BALANCE SHEET

1. Current Assets
    (a) Cash In Bank $_____
    (b) Accounts Receivable (What others owe you) $_____
    (c) Inventory $_____
    (d) Other Current Assets $_____
2. Total Current Assets (Total of 1a thru 1d) $_____
3. Fixed Assets
    (a) Real estate $_____
    (b) Vehicles $_____
    (c) Machinery $_____
    (d) Office Equipment $_____
4. Total Fixed Assets (Total of 3a thru 3d) $_____
5. Total Assets (2 + 4) $_____
6. Current Liabilities
    (a) Accounts Payable (Money you owe vendors,
        suppliers, etc.) $_____
    (b) Credit Card Debt $_____
    (c) Salaries $_____
    (d) Taxes $_____
    (e) Interest (Short-term loans) $_____
7. Total Current Liabilities (Total of 6a thru 6e) $_____
8. Long-term Liabilities
    (a) Mortgage $_____
    (b) Equipment Loans $_____
    (c) Bank Loans $_____
    (d) Other long-term Loans $_____
9. Total Long-term Liabilities (Total of 8a thru 8d) $_____
10. Total Liabilities (6+9) $_____
11. Equity (assets—liabilities) $_____
    (a) Contributed Capital (Common and Preferred Stock) $_____
    (b) Retained Earnings (Net profits/losses
        from current and prior year) $_____
12. Total Equity (11a + 11b) $_____
13. Total Liabilities + Total Equity (10 + 12) $_____

Note: Total liabilities plus total equity should equal total assets.

Use your business plan as a guide for the fiscal year the company is working in. Revisions ought to reflect industry changes as it affects your market share.

Every new fiscal year, add elements to the plan's executive summary on what's happening politically, socially, and economically as it pertains to your business. Unless you monitor and record ongoing changes in your market, it's impossible to chart your company's future.

TODD ALEXANDER, PRESIDENT OF VENDEMMIA, INC.

Aficionados of fine wine in Atlanta are increasingly satisfying their palate with delicate, full-bodied wines from Italy imported by Vendemmia Inc. Four of the largest wine and spirits distributors in the United States are located in Georgia, and the five biggest distributors have cornered the market. Unlike other small companies which bow out in an industry that is crowded with deep-pocketed competitors, Vendemmia is holding its own. The company's 30-year-old founder, Todd Alexander, sums up its success with one word: quality.

I hold my margins by competing on quality and carving out niche markets. Once I created a market for wines that only I have, then they were mine to sell from here on out. As you start to grow, opportunities come from out of the woodwork.

Vendemmia, which means "harvest" in Italian, sells 60 percent of its prized wines to retailers, while the remaining portion is sold to local restaurants. In 1996, the company grossed $1.2 million in revenues and Alexander's estimates for 1997 were $2 million.

Alexander is driven by the fact that he is getting paid for his passion. He developed a love for Italian food, wines, and culture from his travels to the country he first visited as an exchange student in high school. In his junior year as a marketing major at Cornell University, he decided to take a semester off and go to Florence to attend a language school.

Ann States

TODD ALEXANDER

It was during that trip that he became a connoisseur of fine wines and realized it was the industry in which he wanted to work. Upon graduation, Alexander sent out 30 resumes to wine companies in search of a job. Only one company—a small wine import and distribution firm in New Jersey—was willing to give him a shot.

The owner of the company hired me because I was enthusias-

tic about Italian wines and I actually spoke fluent Italian. And I was willing to learn the business. For a year, I became a jack-of-all-trades. I was doing everything from working in the warehouse, to making point-of-sale materials, to going out on sales calls, to helping sales managers track sales reps.

The job, however, became bothersome. There was no one thing that Alexander could sink his teeth into. So, he decided to take a job in the retail side of the business. He went to work for one of the highest-grossing outlets in New York City. In his previous position, Alexander dealt with vendors—store owners, restaurants, and hotels. His new job enabled him to see the actual buying patterns of the end-consumer.

But after a year, Alexander left the retail business to travel back to Italy for three months to write a comprehensive book on Italian wines. The one area he had not been exposed to was how the wine was made. He had never seen a cluster of grapes or a vineyard before. Now here was his chance.

Halfway through the trip, I decided I was going to import Italian wine because wine vintners were dissatisfied with their U.S. distributors or they were not represented at all. Being able to pick up the phone and speak the language allowed me to start as quickly and as efficiently as I did.

This was in 1992 and Alexander was only 25 years old. Entry into the market was fraught with problems. He took labels of the 60 brands he planned to import, attached a check for the registration costs of each—$10 to $20 per label—and filed the appropriate forms with state and federal governments. Instead of the three months he originally anticipated, it took Alexander 10 months to obtain a license.

The forms were basically name, rank, and serial number in 800 different ways (including a series of personal and financial background checks). There was just so much redundancy in the paperwork and bureaucracy dealing with three different levels of government. Historically, the wine business in this country has grown out of bootlegging. The Bureau of Alcohol, Tobacco, and Firearms still thinks there is a lot of money laundering and other underhanded activity. The industry is heavily regulated. There may have been added suspicion because I was African-American and I was young.

The long wait did give him time to work on his business plan. He was able to launch the company in 1994 with a $50,000 loan from his mother. But Alexander soon learned that fine wines and financing do not the business make.

I went about my business plan in a backwards way. About 95 percent of it was written out of gut instinct, and not market research. I discovered that Atlanta did not have a developed wine market like New York, Chicago, and San Francisco. Store owners were reluctant to shell out top dollar for premium wines.

This error proved costly. Alexander landed his first container of wine (over 1,000 cases) in January of 1994. He was able to sell some vintages, but realized about 250 cases of premium wine should have never been shipped to the States. These were wines that he personally liked, but had little to do with the market dynamics.

Undaunted, Alexander reworked his business plan—this time putting an emphasis on market research. He spent a great deal of time knocking on restaurant doors to solicit buyers. Eventually, they began to open.

I had to go around and educate potential clients. I would take my wines and pour them next to my competitors and show them why mine were more expensive. By the end of the conversation the (store owner or restaurateur) was willing to pay more for premium wines. In turn, they were able to educate their customers as to why they would want to pay more—the added value.

Alexander is fully aware of the ways businesses can compete against each other: Price, location, service, quality, customer relations, and track record. He couldn't compete on price with the big wine and spirits distributors, who have deep pockets.

If you try to compete with them on price alone they will beat you each and every time. A number of people have tried to enter this market and tried to be a "me-too" wholesaler. They were put out of business within two years because they were offering the same products but they could not afford to give a better deal when the big distributors started lowering their prices.

More people are familiar with Vendemmia's wines now. There's also an influx of people moving to Atlanta from markets that are more wine savvy, and the number of Atlanta restaurants is growing. Today, Vendemmia has grown from a one-man show to a five-person staff, including three sales reps and a delivery driver. Alexander no longer races from restaurant to restaurant in his Ford Bronco to deliver cases. While he has just one truck, Alexander has no interest in owning a fleet right now. His business delivers a truckload (200 cases) a day.

Since launching the business, Alexander has repaid the loan from his family and expanded his wine portfolio to include higher-end Italian and French wines. He continues to keep overhead low using free office space in a building his mother owns, and the basement, which was converted into a wine cellar.

The unflagging entrepreneur still contends with the rigors of the industry, such as grape shortages and the mind-bending paperwork that comes with importing. He relies on a customs broker that he found through his old employer, as well as a company that specializes in consolidating freight shipments.

This takes a coordinated effort between three parties to make this run smoothly. The idea is for me to put in an order to Italy for the wines, have them consolidated at the port, put in a container, shipped to a port here in the States, and delivered to my warehouse with as little delay as possible.

In the beginning, Alexander did everything from unloading shipments to mopping floors. These days, he spends much of his time traveling back and forth to Italy trying to expand his band of wine growers. The growers he works with are usually very small wineries, with limited amounts of wine that they can sell.

He asserts that slow growth and his repertoire of quality wines will steer him to even higher gains. Long-term goals are building the company into a $4 billion business. Alexander urges would-be entrepreneurs to learn as much as they can about their industries. He also advises to do what you love. He wasn't bringing home a salary the first two years in business, which is why he believes it's important to be in business for reasons other than money.

This whole thing is a lifestyle choice. I decided when I was in college that I wanted to get paid for something that I would do for free. How could I go to Italy a lot, drink good wine, eat good food, and get paid? This was the obvious choice. All I knew about wine back in college was that I liked drinking wine. It surfaced only after a few years of pushing hard toward what was then a ill-defined goal.

JULIE MARTINES, FOUNDER AND PRESIDENT OF WILL RENT, INC.

When Julie Martines decided to launch her business eight years ago, she had some personal savings and a $50,000 bank loan to get it off the ground. It was just enough money to open the doors to Chicago–based Will Rent, Inc., but it wasn't ample enough to cover the upstart's inventory. Martines, who was 24 years old at the time, wanted to start a construction equipment leasing firm—an enterprise that requires substantial start-up capital and has significant overhead.

She applied for a general Small Business Administration 7(a) guaranteed loan for $250,000. Under this program, the SBA guarantees bank loans up to $750,000 if other financing isn't available. The money isn't actually given by the government but is loaned by a commercial bank or other financial institution.

The borrower submits a loan application to the bank, which reviews it and sends it to a loan officer at a local SBA branch office. If approved, the bank processes the loan and the SBA covers a substantial portion of the risk by guaranteeing up to 75 percent of the value of the loan. The interest rates are negotiable between the borrower and the lender, but generally range from 2 percent to 3 percent above the prime rate (as listed in *The Wall Street Journal*).

That SBA loan was the only way I could start my company. I needed to be able to purchase the construction equipment, otherwise, I would have no business. I was a brand-new business with no track record. It would have been impossible to get a traditional loan. I needed that guarantee.

But getting that loan was not an easy affair. The key was persistence. It was Martines's local banker who suggested she work with a consultant who had expertise packaging this type of government loan, and putting together a winning business plan.

They made sure that the documents I submitted to the SBA were done right the first time, instead of my doing a poor job and having to go back and fill in information. It's not an easy thing to do on your own [applying for a government loan guarantee]. It took about a good six months to put that package together.

It took eight months altogether from applying for the loan to actually winning it. Once the loan came through, Martines was able to lease a building on an acre and a half of property where 10,000 square feet was used to stock inventory and the rest devoted to office space.

Since that time, Will Rent, Inc., has grown into a company that rents some 200 pieces of equipment. Over a year's time, the company has had between 300 and 400 clients, including large contractors, municipalities, and smaller construction companies. The firm's revenues at the end of 1997 were $2.5 million.

Financing is a familiar challenge for many small businesses, but Martines also had to contend with other more personal issues. The young entrepreneur had to combat some people because of her age or race—she's of Mexican descent. But her greatest challenge was fighting the long-held belief that the construction business is man's work.

This is still a male-dominated industry. You find most women who are in the construction industry learned about it from a family member or close friend who has given them the opportunity to understand the business. It was challenging being a woman in this industry when I first started out. People tried to challenge me. They would come flat out and say "what do you know about construction equipment?"

Actually, Martines knows quite a bit. Equipment leasing has been in her family for decades. Her father has run his own construction leasing firm for the past 25 years. While the senior Martines's company primarily rents large-scale equipment, Will Rent, Inc. focuses on smaller scale machinery. The company rents, sells, and services light construction equipment, such as air compressors, skid steers, and aerial work platforms.

My father's business was doing very well. But there was really no one pursuing the light end of the business. So, I felt there was an opportunity here for me. Of course, there was the question about being able to keep the business open and stocked with inventory. This is a capital intensive business. The reason people like to rent construction equipment is because contractors don't want to take on the debt of owning the equipment, which can be very expensive. They use the equipment only when they need it.

Another formidable task for Martines—and any other new entrepreneur—is finding and retaining qualified, energetic, and loyal employees who have the desire to grow with the company. She developed her business skills while working as a designer, before realizing that her greatest strength was problem solving.

Martines holds a degree in design from the University of Wisconsin and has two years experience with an architectural design firm. She worked hand in hand with real estate brokers who were trying to lease space in classy commercial buildings in downtown Chicago. Martines would create construction drawings and space plans for prospective clients. It was the downturn in the real estate market that finally prompted her to set up her own business.

It was definitely a bad time in that industry. I would go to work and every day there would be another body missing. I decided it was better for me to move on instead of going to work one day and finding out I was the next body to go. I have always had the desire to go into business for myself. My mind lent itself more toward the business transaction end of the industry (helping vendors and customers identify and satisfy their needs), more so than sitting down at the drafting table.

Financing continues to be a challenge. Martines points out that managing the company's cash flow can be particularly onerous. Clients tend to pay her in 60 days, but she must pay her banker every 30 days. She is always taking on new debt and new inventory. She recently added $300,000 worth of top-of-the-line equipment. Martines also has a good relationship with her banker and other sources of financing.

Every year when I go to the bank for additional financing, I have to present my plan for growth. Which means every year, I update my business plan. I am also 8(a) certified [an SBA program that sets aside a portion of procurement contracts to qualifying socially disadvantaged businesses]. For that program, you have to prepare an in-depth business plan. You learn a lot by physically putting together a business plan. You may be very knowledgeable about your business, but to actually put it down on paper and show trends in the market, gives you more clearcut information.

For Martines, increasing the size of her business right now means more money, more sales reps, more equipment and—hopefully—more customers. She is bringing in new business by networking and soliciting clients.

Attending networking functions and association meetings has helped me tremendously in terms of identifying leads. It is a lot easier to follow up with people from a social gathering than by making cold calls over the telephone. I spend a lot of my time associating myself with construction trade groups, people who own construction companies, or construction-related firms. These are my clients. I put myself in the mix of people who can possibly lead me to some new business.

Although Martines faces stiff competition, she has managed to make her company stand out by emphasizing customer service. Will Rent also supplies the latest equipment compared to older models offered by competitors. For Martines, a crucial task is maintaining the apparatus.

I have mechanics who work both here in the shop and in the field. We have a very stringent maintenance list. We thoroughly review each piece. When and if it does break down, we are prepared to respond to the problem very quickly. We can't have construction workers standing in the fields twiddling their thumbs and getting paid $30 an hour because our equipment broke down.

Will Rent establishes its prices for rental rates dependent upon what's consistent with the market. There are daily, weekly, and monthly prices for customers who may need to rent a piece of machinery for just one day or as long as six months. Will Rent has pieces of equipment with a purchase (or retail) price of $800; some machines cost well over $100,000.

When Martines looks at today's young CEOs, she sees eager and ambitious individuals, who are smart enough to learn from those who are more experienced than themselves. These are the people she sees carrying the torch into the twenty-first century. The key to success is for new entrepreneurs to stay focused.

New entrepreneurs must be focused and innovative. You are going to have to focus 200 percent of your time on your business. Other areas in your life will have to wait [she's single as are many of her entrepreneurial counterparts]. When I first started out, I was putting in 10 to 12 hours a day, seven days a week. I was there until all wee hours of the night. My family and friends called the office begging me to go home.

4

WHERE'S THE MONEY? FINANCING YOUR BUSINESS

> Your crown has been bought and paid for. All you must do
> is put it on your head.
>
> —*James Baldwin, author*

It takes money to make money. This is the plain and simple truth in business. What prevents a company from becoming successful? A lack of a strong management team, a mediocre business opportunity, and shortfall of capital are the most commonly cited reasons.

Before becoming your own boss, you need to know three things: how much money you need, what you are going to use it for, and where do you plan to get it from. To thoroughly answer these questions, you must understand the pros and cons of different kinds of financing: debt (loans), equity (investors), assets, and other sources.

How much money is required to run your business may dictate the financing source. For instance, if you need to raise over $10 million, venture capital may be the only way to go. From $1 to $5 million, you'll probably have to scout for angels (private investors) or do a private placement (shares of the business are offered for sale to a small group of investors). If you need $50,000 to $1 million, consider lines-of-credit and commercial bank loans, suppliers, customers, and SBA Low-Doc loans. Any would-be entrepreneur who is shopping for less than $50,000 will have to turn to family and friends, credit cards, personal sources, and SBA-sponsored micro loans.

In addition to how much you need, your risk tolerance and level of comfort are critical factors. Ask yourself: How much debt am I comfortable taking on, and do I want to have to make payments every month regardless of my business making money? Or am I willing to hand over a piece of my company in exchange for money from someone I don't know?

BORROWING MONEY: DEBT FINANCING

Whether the money comes from your family or a bank, when you borrow money you are relying on debt financing. Since getting seed money from a commercial institution is nearly impossible, most businesses are started with money from friends and relatives. Others are financed with credit cards. Each has its own set of risks and rewards.

Friends and Family—The great thing about loans from relatives and buddies is that they are inexpensive and you don't need collateral. Your relatives can give you up to $10,000 each year (as a gift) without fretting about paying taxes.

Of course, borrowing money this way, you run the risk of straining family ties. People often get touchy about their money. They may start acting funny and interfere with how you run your business by putting in their two cents or demanding their money back. To lessen that chance, make this a formal deal. Treat a personal loan like any other business transaction.

Draw up a promissory note outlining a repayment schedule and an annual rate (interest charged). You can get preprinted forms at most office supply stores. Document the amount of the loan, the interest rate, and the timetable for repayment. Have all parties sign it.

When drawing up a promissory note, make sure your family

charges you an interest rate that is applicable to federal rates. Each month the federal government sets minimum rates that must be charged on short-term, mid-term, and long-term intrafamily loans. If your relatives charge you less than the going rate, the Internal Revenue Service could tax them on the interest they should have collected. The average interest rate for small business loans is around 9 percent.

Credit Cards—Many entrepreneurs use credit cards as a source of start-up money. It is a way to get several thousand dollars quickly without the hassle of paperwork—most banks and investors require three years of financial statements. If you have four credit cards with a $5,000 limit, that's $20,000, which is much easier to get your hands on than a bank loan for that amount.

Comedic actor Robert Townsend is a regularly cited example of someone who used credit cards to finance a major project. In Townsend's case, he used over $50,000 in credit cards to finance his first movie, *Hollywood Shuffle*.

But using credit cards for start-up funds, working capital, or expansion money may be damaging to your business in the long term if not done carefully. Too many credit cards may interfere with your ability to get a loan at a later date in time. By using your credit cards, you risk destroying your credit rating. What happens if your business doesn't generate enough money to pay for your debt? It is easy to get overextended.

This is why it is best to use credit card financing as a short-term solution for raising money and paying for certain business expenses. Sometimes it's easier to document expenses that are charged to a credit card for entertainment, business travel, and rentals. Plan your cash and credit use carefully, meaning don't charge things that are unplanned for or unnecessary.

If you have to charge emergencies, pay off the amount when the bill comes. Most experts advise you to time your transactions so that you charge items at the beginning of your billing cycle, allowing your business time to collect on receivables that will help pay your credit card bill.

Stay away from high interest rates—anywhere between 12 percent and 18 percent. This can eat up whatever profit you are making. Try to get the lowest rate possible. You may be able to switch to cards with lower introductory rates and fees. Use separate cards for business and personal use.

Banks—Most business advisers suggest borrowing money when you don't need it. A bank wants to see how you pay your bills. So, before you start your business, take out a personal loan for about $2,500 to $5,000 (if necessary with a cosigner). Over the next six months, pay off the loan. Starting this way helps you establish a lender/debtor relationship and gives the banker confidence you'll fulfill your obligations when you later apply for that small business loan or line-of-credit.

When you are ready to request a small business loan, make sure you have a solid business plan and financial statements. It doesn't matter whether you're asking for $10,000 or $1 million. Bankers need the same information whenever a loan application hits their desks.

Here are three key questions—how you answer them can make or break your loan request:

1. How much money do you need? Never ask how much the bank is willing to lend you. If you want to borrow $50,000, be specific about it. Assemble the most precise calculations you can to explain why you need that amount.

2. How will the loan help your business? Banks want to see that the loan will result in additional cash flow, higher sales, or cost reductions, not to beef up your salary.

3. How will you pay back the loan? The primary sources of repayment are business proceeds, conversion of assets, or cash flow. You must prove the business has lasting earning power, which is reflected by a year-long monthly cash flow statement and quarterly projections for the term of the loan.

A banker's decision to accept or reject a loan application is primarily based on the five Cs: character, capital, credit, collateral, and capacity. Other considerations are management, banker/applicant relationship, and economic conditions.

- *Character*—Businesses don't pay banks back, people do. A banker wants to know how credible you are, and will look at how you present yourself. Get people who can speak on your behalf—your lawyer, accountant, mentors, associates you have worked with, community leaders, or religious heads (i.e., rabbi, priest, or pastor). Attach their letters of recommendation to your application.

- *Capital*—The bank wants to know how much money you are anteing up. Too often prospective borrowers fail to bring some cash to the table. Banks like to see you foot at least 20 percent of the total bill. Most commercial banks lend the maximum of three times the amount of capital in a business. So, if you want to borrow $30,000 from your bank, you must have contributed at least $10,000 of your own personal cash and assets to the business. The more you put into your business, the more favorably a bank looks on your application. The bank believes that if the entrepreneur has a substantial stake in the business he/she will be less likely to head for the hills when trouble arises.

- *Credit*—Clean up your personal finances. Banks want to know that you are going to pay back the loan. They will check to see if you have a good credit history. Get a copy of your credit report so you know what it says. If there is anything to your discredit in the report, be upfront and explain the situation to a banker and assure him/her it isn't going to happen again.

- *Collateral*—Banks want to know what property you are willing to pledge as a secondary source of payment. If you get an unsecured loan, then collateral doesn't apply. Even though a bank will have liens on all your business assets, it wants to feel comfortable that enough free cash exists to repay the loan and interest when due. The banker refers to free cash as the money remaining in your company's bank account after all expenses and obligations are paid.

- *Capacity*—Bankers want borrowers who have demonstrated the capacity to meet their financial obligations. How will you repay the bank if things don't pan out? The typical response is "collateral." While banks look at what the property is worth at liquidation value—how salable it is—they are not that keen about liens. It's important to have a contingency plan for situations beyond your control, such as an economic downturn in your industry.

- *Management*—Without a track record, all the banker has to go on is you. A decision will be based on a banker's perception of how well you will manage your business and turn a profit. The bank wants to know what qualifies you to run a business, and will review the management section of your business plan for a complete description on key personnel.

- *Banker/Applicant Relationship*—Having an ongoing relationship with a bank can work to your advantage. Use a bank's services as often as possible—savings account, checking, credit cards, safe deposit box, travelers checks, money orders, certificates of deposit, and notary public. Each use makes you a valued client rather than just another bank account number.

- *Economic Conditions*—Banks will look at current and near-term projected economic conditions. Are we heading for a recession or a boom? If the economy has a clean bill of health, bankers are usually eager to lend money to a good candidate. Are you entering an industry that is growing or declining? Is your industry saturated? Is there tremendous growth opportunity in your business?

You can apply for lines-of-credit from a bank. You can also arrange lines-of-credit with suppliers. With a revolving line, you can borrow as little as $5,000 or as much as $1 million. You can draw on and replace the funds as needed. A line-of-credit is a short-term loan usually written for a year—that extends the cash available in your business's checking account. You pay interest on the actual amount advanced from the point in time you take the money out until it is paid back.

Most financial institutions offer both seasonal and revolving lines. If you need money to prepare for a product that won't generate any income until much later in the year, a seasonal line could help you maintain an even cash flow between periods. A revolving line-of-credit can tide your business over during crunch times.

Generally, lines-of-credit are used to expand or maintain an existing business, not to start a new one. There are exceptions though. An entrepreneur who has been in business a short time could go to a lender and say, "I produce lawn chairs and I need to buy 1,000 pounds of aluminum. I already have the contract order for them. But it will take me two months to build the chairs before I can get paid." A banker would look favorably upon this loan request. You still need a business plan to qualify for a line-of-credit. And you have to satisfy the five C's of lending.

SBA—The Small Business Administration is perhaps the best known federal agency for helping start-up businesses. The SBA offers direct loans and guaranteed bank loans.

General 7(a) Guaranteed Loan: Under the 7(a) Guaranteed Loan Program, a bank or other financial institution loans money to eligible entrepreneurs. The SBA guarantees 75 percent to 90 percent of loans up to $750,000. So, if you default on your loan, the SBA will compensate the bank for 75 percent to 90 percent of the loan. The SBA won't consider a loan application unless you have been turned down by a bank. Seek out SCORE (Service Core of Retired Executives) counselors who are trained at putting together 7(a) loan packages. As you recall from Chapter 2, your local SCORE office can match you with an executive to help review your business plan and offer management advice.

Low Doc: The Low Doc Loan Program offers a one-page application and three-day turnaround for entrepreneurs seeking loans up to $100,000. The loan-decision process relies heavily upon the strength of the principals' character, credit history, and business experience.

Microloans: Under the Microloan Program, the SBA funds nonprofit groups, who in turn make loans to eligible businesses in amounts as small as $100 up to $25,000 (the average loan size is $10,000). The SBA has contributed as much as $2.5 million to more than 101 approved economic organizations across the country. Applications generally take one week to process. Each nonprofit lending organization has its own loan requirements.

Most types of businesses can apply for SBA loans, including manufacturers, retailers, wholesalers, service firms, and exporters. SBA loans can be used for such business purposes as to purchase real estate (office building); the construction or renovation of business facilities; and to buy furniture, machinery, equipment, and supplies (inventory). The money can't be used to pay off current debtors, existing debt, or to pay back loans from relatives and friends.

SECURING INVESTORS: EQUITY FINANCING

With equity financing you are actually selling off a portion of your business to investors who may or may not actively participate in the management of the company. The main concern with equity financing is how much control you will have to give up. In the early stages of the business, you may have to give up as much as 50 percent of the equity in the company.

Angels (private investors) — Private investors, called angels, are viable sources of money for fledging companies (though they are hard to find). Typically, angels are wealthy individuals and successful business owners. But they can be relatives, neighbors, associates, or anyone who has the cash to finance your business.

Generally, entrepreneurs find angels through word-of-mouth. However, several business groups and universities, including the Massachusetts Institute of Technology (MIT) in Cambridge, Massachusetts, have created database networks of angels. These networks run pretty much like a computer matchmaking service. Entrepreneurs provide short profiles, plus a business plan and financial projections. The profiles are generally based on the industry the company is in, its size, and its capital needs. Investors also submit profiles describing their investment interests and criteria. Both profiles remain anonymous; only the company profiles are sent to potential investors. If the investor likes what he/she sees, the two parties are formally introduced. Most transactions are anywhere from $100,000 to $1 million.

Some angel databases are strictly local gigs. MIT's Technology Capital Network (617-253-7163) serves mostly the northeast. One national database is The Capital Network in Austin, Texas (512-794-9398). Many, but not all, of these networks charge a fee. It could cost you $35 for a few months to $350 for a full year. The fee only gets you into the system. There are no guarantees that you will get the money you seek, even if a match is made. Capital networks simply introduce you to an investor.

National online sources include the SBA's Angel Capital Electronic Network (ACE-Net; www. ace-net.sr.unh.edu); Norwalk, Connecticut–based Money Hunt Properties (www.moneyhunter.com); Irvine, California–based America's Business Funding Directory (www.businessfinance.com); Milford, New Jersey–based Capital Quest in Milford (www.usbusiness.com/capquest//home.html); and Princeton, New Jersey–based The VINE (The Venture Information Network for Entrepreneurs; www.thevine.com).

Companies searching for money still outnumber the angels who give it. According to the SBA, the average angel seriously considers a third of all the opportunities he or she discovers and invests in one-third of those considered. Most angels look for an annual return between 15 percent and 20 percent over four to five years.

Iris Lorenz-Fife's *Financing Your Business* (Prentice Hall) outlines all of the issues the angel may wish to consider when reviewing your business plan:

- *Financing*— You must include a clear description of anticipated financing from start-up to maturity. You may be looking for just one angel at the beginning, but you should spell out the additional amounts and the number of investors to whom you are willing to sell equity.

- *Strategies*— One of the problems angels report is that too often business plans are single-dimensional, assuming one, and only one, set of circumstances and responses. Most sophisticated business plans include alternative strategies, such as, "If advertising doesn't generate such and such results, we will do this, and this, and then that." Angels like to see these alternatives because they provide information on the business venture and prove that you are sufficiently flexible to respond constructively to whatever happens.

- *Management*— Angels often turn down entrepreneurs because their plans don't demonstrate they have the experience or talent to succeed. The personal section of your business plan should contain enough personal history to fully describe each key person in your business. Early in the angel's consideration of your business venture, you should also provide the opportunity for the angel and your key people to meet. Making yourselves directly available so that the angel can assess your character and motivations may be the difference between a committed and valuable partnership and no deal.

• *References*— Include the names of associates who have worked with you on various projects and who have experienced your abilities to organize, inspire, and solve problems.

• *Growth*— It is better to be bullish, without stretching the facts, on your firm's chances for growth, the talent and managerial experience of key people, and why it is a good investment at the proposed price.

An angel will provide either a specific amount of money on signing the agreement or a series of investments over a period of time. Be aware of a "devil in angel's garb." A devil wants your business. Never lose sight of the fact that it's up to you and your lawyer to negotiate an agreement that will lead to a business marriage made in heaven.

Venture Capital—A venture capitalist is a company, or individual, that invests money in a business. They see themselves as partners, not merely investors. A venture capital firm is run exclusively for profit; it will back a good idea that will make money for both parties.

There are essentially three things at which venture capitalists will take a close look:

1. Do you and your management team have relevant prior experience? Venture capitalists like to be consulted from time to time, they don't want sit around and advise you on how to make day-to-day decisions—that's on you and your managers.

2. Does your product have a competitive advantage? In what way is your product/service unique? What are the barriers to entry in your industry? Venture capitalists like to invest in innovative products that are the next-generation—say, an add-on technology or technique.

3. Does your company have the potential to generate revenues of $100 million—or whatever is your industry's standard—in five years? In general, venture capitalists want a high return on investment (ROI). They hope to get back five times the amount they invest.

Venture capitalists will define your business according to a set of categories:

1. *First-round financing (start-up funds)*. It is hard to communicate a new money-making idea to a venture capitalist. A start-up is viewed as an idea with no prototype product. It usually takes two to three years before a company breaks even (sales equals costs). Venture capitalists investing in start-ups are taking a huge risk and want a big return on their investment.

2. *Second-round financing (development funds)*. Once you have proved your idea can work by means of a prototype, an economic study, marketing analysis or some other means, you are in a position to have a good shot at obtaining financing from a venture capitalist. But you have to show that your prototype can be brought to market and make a profit.

3. *Third-round financing (expansion funds)*. At this point, your company has created a product or service and is marketing it with some degree of success, but is not yet profitable. You need additional funds to grow the business. You will be in a better position to negotiate a deal without having to fork up as much control as in the start-up stage. Much of the financ-

ing the venture capitalist community provides is expansion money.

4. *Fourth-round of financing (growth funds)*. The company is starting to generate a profit and you need additional capital to keep the business going strong. Maybe the business is growing faster than it can meet demand. A venture capitalist will be anxious to give you the funds.

This may also be the stage of your business where you consider a public stock offering—going public—instead of seeking venture capital. Making a public stock offering means selling some of your firm's equity to many small investors using an underwriter (investment banker). Hence, you are going public with your firm's stock. An unwritten rule is that a company shouldn't go public until it reaches $1 million in profits on $10 million in sales. The disadvantages to going public: First, you no longer call all the shots. Shareholders have a say in how the business is run. Second, the Securities and Exchange Commission (SEC), the government agency that regulates the sale of public stocks, requires all public firms to disclose financial and management information to potential investors.

A well-prepared business proposal is the only introduction you need. Unfortunately, most firms complain of getting incomprehensible business proposals, asserts David Gladstone, an executive officer with Allied Capital Corp., a venture capital firm in Washington, D.C., and author of *The Venture Capital Handbook* (Prentice Hall). A two-page summary won't cut it. Gladstone notes that the average venture capital firm will get 100 proposals a month but only ten draw enough interest to get read. Of those, says Gladstone, two or three receive further attention. In the end, only one may get funded. It may take anywhere from three weeks to six months to obtain venture capital funds.

Private Placement Memorandum—There may come a point where you have a great product or service that is in demand, yet, you are short of the funds needed to continue to grow the business. An alternative to banks and venture capitalists is to raise expansion dollars though a private placement, where you offer stock in the business to a small pool of investors. As long as you maintain control of the business (51 percent equity stake), a private placement can be a viable option. Normally, a company will sell ownership between 20 percent and 35 percent and offer a greater than 20 percent return on investment (ROI).

You can write a private placement memorandum yourself or with the aid of an investment bank. Selling stock in your small enterprise is no different than selling stock on the New York Stock Exchange in that the price is determined by profit potential, not asset value. If individuals believe they will make an attractive return on their investment, they will buy stock at whatever price they feel is a good investment.

Many companies use the Small Corporate Offering Registration (SCOR) form, which is a standardized question-and-answer disclosure document. SCOR guidelines fall under the Securities Exchange Commission's Regulations A and D 504. Under Regulation D 504, you may raise up to $1 million within a 12-month period. You don't have to report the sale to the SEC, but you must obtain clearance to sell in the state. There are no limitations placed on the number of people purchasing shares. And solicitations may be made through traditional advertising.

Under Regulation A, entrepreneurs may raise up to $5 million in any 12-month period and must file certain disclosure information with the SEC and every state in which the company hopes to sell securities. Typically, SCOR offerings are priced between $2 and $5 per share and most companies require a minimum investment between $500 and $1,000. Shares can be offered as common stock, preferred stock, or debt securities (loans).

There are at least three steps you'll need to follow to do a private placement:

- *Step One:* Update your business plan. You must have all the key elements, including a mission statement, product/service description, competitive analysis, market potential, management plan, income statement, balance sheet, three- to five-year projections on cash flow, and profit and loss.

- *Step Two:* Create a financial budget and marketing plan. Expect to spend at least $15,000 to $50,000 for a small private placement to raise up to $1 million. You'll need to send direct mail pieces to interested parties and host seminars where you make a formal face-to-face presentation.

- *Step Three:* Write a prospectus document. This memorandum must be given to each prospective investor and must spell out how the stock is to be sold and how the money will be used to achieve the objectives of the business plan.

Be sure to assign someone the task of making follow-up telephone calls or sending letters to potential investors. Don't underestimate the time and energy required to raise money. Expect your money quest to take at lease six months.

To find out more, contact your local secretary of state or state department of banking and finance. Other resources are *The SCOR Report* (972-620-2489), a Dallas-based newsletter that tracks small company stock offerings, and Santa Monica, California–based Direct Stock Market, Inc. (www.directstock market.com), which allows companies to post private placement memorandums and public offering documents.

Before attempting to raise money from any source, you must ask yourself some basic questions: What do I hope to gain monetarily from company operations? What percentage of my company am I willing to sell to achieve my long-term goals? What method of funding will best serve me in my efforts to attain long-term goals? You should learn as much as possible about available funding options and strive to make the search for funding an ongoing and standard part of doing business.

BO PEABODY, PRESIDENT AND CEO OF TRIPOD, INC.

In six years, Tripod (www.tripod.com) has positioned itself as the ninth most popular site among Web users. It is homegrown online community where around two million members get the news, chat with one another, retrieve e-mail, buy and sell products, and create their own Websites. The Website is the central property of Williamstown, Massachusetts–based Tripod, Inc., a wholly owned subsidiary of Lycos, Inc., a leading Web search engine.

Tripod is the brainchild of 27-year-old Bo Peabody, president and CEO, and college professor Richard H. Sabot, chairman. It started in 1991 as a poll about why students had no idea how to prepare for what comes after college, and grew into a full-fledged company.

Peabody, a 20-year-old freshman attending Williams College at the time, went around to many of his friends and associates and started asking them what were some issues they were facing. He noticed some similarities between himself and his peers, especially in the areas of careers and finance. Taking his findings a step further, Peabody conducted a survey in class for his college economics professor, Richard Sabot.

At the time, the project was academic. We were trying to probe why the United States had such a low savings rate. Our hypothesis was that young people didn't know how to manage their money. We broadened the concept to focus on other real world things that they didn't understand.

The tallied survey results showed that about 85 percent of the students said that college was not preparing them for the future. They felt they were not receiving ample guidance in managing personal finances, investing, health care, career planning, and other important life issues.

We decided to commercialize the concept and to conduct a nationwide market research with Roper Starch Worldwide [in 1992]. We were able to get Dow Jones to fund a good portion of the national survey. From the time that we did the research at Williams until the time we finished the nationwide market research, we felt that we had a solid business concept.

It's inconceivable that Peabody's application to Williams was rejected in 1989. His doggedness got him into the school a year later; he earned a bachelor's degree in political philosophy and sociology in 1994. Peabody knew he could reach his peers through books or magazines. But he wanted his company to provide interactive communications. He started looking at the evolving electronic medium. The Internet seemed like the ideal outlet. Enlisting people from Rensselaer Polytechnic Institute and Williams College, Peabody designed the site in-house.

I came up with the content based on the research. We took advantage of what the Web as a medium had to offer. We didn't just shovel magazine content up there like large corporate sites. Ours is very interactive. It's a place where people can hang out.

During the early years of the business, Peabody and four other colleagues worked out of a small office space. When Peabody graduated in 1994, he moved Tripod into a mid-nineteenth century Greek Revival house near the Williams campus. The business recently moved into a 16,000-square-foot converted mill space that the Tripod crew renovated themselves.

A handful of staff working in advertising and editorial are housed out of a small New York office. A key part of Tripod's staff is its sales team, which makes up one quarter of the staff. In the spring of 1997, Peabody hired a vice president of advertising sales, with over 20 years of experience.

During Tripod's start-up years, Peabody raised $14 million in capital. In fact, Tripod went through three different stages of financing. To jump-start the company, Peabody raised about $1 million from angels (which took about four months). He prevailed on Professor Sabot to help him locate investors, including Pete Willmott, chairman of the board of trustees at Williams College, former chief financial officer of Federal Express and current CEO of Zenith. With Willmott's financial backing, a solid business plan, and nationwide market research, Peabody was able to attract other high-net-worth investors.

The second round took two months to raise about $3 million, because Tripod had a track record. Peabody looked at 30 different venture capital firms, attending a total of 100 meetings to discuss the deal. After about eight meetings with New Enterprise Associates (NEA), the nation's largest early-stage venture capital firm, Tripod made a deal with them. There were three things that NEA reviewed—Tripod's management team, business strategy, and whether it was in a hot market.

Tripod posted its first sizable revenues in 1996: about $200,000 in ad sales generated by the debut of *Tools for Life*, a 40-page magazine whose theme was "live smart, work smart, street smart." *Tools for Life* (which was discontinued in 1997) was distributed each semester to 1 million students on U.S. college campuses, and was poly-bagged with textbooks from publisher Prentice Hall, which originally approached Tripod about doing Web-based material.

Raising the third round of venture capital, which was $10 million, was the most difficult. The market was not very hot on content companies and plus we were asking for a lot of money. We had over 175 face-to-face meetings with different financiers. It was a grueling eight-month process. For us, they wanted to know how much traffic we had on our site. At that point, that's what companies were really looking at, in terms of investing in Websites.

The Interpublic Group of Companies, Inc., one of the world's largest advertising agency and marketing communications holding companies and Rho Management, a New

York–based venture capital firm, purchased minority interests in Tripod, Inc. Investors were pleased with the "virtual community" Tripod had built.

Characteristics of the people on our site are young urban professionals, who are highly motivated, educated, Web-savvy, and somewhat cynical and media-savvy. They are looking for guidance, but not in the traditional way most media have provided it. In many ways they are looking for guidance from their own peers.

Initially, Tripod was created as an interactive source of information services for 18- to 34-year-old members. Peabody envisioned a site where about 75 percent of the content was generated by Tripod and 25 percent by users. However, the site is actually the opposite; it is largely composed of content generated by members—special interest groups called "Pods." Tripod has more than 100 Pods, each has its own distinct look and feel, and offers a regular newsletter, live chats, and message boards.

Responding to feedback from its members, advertisers, and extensive market research, Tripod underwent its most ambitious redesign in the company's history. The Internet site was recently organized into four main sections. Build allows members and visitors to search through Tripod's 14 Zones in order to view homepages about entertainment, computers/Internet, women, jobs/career, home/family, society/culture, health/fitness, money/business, teens, shopping, cars & trucks, fun & games, travel, and sports. One of Tripod's fastest growing areas is Interact, which is the home of the "Pod" user-groups. Emphasizing the role of electronic commerce, the Buy/Sell section enables Tripod users to get discounts on music, books, and software. Moreover, members can earn cash or credit by building their own "online stores" and selling products through Tripod.

Tripod has been defining the concept of online communities and leading the homepage building revolution since the get-go. Our redesigned site makes it easier for members to find activities or content of interest. We are always seeking new and different ways to offer the best services to our members and partners. The new design simplifies what Tripod has to offer, creates a stronger sense of community, and caters to each individual's reason for being online.

The average age of the 45-employee company is 27, which matches the average age of Tripod's members. The Website has over 2 million members (at a rate of 210,000 new visitors per month). Sources of revenues: advertising sales, e-commerce, transaction fees, and subscriptions for premium services.

Advertising by far is the largest contributor of revenues for us—about 90 percent. Initially, we were going to build the site as a subscription model (Tripod recruited representatives from over a hundred college campuses, who helped register some 50,000 members). But everything on the Web was geared toward advertising revenues. So, we switched to that model in 1995, making a limited portion subscription-based and offering all other information for free. I hope in the long term to increase our subscription base and have ads account for 60 percent of revenues.

Tripod has received tremendous support for its Website from more than 50 advertisers, including AT&T, Fidelity Investments, Ford, Kodak, Microsoft, MTV, Northwest Airlines, Sony, Fleet Bank, Yahoo!, Visa, HotWired, Earthlink Network, and The Discovery Channel.

The biggest challenge is building Tripod as a brand, positioning it properly, and making it relative to people's lives. Next, it's striking up relationships with advertisers, getting the right distribution arrangements, and continuing to build traffic on the Website. There is only a small handful of sites that have the level of traffic we have on our site. We are competing with the big search engines, not the overnight sites that crop up. Advertisers have so many choices with respect to Websites.

In February 1998, Peabody sold Tripod for $58 million to Lycos in Waltham, Massachusetts, a three-year-old online service that helps users locate and retrieve information. Peabody, who retained his CEO status, saw the potential of the technical and product synergy between the two flagship sites. Indeed, Tripod skyrocketed 40 percent in reach to new visitors since it was acquired.

To further build the Tripod brand, Peabody eventually plans to put out a magazine that can compete on the newsstands with such publications as *Swing* and *P.O.V.* Moreover, Tripod has created TV programming for CNN, and bookstores offer Tripod's *Tools for Life* (Hyperion), which Peabody describes as a definitive world guide to making it in the new millennium.

Even though he puts in about 60 to 70 hours a week, Peabody tends to live the same life he did in college—"which is work hard, play hard." As chairman, Sabot oversees the board of directors, helps with the strategic financing, and serves as a sounding board for company executives. (He also sits on Lycos's board.) As CEO and president, Peabody runs the day-to-day operations of the business and develops the strategic relationships with other companies.

We set a goal of how we wanted to build the business, which was through strategic partnerships. We look for partners who have products or services or know things that we don't. We go to them hoping to form a win-win situation.

Peabody attributes his success to good support systems, mentors like Sabot and his parents (his father is a high school teacher and his mother a tech company executive). The advice he gives to young would-be entrepreneurs is simple:

Know what you don't know. When you create an idea, understand the efforts of that idea you can contribute to. Then surround yourself with people who know what you don't know, or have the expertise you don't have, to help guide you. So many entrepreneurs think they know everything and that's what limits them. Get totally involved in your industry, find out where those people are who can contribute to your business, and seek them out.

MICHAEL RUBIN, PRESIDENT AND CEO OF GLOBAL SPORTS, INC.

As early as age nine, Michael Rubin was involved in one entrepreneurial project or another, from selling personalized stationery (printed on his Apple computer) door-to-door to hiring
five friends to help with his snow removal business. Just back

MICHAEL RUBIN

from ski camp, a 13-year-old Rubin followed a friend's suggestion to open a ski-tuning shop.

Taking $2,500 in gift money from his bar mitzvah in 1985, he set up shop in his parents' basement, tuning skis and later selling equipment and apparel (on consignment). He soon outgrew that location and moved into a local strip mall near his Lafayette Hill, Pennsylvania, home.

I did about $25,000 that first year. I wanted to open my own retail ski store, so I found a place that was about five minutes from my parents' home. I was allowed to lease the space month-to-month, so there was no long-term commitment. Also, I could get rides from school pretty easily—I was still too young to drive.

Rubin's father, a veterinarian, co-signed the lease although his mother, a psychiatrist, questioned her son taking on such a responsibility at an early age. School authorities allowed Rubin to join a cooperative education program where students divided their day between school and work. By the time he was 19, Rubin owned five retail ski and sporting goods shops, generating $2.5 million in revenues.

Today, the twenty-six-year-old whiz kid is the CEO of Global Sports, Inc., in King of Prussia, Pennsylvania, a $130-million public company that manufactures and markets athletic, casual, and outdoor products worldwide. In 1997, Rubin combined KPR Sports International, Rykä Inc., Apex One, and Yukon to form Global Sports. KPR (the name is from his parents' initials, Ken and Paulette Rubin) is a wholesale company that buys discounted athletic and casual footwear, apparel, and sporting goods from manufacturers and resells them to retailers. Rykä is the only brand of performance footwear made exclusively for women. Apex One markets moderately priced athletic footwear and apparel. And Yukon is an exploding manufacturer of performance outdoor footwear, including hiking boots. In 1998, Rubin acquired Gen-X Holdings, Inc. and Gen-X Equipment, Inc., a Toronto, Ontario–based wholesale distributor of off-price sporting goods and equipment, such as in-line skates, snowboards, and skate-boards.

Among several major decisions Rubin made in 1997 was to take his company public. He cautions that a company needs to have several reasons for going public—it's not just a way to raise capital; it is a major change in lifestyle with both pros and cons.

The downsides are that you are in the public eye every day. It's difficult to get internal problems in the company fixed before it gets out to the rest of the world. Everything you do is public information and that's not an easy thing to cope with. We have always grown quickly. Cash flow has always been a major issue for us. We raised $5 million for Rykä in a private placement [in 1995] and plan to raise another $25 million in the future when the timing is right.

Rubin vividly remembers his early experiences with money and banking. He was 15 the first time he applied for a $25,000 line-of-credit.

The bank told me they needed a couple of things to finalize the line-of-credit. They wanted me to put up $25,000 in a letter of credit or CD. I said, "Let me ask you this: if I had $25,000 to give you, why the heck would I be coming to you for a loan?" That's the first time I ever understood banking. They came to me and basically said we will give you money if you have money. I will never forget that day.

Rubin learned a big—and costly—lesson when he was 16½. He was overextended in debt. He undercut other ski-shop own-ers' prices. But in his exuberance, he slashed prices too deep. After one particulary bad ski season, he found himself in serious financial trouble—$180,000 in debt and $80,000 in assets, and heading for bankruptcy.

His father came to his rescue with a $37,000 loan, enabling him to work out repayment deals with creditors. Rubin Senior didn't want the people his son owed money to get screwed. But there was a catch—Rubin had to go to college. He enrolled in

Villanova University, however, cutting undergraduate studies short by quitting after all of six months.

. In 1991, one of Rubin's stores was selling soccer shoes for a great price. He then bought the overstocked inventory for $60,000 (which he borrowed from a friend) and sold it for over twice that amount making a $75,000 profit in a few days, paying back his father and his friend. That's when he discovered the closeout business and launched KPR Sport, turning his attention to buying large quantities of off-price footwear and apparel and reselling it to major retail chains such as TJ Maxx, Ross, and Modell's, as well as thousands of other accounts.

I liked the wholesale business—buying and selling things in large quantities—a lot better than the retail business, where you buy the merchandise for your store, building a desirable mix of products that you sell to each consumer one at a time. I started soliciting all these big brands to sell me at closeout. I went through directories of the major sporting goods companies and made a list of different people to go after. It was a fairly small list of top sporting goods, apparel, and footwear brands. I would get samples of products and show them to retailers, and then try to get their commitments before I actually went out and purchased the merchandise.

Armed with a solid business plan, Rubin finally managed to get a line-of-credit for $250,000 with Continental Bank. He sold off one of his ski stores and closed out the others. KPR International grew from $3 million in sales in 1992 to $45 million in sales in 1995. When manufacturers had canceled orders, too much stock, or unpopular sizes, they called on KPR Sports, which stocked about 1.5 million pairs of shoes and tons of assorted sports apparel..

By that time, KPR had secured a $15 million line-of-credit. Over the years, Rubin had developed a rapport with his bank, where he kept separate personal and business accounts. He also established lines-of-credit with all of his suppliers—in excess of $10 million with some vendors.

In the beginning, I managed the company's cash flow. As we grew we got better resources. Deloitte and Touche LLP is now our accounting firm. They have been a key player in helping us grow. One of the things I strongly recommend to start-up business owners is to surround themselves with the right kind of professionals to help them grow the business. Your job is not to know everything yourself but to build a great team of people.

Rubin notes his company was always severely undercapitalized. And that a necessity in growing the business has been raising more capital. This has presented a big challenge over the years, in part, due to some early advice Rubin received.

I was advised not to take any partners to raise capital and told that I should rely on bank financing and build the business that way. As we started to get more involved in the branded business (with Yukon and Rykä) and moved away from the closeout business, KPR Sports, our performance on paper was not as good. This caused us problems with the banks. Our financial situation became even more difficult.

In 1995, Rubin acquired Rykä, Inc., a Norwood, Mas–sachusetts–based firm. Rubin contacted the seven-year-old company's founder, Sherie Poe, who was in her twenties when she suffered from bulimia. As part of her treatment, a doctor told her to work out. But she couldn't find a pair of athletic shoes that fit her comfortably. That's when she decided to start Rykä — the only brand of athletic shoe-wear that is made exclusively for women.

Rubin put together an $8-million financing and equity package to acquire 40 percent of Rykä. The $9-million company was reportedly struggling under poor financial management. Rubin wanted to capitalize on Rykä's brand name and niche, even though it had never made a profit, was $2 million in debt, and in jeopardy of going bankrupt.

I merged and acquired other businesses to grow. I had built a $45-million business by selling excess inventory. The next logical step for me was to own my own brand. I wasn't content just buy-

ing and selling other people's merchandise. So, I created Yukon in 1994. Then I acquired Rykä. In 1996, I acquired Apex One. I want to do what Nike and Reebok did—build their reputations by creating their own line and getting people excited about their products. The brand business now makes up more than 40 percent of our overall company volume.

However, acquiring Rykä was no easy task. Rubin had to erase Rykä's debt before he could get a bank to underwrite the deal. He was able to have $1.65 million of debt forgiven by offering creditors a favorable term. With $1 million of his own money and another million from investors, Rubin brought Rykä into the black. Rubin retained Poe as director to maintain the brand's identity.

To make sure he is satisfying consumer needs, Rubin conducts market surveys and focus groups. He recently invested $5 million in a marketing campaign to promote his Yukon and Rykä brands. Division managers are responsible for building the company's marketing plan each season. Rubin's long-term goal is to create a $1 billion enterprise, and to give Nike and Reebok a run for their money—which combined rake in $14 billion a year.

Global Sports employs about 100 employees—housed in 80,000 sq. ft. of warehouse and office space. Like many young entrepreneurs, Rubin has a hands-on, yet altruistic management style. He believes in motivating employees through merit raises and stock options. He enjoys shooting hoops with his workers—who get to wear jeans to work—on the company's half-size basketball court. His black Labrador retriever, Willow, accompanies him to work. Moreover, Global Sports sponsors a youth entrepreneurial program, where high school students from around the country submit business plans and compete for $2,500 cash awards.

We have attracted a great group of people who have helped grow the company to where it is today. Right now, Yukon and Rykä are our flagship brands. We want to build each one of those to be a substantial player in their niche. Yukon's competition is Timberland and Rockport, and Rykä's competitors are Nike and Reebok. The key to having a successful brand is to first start with great product. But alone that means nothing. You need great marketing, great sales, great service, and a great foundation to build upon.

5

TO INC. OR NOT TO INC.:
YOUR BUSINESS'S LEGAL STRUCTURE,
NAME, AND IDENTITY

Opt for the best possible hand. Play with verve and sometimes with abandon, but at all times with calculation.
—*L. Douglas Wilder, former governor of Virginia*

The best strategy of any game plan is to anticipate what your
opponent will do—to think ahead. If you don't want to leave
yourself wide open to a legal battle down the road, give some
earnest thought to the legal structure of your business. You'll
need to choose a legal structure according to potential tax liabilities, administrative costs, special licenses, and regulations.

Remember, the objective of your business is to make money.
If you think you are going to have losses in the early years, you
may not want to incorporate—or at least not right away—
because you can't take tax losses against your personal income.
What incorporation does do is give your company protection
against legal liability. What if you have a personal service business or a consulting firm? You may not get the legal liability
protection since you are the main person performing the
work—you can't hide behind a corporate shield—"Don't sue
me, but my company instead." If you have a lot of people work-

ing for you and representing your company, then incorporating for liability protection makes sense.

Still, there are no fast, hard rules to incorporating. It depends on the type of business you run and what you want to accomplish. This is why it is important that you clearly define your business operations before you rush out and incorporate it. Moreover, incorporating involves a lot of legal paperwork—articles of incorporation and bylaws. You have to file and prepare a whole set of tax returns in addition to your personal income tax return. For a small business, it may not be worth it to incorporate right away just based on administrative costs.

To run a legal and legitimate business, you need to choose one of eight different legal forms of operation: sole proprietorship, general partnership, limited partnership, limited liability company, corporation, professional corporation, closely held corporation, or a subchapter corporation. The following outlines the advantages and disadvantages of each.

Sole Proprietor. Declaring yourself as a sole proprietor ("doing business as" or DBA) is the simplest and cheapest legal business structure you can start. You simply need to fill out the right forms, available at the county clerk's office. Expenses, licensing fees, and filing fees are minimal.

As sole proprietor, you are in charge, maintaining total control over the business. There are no altercations with partners or authoritarian board members when decisions need to be made. All profits are yours for the taking. You can use losses in the business to offset other income on your personal income tax return.

There are two very notable things about sole proprietorships:

1. On the plus side. It has one of the lowest tax rates. You are taxed only on your personal income—15 percent if you earn less than $20,000.

2. A disadvantage. It has high personal liability. You alone are accountable for all transactions of the company, any losses and legal actions.

As the individual owner, you and the business are one and the same. For tax purposes, you will report all income and expenses on that same individual tax return—Form 1040—that you filed when you were an employee. The difference is that you will attach a Schedule C or C-EZ. Schedule C states your profit or loss for the year. It must be filed if you have gross receipts over $25,000 and expenses greater than $2,000. Form C-EZ lists gross receipts, total expenses, and net profit. You must gross less than $25,000, report expenses less than $2,000, use a cash method of accounting, and have no business inventory that first year and no net loss from the business. Since all the money you make from your business is considered personal income, you can take business deductions and write off financial losses, which translates into tax perks.

Since taxes aren't withheld from your business's earnings, you have to pay self-employment tax. You can use your Social Security number as your tax identification number. But you will have to get an employee identification number (IRS form SS-4) or federal and state payroll ID number if you plan to hire employees or if the companies you plan to do business with require you to have one. (Manufacturing companies must register with the labor commission.)

If you operate the business using a name other than your own, you must file a "Certificate of Doing Business under an Assumed Name" form. Some states also require you to have a fictitious name statement published in the local newspaper to identify to the public the business ownership.

Operating a business by yourself also means that you are relying on your experience and knowledge. The money to finance the business comes out of your pocket—putting your personal assets on the line (consider getting general or product liability insurance, just in case any legal actions are brought against the business).

Partnerships. You may feel that two heads are better than one when it comes to forming the company—plus two sets of shoulders to bear the workload and bank accounts to finance the start-up. Partnerships may be perceived more favorably by bankers, investors, and suppliers as well.

The decision to go into business with one or more individuals to form a partnership should not be taken lightly. Many a friendship or business relationship has been destroyed because the parties didn't see eye-to-eye, or someone wasn't pulling his or her own weight. You and your partner should complement one another. The decision to work together should be based on the skills, knowledge, experiences, and contacts each of you brings to the table. You want to pool acquired and innate skills (refer to the personality test in Chapter 2). Be wary of family ties, which could sever quickly under pressure.

Under a general partnership, each partner has the authority to enter into contracts and to make other business decisions, unless the partnership agreement stipulates otherwise. Each partner is liable for all business debts and reports partnership income on individual tax returns. The business does not pay any taxes as its own entity.

Putting the partnership in writing isn't mandatory but it is highly recommended. You can draw up some very simple preliminary documents, such as a letter of intent, which would state the name of the business, principals, initial investment, partner's equity and date of operation. But there are some ground rules you need to cover regarding division of labor, distribution of profits, and restrictions. It's in the company's best interest to have an Articles of Partnership. Ideally, the agreement should be drawn up by an attorney and signed by all parties. This document includes:

1. Name of the partnership

2. Date of the formation of the partnership

3. Business address

4. Purpose of the partnership

5. Names of each partner

6. The amount and type of capital invested by each partner

7. The sharing of profits and losses, including any salary arrangements for working versus nonworking partners

8. Distribution of assets at the time of dissolution

9. Specific duties and responsibilities of each partner

10. Limitations on outside activities

11. Admission of new partners

12. Banking and check signing privileges

13. Noncompetition clauses for departing partners

14. Buy-sell agreements and life and disability insurance

15. Settlement provisions for the voluntary or involuntary premature withdrawal of any partner to assure the survival of the business

You legally form a partnership by registering it with the IRS and getting a partnership identification number. If you operate under another name, you must file a "Certificate of Conducting Business as Partners" form. When it comes to running a partnership, every partner is personally accountable for the business. The greatest benefit of a partnership is that both parties share the responsibilities and liabilities. In addition, there are tax advantages. The partnership files a separate income tax return that states profits or losses, and how the money was appropriated.

Limited Partnership. A variation of a general partnership is a limited partnership. A limited partner is basically an investor, while general partners handle all management duties and daily operations of the business. General partners sell shares in the business to limited partners in order to raise capital. Limited partners pay a set amount in exchange for a percentage of company profits over so many years. Limited partners have no personal liability except for the amount they invest in the business. General partners are personally responsible for liabilities, thus, limited partners cannot be sued for actions of the business.

To form a limited partnership, you must file the necessary paperwork through your local secretary of state office. Limited partners report their share of income or loss on their individual tax returns. An exiting limited partner does not dissolve the business, but a general partner pulling out might, unless the partnership agreement states otherwise.

C-Corporations. A general corporation (technically referred to as C-corporation) is often formed by companies that need to raise significant amounts of capital at various stages throughout the business's growth. When you incorporate your business, you create an entity separate from yourself, meaning that you are an employee and stockholder, rather than the personal owner.

In forming a corporation, there are three tiers: shareholders, board of directors, and officers. Stock is issued to shareholders in exchange for cash or other assets. Shareholders, the number of which is unlimited, have nothing to do with day-to-day operations of the business. You are legally required to establish bylaws and hold stockholders' meetings. Earnings are paid to shareholders as dividends in proportion to the number of shares owned. The state in which you incorporate will require an annual declaration of stockholders and directors report. Failure to do so could result in fines and penalties or even the company's eradication.

Board members appoint corporate officers, but they have supremacy over policies, personnel, employee compensation, delegation of dividends, and general supervision of corporate activities. The board may meet once a year or once a month to discuss company affairs. Officers (president, vice president, secretary, treasurer, etc.) carry out day-to-day business operations. If you are the only person forming the corporation, then you are the sole shareholder and can appoint yourself to the board of directors as well as anyone else you deem appropriate.

An advantage of a corporation is potential limited personal liability, as you have separated yourself from the company. The corporation can buy, sell, enter contracts, sue, and be sued. The business entity is responsible for its activities. The stockholders or owners only lose their financial interests and investments, not their personal assets. Of course, there are no absolutes. Owners have been found personally negligent in suits involving their companies.

Another advantage is that because the corporation is its own legal entity, it can survive the death of owners, partners, and shareholders. A disadvantage is the tax double whammy. Since you and the company are two separate entities, both must pay taxes. The company files a separate income tax form 1120 and you file your personal tax returns. Equally, shareholders must report their shares of corporate profit or loss on their individual tax returns.

A corporation pays taxes, separately from owners, on profits before dividends. Working owners or shareholders can deduct their salaries. But they pay taxes on dividends distributed from corporate profits, thus, causing a form of double taxation since the corporation must pay taxes—15 percent on the first $50,000; 25 percent on $75,000; and 34 percent on all taxable income over $75,000.

These days, for about $300, you can get a corporation kit online, which would include an Articles of Incorporation form—the official record of your business's name and location, corporate purpose, shares of stock, and capitalization. The Articles of Incorporation identify the key players, such as the president, vice president, other officers, and board of directors. You may want to consult a lawyer about forming your corporation, which could cost you around $500 and take a couple of days or a few weeks to get off the ground. Also, most states require you publish a corporation announcement in local newspapers.

Closely-held Corporation. Another corporate structure is a closely held corporation—which is traditionally associated with businesses formed by family members. The company's voting shares are held by a single shareholder or a closely knit group of shareholders, who limit the transfer of stock. It operates like a partnership but has the same corporate structure protection against liability. A closely held business bypasses the process of holding an election of a board of directors or holding annual shareholders' meetings.

Professional Corporation. Every state allows groups of professionals or firms that have a sole principal and associates to set up a professional corporation (PC), also known as a professional association or service corporation. A PC pays taxes on earnings; the owners pay tax on the money once it is distributed by way of salary. This legal structure was established specifically for such groups as lawyers, doctors, architects, and accountants.

Organizing a professional corporation works for small business owners who form partnerships or in cases where colleagues work closely with each other but don't shoulder liability for another person's negligence. In essence, a professional corporation offers corporate tax advantages and the protection of corporate state law for activities that are associated with partnerships or proprietorships. A PC files and prepares a set of tax forms in addition to individual tax returns. Accordingly, you'll need a certified public accountant (CPA). For this reason, the PC may not be worth the administrative costs to a small business. On the other hand, you get what you pay for, if you do it yourself.

Sub-chapter S. If you have no intention of selling stock to the public and plan to have less than 75 shareholders, consider forming a Sub-chapter Corporation (a.k.a. S-corp). S-corps were originally created to enable small and family-owned businesses to enjoy the limited personal liability protection of a C-corp. and the tax status of a proprietorship or partnership. Translation: You only have to pay taxes once and you can benefit from certain tax deductions.

An S-corp. is incorporated under the same rules as a regular corporation, but it is taxed like a partnership. Shareholders declare all earnings as salary or dividends and the corporation does not pay corporate tax, because all activity is reported through the owners. Income and losses must be declared and distributed to shareholders in the year in which they were incurred.

Limited Liability Company. The newest and most closely watched form of operation is a limited liability company (LLC), which offers tax breaks and liability protection to small businesses. Not all states recognize LLCs. Up until 1997, you had to have at least two owners to form an LLC. At least 31 states now recognize one-owner enterprises. You'll have to file an Articles of Organization with your secretary of state's office.

Like S-corps. and partnerships, LLC partners have complete authority over the business, and report any loss or income on their individual tax returns. The owners can't be forced to use their personal assets to pay business debts, and any losses can be used as tax deductions against active income. LLC owners can determine what share of the firm's profits and losses each member will receive. S-corps, however, dictate that the gains and losses must be divvied up based on how much stock a member owns.

Another notable difference is that with an LLC, you can offer different classes of stock. An unlimited number of individuals, corporations, and partnerships can participate as shareholders. There are some restrictions on transferring ownership interests. Also, state laws vary regarding the continuity of LLCs. Unless specified, the company dissolves when an owner leaves the business.

NAMING AND PROTECTING YOUR BUSINESS

Two important tasks in starting a business are giving that entity a form and a name. The form determines the company's operation, while the name gives the company its identity. In fact, your corporate identity is the combination of words and symbols that represent the distinctive character of your organization.

Give some careful thought to your business name, which cannot resemble that of an existing corporation in the same jurisdiction. However, you may be able to operate a store in New York under a name similar to that of a store in California, if it is not in direct competition with your product. Your state agency can notify you as to whether a name is available. If it isn't already taken, you can reserve that name for up to 120 days.

The best name for a company is often one that tells what the business does or sells. Just as well, namesake companies should have a qualifying adjective that describes what the business does (i.e., Jim Taylor Accounting Services, Inc.). It must also include a corp., co., inc. or ltd.

What's in a name? Everything, when it comes to business. If you need convincing, just roll these off your tongue—Kleenex, Vaseline, and Jell-O. These common household brand names are interchangeably used when referring in general to tissue, petroleum jelly, and gelatin. But more important, they are examples of a trademark or service mark.

The name under which you do business is your trade name. The name you use for the business as well as your products or services is a valuable asset you should want to protect. The best way to safeguard your assets is by registering them as a service mark or trademark. When you use the name of your business publicly or sell products with a brand name, you are using it as a trademark. A trademark can consists of words, letters, a symbol, graphic design, or slogan that distinguishes your product or service from the competition.

In this day of national catalog sales, chain stores, and franchise mania, you need to be extra careful. Say, another business is using the same name as your company name in another part of the country without your knowledge. Should that business decide to expand its operations nationwide, you may be forced to change your name.

To avoid such a hassle, conduct a nationwide name search and reserve your mark with the U.S. Patent and Trademark Office (703-308-4357) in Arlington, Virginia. You're not legally required to register your trademark; previous use affirms legal ownership. But national registration protects you by serving notice to other entrepreneurs the name belongs to you. Once it's on the books, no one else can use it—at least not without paying you for it. The ® signifies that you registered federally with the PTO. You may also use a ™ (trademark) or ℠ (service mark).

Unfortunately, you can't protect your ideas. This puts you in a bind while you are in the development stage, because you may need to talk to investors and business associates about your business. A good way to cover yourself is to have people sign a nondisclosure document stating that you are the originator and that they didn't have anything to do with the development of the idea. This way, they are forewarned that they are not to use your idea or discuss it with anyone without your authorization.

To protect a unique product you have invented—even if it's something as simple as the Slinky—you need a patent. Whether you plan to sell it yourself or authorize others to make it, use it, and sell it, you need a patent. Once your product is registered with the PTO, you gain exclusive rights to manufacture and distribute it throughout the United States. Again, you can't get a patent for an idea, your product must be fully developed and working.

Yes, getting a patent is a convoluted legal process that may take anywhere from six months to two years. But failing to do so could prevent you from fully profiting from your invention. If you put your product out on the market for more than a year without obtaining a patent, it becomes part of public domain, so anyone can use it.

Literature, music, art, and computer programs can all be copyrighted (this also applies to unpublished works). You can register your material with the Federal Register of Copyrights by filling out an application, paying a small fee, and attaching two copies of the work. Your material should appear with the symbol © along with the first year of publication.

PERMITS, LICENSES, AND TAXES

Every local and state organization has different requirements for business licenses and permits and different local tax rates. In some states, you have to pay quarterly local government taxes. Contact your local government office on taxes and finance or county clerk to find out what is required to start a business in your area. Ask them what products or services require permits and licenses. Look into state statutes governing your line of work, which may require professional licenses. If you plan on setting up an office in more than one state, you will have to get the appropriate licenses for each location. This may still apply, even if you're not going to physically work at that location, but plan to do business within that state's jurisdiction.

Equally, your business is automatically considered a domestic company. But should you decide to extend your business to other states, you will have to apply for a foreign corporation status in each of those states. If you are selling a product, you're going to have to charge a sales tax and, of course, the business will have to pay taxes each year you are in business. Again, if you have a C-corporation you will also have to pay personal taxes in addition to business taxes.

As a business owner, if you make a net profit greater than $400, you have to file a self-employment (SE) form. If your company hires independent contractors, you must report any payments made to them with a 1099 form. If you hire full-time or part-time employees, you must file a W-2 form for each one. It's important to consider how many people are going to be involved in the business. Is it just you and a partner or several employees? The mere fact that you say someone is an independent contractor doesn't make it so.

Anyone who works for you out of your office using your resources will most definitely be considered an employee—even though you pay a flat rate, but not benefits, FICA, unemployment taxes, and payroll taxes. If the person works part-time or on a project basis, has his or her own tools and discretion as to how he or she does business, then you are okay.

Obviously, this is a hot issue right now, which was played out by the UPS saga. UPS used a lot of part-time employees, because it was economical. Be careful, try to avoid the trap of bringing people in-house and paying them as independent contractors or part-timers. Outside of the tax issue, it could open your company up to greater risk or exposure.

The IRS provides a toll-free information line (800-829-1040) or you can get free information from a local representative. Some IRS publications you'll find useful are: *Tax Guide for Small Businesses*, pub. # 334; *Tax Withholding and Estimated Tax*, pub. #505; *Self-employment Tax*, pub. #533; *Business Expenses*, pub. #535; *Employment Taxes*, pub. #937; *Taxpayers Starting a Business*, pub. #583; and, *Business Use of Your Home*, pub. #587.

Attempt to get as much free legal and accounting advice as you can. Even if it costs, you can say you spent peace-of-mind money by complying with all federal, local, and state laws and regulations. When you decide the type of entity and the method you are going to utilize, take into account your overall situation. Don't make a decision about your company in a vacuum. You have to view your business as one more component of what you do and who you are.

DEXTER WIMBERLY, CEO, BARNEY BISHOP, PRESIDENT, OF AUGUST BISHOP LLC

"Don't be a pawn, and let strategy be an asset," are two statements that serve not only as company mottoes but rules of conduct for August Bishop, a cutting-edge marketing firm, specializing in publicity and promotions for young fashion designers. The young men at the helm of August Bishop are 24-year-old Dexter Wimberly, CEO, and 26-year-old Barney A. Bishop, president.

Bishop is quick to point out that his namesake company is strategic from its name and legal structure to its financial and operational systems. Besides being a combination of the month Wimberly was born in and Bishop's surname, August Bishop has a deeper meaning.

August as an adjective means awe-inspiring and majestic. Bishop is a mitered-shaped chessman that can move diagonally across any number of unoccupied spaces of the same color. We combined these two ideas, because they seemed to really fall in line with our company's business ideology. In our line of work, and in life in general, we know that strategy plays an important role in separating the winners from the losers. We wanted a name that would open doors instead of limiting our possibilities.

Prior to their endeavor as business partners, the duo were responsible for handling publicity and promotions for Maurice Malone Designs, a young men's sportswear collection that rivals top fashion labels such as Tommy Hilfiger, Nautica, and Polo Sport in the urban market. (Malone also owned a Detroit-based retail store called the Hip-Hop Shop, which sold apparel along with music and art.)

It was in 1991 that the enterprising New York natives first met at Brooklyn College, where Bishop majored in radio/television and Wimberly studied political science. While handling promotions for local night clubs, Wimberly was introduced to Maurice Malone, for whom he later worked as an intern.

Wimberly, who originally planned to become a lawyer, went to work full-time for Maurice Malone in 1994. Bishop came on board shortly thereafter. It was in 1995 that the two friends— Wimberly was 22 at the time and Bishop 24—decided to pool their talents and resources to start their own business. Wimberly notes that they made their boss the company's first client.

We had to educate ourselves in ways that our formal educa-tion didn't do. We looked at what marketing, promotion, and publicity really entailed, beyond words. For a service business, the hardest part was putting together the structure. We were not manufacturing anything; our real asset was our minds.

When it came time to hire a lawyer for the firm, Wimberly's internship gigs again proved beneficial. He called on an attorney for whom he had once worked to help set up the company's legal structure. The partners decided to form a limited liability company.

A limited liability company was still fairly new. Our attorney felt that this was the best legal structure for us. With an LLC, the taxes are passed through the partners, whereas with a regular corporation, the company gets taxed on its earnings and the partners get taxed on their personal income. We didn't want to file as a S-corp., because it's limiting; you can't grow past a certain size (maximum number of shareholders allowed). We didn't want to get in a situation where we had to undo our legal structure to accommodate the business's growth.

August Bishop's initial overhead was very low—no security deposit, no office equipment, no utility bills—since they shared office space with their attorney. This allowed the two comrades to have free access to telephone lines, fax machines, copiers, and a conference room. August Bishop was launched with hardly any start-up capital.

We had about $1 in the bank. We both lived at home with our parents starting out. Our families didn't invest money in the business. But at the same time, living with them kept us from having a tremendous amount of expenses, so that we could concentrate on our business.

August Bishop also reduced its costs by using independent contractors instead of hiring a staff, including Publicity Coordinator Carmelo Cherubin, 22. In addition to legal counsel, Wimberly and Bishop hired an accountant, mainly to handle their taxes (the partners report their earnings and losses quarterly). Wimberly handles the company's bookkeeping.

The young marketing entrepreneurs believe their strength is that they are more in tune with popular culture than most people in their field. They are using this as a competitive advantage to carve a niche for their company. Looking back, the partners believe their company would be drastically different had it not developed the way it did. The foundation of their business hasn't been based on luck though. It's about timing.

After a little over two years in business, we are where most people said we needed to be when we started out. We now have our own office space—1,200 sq. ft., a reputation in the industry, money put aside or a cash reserve for an emergency, and a business plan. These are all of the things we needed in place to run a business. All this means now is that we simply can take our business to the next level.

To grow the firm, Wimberly and Bishop will eventually have to work with companies with larger budgets allotted to public relations, marketing, and advertising. Most of their clients are themselves small business owners.

Our livelihood is based on the aggressive acquisition of clients—and being able to leave a client where there was no money and to grab a client where there was money and growth potential to keep the ball rolling. As a company, we can't afford to be complacent. There is a lot happening right now in the young men's sportswear market (ages 14–25). I think we are going to see a narrowing in this business. August Bishop plans to be one of the companies who will still be around and who will make an impact on this industry.

The twosome's relationship with 12-year industry veteran Maurice Malone (which ended in 1997) paid off in another way. Because the sportswear collection sold overseas in the United Kingdom, South America, and Japan, August Bishop was able to go global after a year in business. The firm met up with a distribution company based in Tokyo that purchases American goods, primarily clothing, for export. Wimberly and Bishop work on a commission basis and serve as marketing representative or agents.

We represent some of the most popular designers in the urban sportswear market. From New York to Tokyo, our clients define what it is to be young, hip, and stylish. We position our clients in ways that increase their visibility, reinforce traditional advertising efforts, and ultimately increase their profits.

August Bishop increases clients' exposure by creating and providing numerous services, including press releases, video news releases, media buying, events planning, print advertisements, in-store promotions, direct-mail brochures, marketing presentations, and customer surveys. As part of the image-building process, the firm utilizes product placement. The firm has placed their clients' clothing on such recording artists as Brandy and the Fugees.

Through the use of contacts within sports and entertainment industries, August Bishop is able to garner promotional exposure for their clients' products through high profile performers, actors, and athletes. It has coordinated artists' wardrobes for concert tours, music videos, magazine interviews, and television appearances on major network and cable shows, including *New York Undercover* and *Yo! MTV Raps.*

A significant marketing tool for Wimberly and Bishop has been fashion industry trade shows, such as Magic, held in Las Vegas and the Super Show, in Atlanta. Wimberly and Bishop come across a lot of potential clients or new business. Thousands of clothing companies and buyers from across the globe attend the big events. To help expand their global presence, Wimberly and Bishop plan to add trade shows held in Paris and Germany to their itinerary.

A mid-size public relations firm can command a $5,000 monthly retainer. August Bishop is profitable, partly because the partners don't take salaries—at least not what they would get paid as employees. In 1997, the firm generated more than $200,000. The duo hope to top the million-dollar mark by 1999.

Making your own decisions in life is the only way you can fulfill your own destiny. Being an innovator, thinker, and using all of the knowledge at your disposal will instantly separate you from the pack. August Bishop will continue to position itself both defensively and offensively in the strategic game of marketing, never sacrificing our integrity, always pursuing victory.

SUJATA PATEL, PRESIDENT OF SUJATA PATEL ENTERPRISES

"In vogue" refers to someone who is fashionable. Likewise, it describes designer Sujata Patel, whose stylish creations have

Jules Allen

SUJATA PATEL

adorned the models in *Vogue, Elle,* and *Glamour* magazines. Sujata launched her accessories business, Sujata Patel Enterprises, in 1993. She began with jewelry, selling handmade pieces. She later expanded her accessory line to include a variety of hats, handbags, scarves, and hair adornments.

Sujata is the classic case of someone who turned a hobby into a business. The self-taught jewelry maker started creating pieces in 1990 as a way to make money to travel. She sold the handcrafted baubles—on and off—to friends, private clients, and local boutique buyers.

I had a lot of friends who were stylists at magazines, and in 1992, one of my friends asked me to create a collection and set me up with Vogue. *I started getting introduced to fashion editors at the other women's magazines. That's when I came out with the piece that really launched my business. It was a choker that appeared in* Elle *magazine. Since I listed my telephone number, I was getting all of these mail-order calls. I was selling to fashion models, magazine editors, and entertainers. That's when I realized I had something great.*

Sujata drew on her fashion design and merchandising background, having graduated in 1987 from The American Intercontinental University, where she spent the first two years in Los Angeles and the last two in London at the school's sister college. Sujata's family, who is originally from Gujrat, India, lived in London until she was four, prior to moving to the States. Patel worked for a clothing manufacturer in L.A., where she gained firsthand knowledge on every phase of production. She learned about overseas operations when she later worked for a company in New York that had factories in Hong Kong.

There is more to designing than just drawing something on paper. There is the whole execution of the item (from concept to design to manufacturing). I had the chance to learn the business side of the fashion industry. I just didn't like that environment (it was too stifling).

Sujata was able to use her creative talents and professional relationships to her advantage in developing her own enterprise. The then 27-year-old took care of all legal matters—structuring the business as a sole proprietorship, getting a tax identification number, filing the business, and registering it with the proper agencies. She went down to city hall and handled all of the paperwork herself.

Sujata financed the business using money she acquired from freelance design projects and her credit cards. She was creating the pieces herself, so she was able to operate from home, needing only a computer, fax, and printer. Whatever she earned, she put it back into the business.

Sujata underscores the importance of protecting one's work. She hired a lawyer and trademarked her name. She couldn't simply get a trademark for accessories in general; she had to register her name in several categories—handbags, beauty products, scarves, gloves, and jewelry.

A lot of times people like myself (young, up-and-coming designers) are offered opportunities by large corporations or independent individuals who want to work with them. If you are already trademarked, then they know going into the deal, they can't con you and take advantage of you. Or try to take your trademark and make it their own.

Still, a trademark doesn't protect one designer from recreating another person's work. Sujata says the laws are "funny" in that you can move a seam over a quarter inch and suddenly a piece is no longer the originator's design.

Essentially, in this business everyone knocks off [copies] everyone else's work, where you see the cheaper version of a design. I've been knocked off before. I saw a knock off version of the choker I did in one department store a month after it appeared in Elle *magazine.*

Sujata has had her share of setbacks, namely, she concentrated all her time and resources on one item. She failed to realize that in the fashion business, even with accessories, you have to change your product from season to season.

Although a particular design might run a long time, you can't count on it being your forever money. Once the trend is gone that's it, you have to have something ready in its place. I overproduced this one piece (the choker). It sold so strongly for two seasons, I was sure that it would do as well in the third season. But it didn't go anywhere and I ended up stuck with a lot of chokers. It was an awakening for me.

The trinkets artisan started out with eight different chokers, then fashion magazine editors asked if she could make hats. Once those designs took off, requests came in for handbags. Those too were an instant hit.

But what happened next was that I lost all the contacts and customers I had built up from my jewelry because I had stopped making those items. Instead, I was creating hats. That next season when my clients wanted to order hats, I couldn't supply them, because I was doing bags. You build up a clientele and then you build off that. You don't build up something and then knock it down and start over again. I know now that's no way to run a business.

Now every season the focus is exclusively on handbags. Sujata changes the styles of her designs, adding totally new creations to her collection. She does keep some items from the previous season with certain modifications (i.e., new colors and materials). These are usually her best-sellers and, therefore, are carried over into the next season.

The magazine press Sujata gained has generated enough orders to cover costs and showcase her goods at trade shows. She purchases her materials wholesale—at about $7,000 per season for supplies to make samples. She uses high-end fabrics, including fur (fake), feathers, jewels, and glitter. Pieces sell from $50-$500.

Another major challenge for Sujata has been fulfilling orders, since she does everything herself. For this reason, she recently signed on with an accessories showroom rep to sell her pieces to boutiques nationwide and overseas (her designs have sold in Japan, South America, and Hong Kong).

Because I create the designs myself, each piece is special and unique—I make up techniques as I go along. That's part of my niche; that's what enables me to cut my competition. I have to get to a point where I make things that are salable, yet cost-effective.

For about a year, Sujata investigated several factories to produce her designs—on a mass-market scale. She wanted to deal with a manufacturer who was as detail-oriented as she was.

I have been fortunate enough to find a good factory that believes in my talent and my ability to launch my line. Therefore, they are willing to work with me at affordable prices. Factory costs can be very high and discouraging to a beginner. I have started to do trade shows. This is how market visibility occurs and people take you much more seriously.

The reason I am taking so long is because I can't afford to send a design to a factory and get back sloppy work. That means the sales agent can't sell it, because the store rejects it. There goes the money I put into my supplies down the tube. Once the fabric is cut and the item is made, you can't redo it. I don't ever want to be in a situation where an order goes unfilled.

Her target audience is still an offshoot of the fashion model crowd. The bulk of her customers are essentially trendy young women between the ages of 25 to 35. Her market also can be found in such department stores as Saks Fifth Avenue, Neiman-Marcus, and Nordstrom.

A department store can actually put a new designer out of business in the early years. Oftentimes, they want markdown money. They have such large buying power that they want a lot of perks. As a small designer if you have one large account that orders so much product from you and then something goes wrong, you are in trouble. But if you have several accounts—say 50 boutiques—that buy in smaller quantities, then it's easier to get rid of your product.

In the past, Sujata has had boutiques sell her products and new samples on consignment. She's now exploring putting out a mail-order catalog on the Internet, which is much cheaper than the traditional print approach. She's also working on a business plan—which includes market analysis for a Website—in hopes of raising venture capital to finance her business expansion.

Your product has to sell and appeal to an audience. You have to do the research—where and what stores sell your type of product? Who else is producing it? Where are they producing it? How much are they selling it for? Then you have to ask yourself—Can I produce it? Can I make it better, cheaper, and somehow cut my competition? How do I get that edge?

6

DO GOOD FOR OTHERS: SETTING UP A NONPROFIT BUSINESS

> The ultimate measure of a man is not where he stands in
> moments of comfort and convenience, but where he stands
> at times of challenge and controversy.
> — *Rev. Dr. Martin Luther King Jr.*

There are scores of nonprofit organizations in America that fight for the human rights of diverse groups; provide much needed services to the poor, elderly, children, and the mentally and physically challenged; advocate religious freedom; foster educational development; support recreational activities; promote the arts and cultural expression; defend consumer rights; and raise consciousness about threats to the environment. The scope of issues addressed by grassroots organizations is tremendous. The amount of good they do for their communities is immeasurable.

The number of nonprofit organizations in the United States is steadily increasing each year. Many conscientious and enterprising young people have founded organizations to help build up their communities. Perhaps one of the most publicized of these groups is *Do Something*, founded in 1993 by a board of young people under age 30, including Andrew Shue, co-star of Fox Television's *Melrose Place*. The national organization provides training courses, community guidance, and financial resources to emerging young leaders.

In conjunction with local leaders, *Do Something* provides funds and grants in several cities, including New York, Boston, Washington, D.C., and San Diego. A major success was Webstock '96, an Internet community-building festival, which brought together hundreds of thousands of young people who wanted to share ideas, learn from each other, and take action to build their communities.

Do Something has been able to leverage its resources—from free office space to marketing materials to public service announcements—thanks to such corporate partners as MTV, Blockbuster, Guess?, Mademoiselle, General Mills, and First USA/VISA. In fact, *Do Something* co-sponsors along with MTV the annual Do Something Brick Award, totaling close to $200,000, which is given to ten enterprising young people heading community-based organizations.

A prime example is the 1997 Brick Award Winner, Joseph Barisonzi, who is the 27-year-old executive coordinator of the Lyndale Neighborhood Association (LNA) in Minneapolis. LNA was founded in 1974 as a social organization, but was incorporated as a nonprofit in 1990. LNA has helped its residents implement over 300 programs and events, including revolving loan funds and the Lyndale Youth Farm and Market, which is about 15,000 sq. ft. of land where teens cultivate crops and sell organic foods to people in the community and local grocers. LNA also helped two residents to write a business plan, find a location, and secure financing for their café.

Since 1994, over $23 million in new investment has been brought into the Lyndale neighborhood from private foundations, government agencies, and philanthropic individuals. Barisonzi oversees a $1.2 million budget and manages some 700 volunteers a month. He also handles fundraising, long-term strategic planning, and maintaining strategic alliances with civic groups and social organizations. Barisonzi, who holds a bachelor's degree in social change theory and a master's in organizational development from Antioch University, is the former director of the International Alliance for Sustained Agriculture, an environmental advocacy organization. He describes himself as a social capitalist who tries to leverage the power of the community.

Many of *Do Something*'s grant and award winners belong to a new breed of do-gooders in the nonprofit sector, referred to as social entrepreneurs, because they attempt to address social ills using private sector tactics and tools. They are pushing their programs based on price and quality of services provided, not on pity or sentimental stories.

These new-generation founders of nonprofit organizations are not much different from the ambitious founders of emerging growth companies. Their objective is to run a profitable nonprofit, channeling the organization's earnings back into its programs. Even though nonprofits are in the business of helping people, they are still impacted by the bottom line. Answering the call, entrepreneurially minded do-gooders are institutions such as the Minneapolis-based National Center for Social Entrepreneurs, which works with nonprofits who want to run profit-generating businesses. Stanford University Graduate School of Business hosted a conference spring 1997 on social entrepreneurship and is planning to integrate its findings into an ongoing curriculum.

FROM TALK TO ACTION

If you have a cause that you want to do something about, start by talking, meeting, and planning with others who share your vision. If you don't need to raise much money to accomplish your goals, you can function as a loosely knit association. To operate as a legal entity that solicits money, you must form a nonprofit organization—choose a name, tax identity, and purpose; devise a strategic plan, recruit board members; hire a staff; and raise funds.

There are several organizations that can assist you in your quest to get organized. For starters, state associations of nonprofits offer technical assistance, educational programs, insurance plans, referrals, and other sources of assistance. The National Council of Nonprofit Associations in Washington, D.C., is a national coalition of nonprofit associations, representing more than 20,000 community-based organizations. The Foundation Center in New York is the authoritative source of information on foundation giving. It has a directory of foundations and grants and publications on fund raising and grant proposal writing. Much of the center's documentation can be retrieved online.

THINK BEFORE YOU LEAP

While the number of people in need and the cost of servicing them is on the rise, state and federal funding is on the decline. Similarly, corporate and individual giving has decreased. Grants are synonymous in the nonprofit world with money raised in the form of handouts. As a result, nonprofits have the stigma of constantly begging for funds.

It takes more than a worthwhile idea to run a nonprofit; you'll need a well-planned and fully defined program that appeals to potential donors who can aid you in your fundraising efforts. You also need to recruit volunteers and organizational members to join your cause.

The following outline will give you a head start:

Forming Your Organization's Mission and Vision: Obviously, you have identified an existing problem, otherwise you wouldn't be forming a nonprofit organization. But how can you rally financial contributors around your cause and convince them it's worth funding? It's important that you gather data to substantiate your target audience and its specific concerns.

Your organization will need to define five areas upfront:

1. *Mission statement:* This tells why the organization exists — its purpose — and defines its target audience.

2. *Vision statement:* This sets forth the long-term goals of the organization. You must be able to clearly convey the organization's vision to your staff, board of directors, volunteers, and clientele.

3. *Goals statement:* This describes the organization's short-term and long-term goals and how they will be achieved.

4. *Needs Assessment:* This spells out the specific need(s) of the target audience your organization intends to the address, what services it will provide, and what circumstances are likely to impact your select audience.

5. *Client Population:* Be specific in selecting and defining your target audience. For instance, a program should not be designed just "for youths," but "young people between the ages 12 and 16, living in urban areas."

Incorporating Your Organization: You have to incorporate as a nonbusiness organization formed for artistic, social, or charitable purposes. In general, the difference with incorporated organizations is that they don't sell stock to shareholders or pay dividends as do business corporations. No one owns a nonprofit corporation.

There are several legal matters that apply to nonprofit organizations, including registering with state and government agencies, filing reports, securing licenses, adhering to employment laws, and addressing tax issues. If your group plans on doing heavy fund-raising directed at several sources (corporations, foundations, and individuals), a solicitation license may be required; check with the county clerk's office.

You can register yourself, but you may want to consult a professional lawyer that specializes in nonprofits or get free legal help through a legal assistance program.

To incorporate you will need:

• *Articles of incorporation:* A nonprofit organization becomes a corporation by drafting an articles of incorporation and filing it with the state. While the information varies from state to state, you need to include:

1. Organization's name and location

2. Mission or purpose

3. Name and address of each incorporating member

4. Board of directors: names, addresses, and tenure

5. Membership qualifications (if applicable)

6. Corporate obligations/personal liabilities

7. How funds will be solicited and distributed

• *Bylaws:* The rules by which your organization operates are the bylaws. This set of rules governs the internal operations, gives structure to the group, dictates who has power and how much, and outlines the group's financial and legal procedures. In general, the bylaws should spell out the specific services to be provided; responsibility and structure of the board of directors; the number of officers, their duties, and how they are appointed or removed from their positions; and membership (individuals or corporations) qualifications, size, and eligibility. The bylaws should also include what is the fiscal year of the organization, how funds will be appropriated, and any specific rules that apply to members. Also, when and who can amend the bylaws.

Filing for Tax Exemption/501C.3 Status: Nonprofit corporations are tax-exempt, meaning they don't pay taxes on their income. To qualify for the IRS 501C.3 classification (form 1023) your organization must offer educational, scientific, religious, literary, public safety, or charitable services. Some nonprofits qualify as social welfare organizations (i.e., civic groups) under IRS code section 501C.4. (Note: you are required to have an employer identification number [form SS-4], which is much like a Social Security number for an individual, regardless of whether or not you have employees.) Attach the bylaws and articles of incorporation to your IRS tax-exempt forms. It can take anywhere from three months to a year for the IRS to process your application. If approved, you will receive a letter verifying your tax status. At the end of your organization's fiscal year, you will file IRS form 990 for organizations exempt from income taxes.

Enlisting a Board of Directors: The size, structure, and composition of your board should be based on your organization's needs. As your organization grows, the composition of your board will evolve. Starting out, you may have a working board, where members do some of the work normally carried out by employees.

Many groups add prominent "names" to their board. Generally, their names are supposed to make it easier to raise funds. However, this could backfire and turn off more prudent financial donors. You want to seek out people with the necessary skills and interests who can help transform your organization's vision into a reality.

The board of directors assumes a governing role. It's responsible for several areas, including finance. The board is accountable for how funds are spent and determines the fiscal policies and controls; reviews and approves long-term goals; participates in fundraising activities; makes financial contributions when possible; reviews and approves operating policies; hires/fires an executive director; and determines staff salary scales. Ideally, you should have at least six people appointed to your board. Some state laws dictate the minimum size of a board.

Choose people who demonstrate competence in finance, management, law, and public relations; who have viable contacts and connections; who are leaders in the community or have access to people of importance; and share your vision for the organization. Social gatherings (or references) are venues for soliciting potential board members. Let them know what is exciting and interesting about your organization. At the same time, find out what they can contribute to the group. A word to the wise: Try to ascertain if any people you are considering have personal issues with one another. Conflicts can't always be avoided, but you'll want to weed out anything that could hinder the harmony of your board. For more information, check out the Washington, D.C.–based National Center for Nonprofit Boards, which is dedicated to improving the effectiveness of organizations' board of directors.

Developing a Strategic Plan: Planning is a continual cycle of thinking, analyzing, monitoring, and evaluating. Every organization should have a written annual plan that outlines specific steps:

1. A set of objectives

2. A list of actions that will be taken to achieve each objective, who is responsible for carrying out each action, when it will start, and how long it will take

3. A list of task assignments

4. A timetable (or deadlines) for the detailed tasks required to complete the actions

5. An organizational budget that takes into account everything you want to do in the coming year and figures out what it will cost

Your organization's objectives should be feasible, measurable, and stated in a way that is clearly understandable to anyone. The approaches you intend to take to achieve your objectives also should be stated in specific terms. For instance, the organization will set up a certain number of workshops, provide counseling to a given number of clients, deliver a certain number of meals to the homeless, sponsor cultural events, or lobby for environmental causes.

After three years of rapid growth, the *Do Something* organization underwent a systematic strategic planning process in 1996 to clarify its long-term goals, which included expanding their in-schools program and launching a membership campaign; participants would receive the organization's *Build* magazine, a series of corporate benefits from sponsors, and programmatic information. In addition, *Do Something* linked up with a major foundation to research strategies on how to strengthen the efforts of local organizations in recruiting and training young people for community-based work.

It's important that your organization monitors and measures its plan. If you can't evaluate how well you achieve something, how can you be sure you have accomplished anything where your constituents are concerned? There are several ways you can evaluate your program, including keeping count of the number of clients served, surveying participants to get their feedback, and comparing your services against organizations with similar programs. The New York–based Nonprofit Management Association helps organizations and individuals better manage nonprofits. The Independent Sector, in Washington, D.C., provides materials on leadership and management, information on trends, and other data relative to nonprofits.

Raising Funds: You need dollars for general operating expenses—rent, utilities, computer systems, administration, etc.—and to run your specific programs. What kind of fundraising strategy will you employ to keep your organization running efficiently and effectively—grants, annual giving, special events, and/or endowment funds? To raise money, you must identify the best sources for each financial need. How will you approach funders—foundations, corporations, other businesses, government agencies, and individuals?

Government funding requires a more formal process in the way of grants or contracts. Some institutional funders provide grants for certain programs. Others give to certain areas, such as the arts, education, environmental protection, or human rights. There are independent foundations that fund small local groups as well as national organizations, including the Ford Foundation, Carnegie Foundation, and Rockefeller Foundation. Some cities have community foundations that distribute to local causes. More and more corporate foundations are being set up by businesses, making contributions in communities where they operate and for causes of interest to their officers or employees. Many companies have direct giving programs as part of community relations or public affairs.

LNA's Joseph Barisonzi compares writing a grant proposal to developing a business plan. It is about selling your concept to someone who is willing to invest in it. It includes a mission statement, program objectives, financial projections, and measures how you are going to prove your results. View grant money as start-up capital. Look at how you will develop and sustain your organization in the long term.

Writing grant proposals, soliciting contributions, and developing other funding sources requires special skills. Most groups have written guidelines on what they will fund. Do your homework to find people interested in your type of program. You can contact private and public funders via letters, personal calls, proposals, and brochures. Your board should play an integral role in this labor.

If another organization services your same group of constituents, you must be able to demonstrate how your program differs. It takes time to develop a track record, but you can begin by building community support for what you are doing. Try to get endorsements from reputable sources. The people on your staff and board will also add credibility to your program.

Recruiting Staff Members: Outline how and if you will use a paid staff, paid consultants, volunteers, or college interns. You may choose not to have paid employees and instead rely heavily on volunteers. Even so, you need to build a competent team. Take time to structure your staff. Determine what tasks need to be done and what skills are needed for each. Develop a list of staff positions. Outline the major responsibilities of each position, and what qualifications are needed. Recruit people through professional newsletters, associations, placement offices at colleges and universities, special interest publications, and local and community newspapers. Some social and professional organizations have their own job bank. Hire people who can do the job, not friends and family members who may be sympathetic to your cause.

Most organizations use volunteers as an auxiliary part of the business. Staff management of an employee-based group is much different than a volunteer-based organization. For instance, when you call a staff meeting, people show up because they know it is a part of their job responsibilities. If you call a meeting for a group of volunteers and the time conflicts with their favorite television episode, they may not show up. You need to understand what motivates volunteers, board members, and private donors.

Developing a Budget: The financial blueprint for your organization is the budget for the fiscal year—the annual twelve-month period that typically corresponds to the calendar year—January to December. The budget tells how much you can expect to achieve in revenues and how much you will spend during the year. In the nonprofit sector, every dollar that comes in is tied to a specific expenditure. In comparison with a for-profit business, revenues are dispersed to meet total costs. Imagine you are running a grocery store. And the money you made from your meat section could only be spent on the rent. Money from the produce section was for the electric bill only. Profits from canned goods must be used to pay for new product development. That's how nonprofits operate. Most foundations and private investors specify where they want their money to go.

Sources of income are grants, government contracts, members' contributions, fees, and donations of services and supplies. Some nonprofits charge fees, for instance, educational organizations charge fees for courses. Funds that are to be raised from special events also should be included in the budget.

Expenses include how much you need to pay staff (whether full-time, part-time or temporary), consulting fees for services, health and liability insurance, Social Security taxes, rent, equipment (leased or purchased), supplies, and other costs of providing services. Your budget should include costs for both fixed (i.e., salaries, insurance, utilities, and rent) and variable (i.e., postage, printing, travel, conferences, and publicity) expenses. Take advantage of resources designed especially for nonprofits. For example, the Telecommunications Cooperative Network provides nonprofit member organizations discounts on long-distance telephone service, fax service, conference calling, and other services.

Don't make the mistake of setting an unrealistically high income goal for yourself. Be reasonable in your expectations. Outline how much you anticipate receiving from outside sources. When the anticipated income from all available sources is added together, the difference between this figure and your expenses is the amount you still need to raise from undetermined sources.

Your budget should be used for financial planning and cash management throughout the year, but be reviewed quarterly. You need to stay on top of cash flow management to ensure that the money is there when you need it. It is one thing to say that you need $50,000 a year to cover your anticipated expenses of $50,000, but will you have cash in the bank to cover your monthly costs? In order to avoid a cash shortfall, prepare a cash flow statement—an outline of money coming in and going out each month. This is where personal savings or a personal loan in the initial stage may come in handy to help offset those periods when your fund-raising efforts are languid.

You or someone on staff should know basic bookkeeping. You may be able to find a volunteer accountant or affordable accounting service to handle your taxes. When the fiscal year ends, the financial odometer returns to zero and funds have to be raised all over again. Make sure your organization emphasizes results: Nonprofits must be accountable to the folks they serve and provide clear goals against which staff, directors, and fundraisers can measure the program's accomplishments.

Those nonprofits that hope to survive in the new millennium must find nontraditional ways of earning income, including developing corporate partnerships, and making better use of resources to bring added value to their communities.

MARIBEL CRUZ, FOUNDER AND
PRESIDENT OF ACTION AGAINST AIDS

In 1995, Maribel Cruz read a newspaper article about a group of inner-city children, whose trip to summer camp was canceled once the camp directors discovered they were HIV positive. The story brought tears to Cruz's eyes. It was then that she decided to shift gears and dedicate her newfound business to take Action Against AIDS (AAA).

A graduate of Johnson & Wales University, Cruz was the former director of sales and marketing at Wondercamp Entertainment, where she was responsible for advertising, corporate sales, field trips, and fund-raiser events. At age 29, Cruz left the corporate world in 1994 to start her own business. However, she had originally developed a recreational program for children. In fact, she had even written a business plan and incorporated the for-profit enterprise.

MARIBEL CRUZ

Once the focus shifted to addressing the needs of children with HIV/AIDS, Cruz changed the New York–based business to a nonprofit AIDS awareness and fund-raising organization. Its mission: To educate teenagers about HIV/AIDS through entertainment by providing an array of educational activities and interactive exercises led by recording artists, sports figures, radio personalities, community leaders, corporate executives, and AIDS educators who are living with HIV/AIDS. Cruz's first step was to hire a lawyer to help her apply for a 501C.3 non-profit status.

It involved a lot of paperwork, including my articles of incorporation and bylaws. It took about six months to get approved by the IRS. I wrote a business plan, but it was very trying, because there weren't really any materials out there tailored for nonprofits. Looking back, I wish I had known then about the Foundation Center and the Support Center of New York, which are the primary sources of information for nonprofits.

AAA assists communities in helping their children and teens become informed about HIV/AIDS through "edutainment"—a combination of education and entertainment. In addition to the All-Star Edutainment Programs, the organization has developed an All-Star Edutainment Fan Club, which is by and for teenagers. The group educates adolescents through newsletters and jam sessions about Health (HIV/AIDS, Teen Pregnanacy, STD's), Education and Career Opportunities, Teen Relationships, Self-esteem, Fashion, Entertainment, and Sports Issues.

When she first started out, Cruz thought it would be easier to sell a product dealing with children and health. She learned through various HIV/AIDS seminars that three million American teens are infected with sexually transmitted diseases (STD) each year—one every 11 seconds. There are two teenagers infected with HIV every hour and approximately 60 percent of all American high school seniors have used illegal drugs. About 75 percent of people living with HIV/AIDS were African-American and Latino (Cruz is of Puerto Rican decent). It is estimated that there are 650,000 to 900,000 people living with HIV and AIDS in the United States and there are 40,000 new HIV infections each year in the U.S. But despite the worthy cause, people weren't buying into it.

I didn't realize I was going to run into so many obstacles in starting this business and raising AIDS awareness in our communities. I had no idea how resistant this society was to receiving HIV/AIDS information and materials and contributing to the "edutainment" programs. I was the new kid on the block with a new organization, mission, and readiness to raise money for school programs. I quickly learned that people were apprehensive about funding new grassroots organizations; they fund the same and much larger organizations each year. I tried to link with other organizations to facilitate access to contacts, funding, and resources, but they were resistant to working with a new organization and sharing their resources and funding sources.

Cruz tried to remedy the situation by hiring a public relations firm to garner some positive press about herself and AAA. That proved to be a mistake: first because she couldn't afford to retain the services of a PR firm and second because she got little publicity for the money she did spend. All together, Cruz spent $38,000 of her personal savings to get AAA up and running.

Like any operation, whether it's a for-profit or nonprofit, Cruz had to recruit people—mostly volunteers—to help run the programs. But it was difficult for Cruz to relay the organization's objectives to her team members. It wasn't until they actually saw the events, that people understood her vision.

I decided to create an edutainment program where kids between the ages of 12 and 19 and from the public high schools would experience a day of education, music, and games. We would invite artists, corporate professionals, sports figures, and AIDS educators to come and talk to them about HIV/AIDS, condoms, abstinence from sex, drugs, and violence as well as the importance of staying in school. The reason I wanted to get musical artists involved is because a lot of kids look up to them as role models. And because music is universal—it transcends color.

It took nearly a year—from June 1995 to April 1996—before Cruz could raise enough money—around $6,000—to fund her first edutainment program. She was able to sign up only two artists and enlist less than half a dozen schools. Through her

pioneering efforts, five high schools and 3,000 teenagers benefited from AAA's programs.

Cruz embarked on an extensive letter writing campaign the
following year to raise funds, friends, visibility, artists, and volunteers. After sending some 150 letters to record labels, radio
stations and other corporations, 12 entertainers, 3 radio stations, and 6 corporate executives signed up for AAA's All-Star
Edutainment Program–AIDS Awareness project for the 1997
school year.

*It is a challenge getting the high schools to agree to host our
events, because of the subject matter dealing with AIDS, sex,
drugs, and condoms. Also, many of the schools are not comfortable with hip-hop music. This forces us to be a little more selec-
tive and to screen which artists we want to approach. It costs AAA
about $3,600 per school to put on one of its programs, which
includes AIDS information packets, transportation, and stage
and production equipment for an audience of 600 kids. All performers and speakers are given scripts on their individual topics
of what they are to say to the kids. This ensures that everyone is
on the same page and delivers appropriate and educational
information.*

Cruz notes one problem is that some performers have tried
to use the same stage gear as if they were performing at a major
concert hall. But they have to adjust their style and format to
the size of the school and age of the kids in the audience. AAA
hosted its AIDS awareness program in 25 schools in 1997, with
Cruz putting in hours from about 5 A.M. until 1 A.M. In 1997,
Cruz took her program national, including a $2\frac{1}{2}$ day event held
at five high schools with 3,500 teenagers in Chicago.

*The hardest task for us has been getting individual donations,
grants, and financial sponsors. We have had companies donate
their products. They want to get involved based on which performers are participating. They lose sight of the fact that this is for kids.*

To help remedy the situation, Cruz retained an events planning management company to help with fund-raising and help

AAA develop different levels of sponsorship packages. But again, that decision proved to be fruitless, because AAA didn't raise enough money to retain the firm's services. Cruz's goal now is to beef up fund-raising efforts in order to sustain her cause and withstand current hard times of cutbacks when it comes to AIDS programs. She is focusing on individual donations as well as grants, merchandising, and corporate sponsorship.

To help us get the funds and establish a track record, we developed a survey for kids to fill out after each program. This was a way to get direct feedback from the kids on our program and measure our strengths and weaknesses.

The response from the youth has been phenomenal. The 33-year-old Cruz's long-term goal is to host national and international edutainment programs and fan club jam sessions for teens throughout schools, amusement parks, concert arenas, and even movie theaters. Her more immediate goal is to put on several Stars of Teenagers Fund-raisers.

Through the efforts of volunteers, AAA retained the services of an advertising agency (pro bono), The Lord Group, to handle a national advertising and fund-raising campaign. Since then, Cruz has secured pro-bono office space, computer, telephone and fax service, and a dedicated team of professionals to help her in her efforts to increase AIDS awareness, raise money, and establish an image and visibility in local communities as well as in the corporate arena.

Despite the initial resistance from some individuals and companies, Cruz has managed to surround herself with dedicated people and companies that want to make a difference. Her team of 15 board of directors, 12 advisory board members, 14 teen P.A.C.T. Fan Club members, 55 volunteers, 10 events planning committee members, and the numerous companies with their financial support and in-kind services are what makes the All-Star Edutainment Programs and Fan Club a success, and most importantly a fun and memorable experience for young people.

Our dream is to bring together people of all ages to fight AIDS with compassion, hope, and inspiration.

MELISSA BRADLEY, FOUNDER OF THE ENTREPRENEURIAL DEVELOPMENT INSTITUTE

When Melissa Bradley graduated from Georgetown University in 1989, she went right to work as a higher education marketing/finance specialist for the Student Loan Marketing Association (SALLIE MAE), where she interned the previous summer. But after just a year on the job, the 22-year-old self-starter took the skills and experience she gained both as a student and employee and applied them to her own consulting firm.

Called Bradley Development, Inc., her firm aided people—mostly parents—in planning how to finance a college education, choosing the best school, and filling out college applications and other necessary documents. She also assisted adults with career planning, which included reviewing their interviewing skills and resumes. She later formed a consortium in order to pool the talents and resources of 10 other small business owners and consultants.

Bradley Development booked $1 million its first year in operation, servicing 150 clients (with fees ranging from as little as $15 to $2,000). Bradley sold the consulting firm in 1992, taking part of the proceeds to launch The Entrepreneurial Development Institute (TEDI). The Washington, D.C.–based organization teaches low-income, at-risk youth how to start and run a business.

I had been involved with the After-School Kids Program at Georgetown since I was an undergraduate. One day the kids asked me if I was unemployed. I tried to explain I was an entrepreneur. They couldn't identify. Some of them couldn't even spell the word. Many of them didn't even go to school and were juvenile delinquents that had been put on probation. I realized that not every kid in the program would become an entrepreneur, but at least [he/she] could benefit from learning entrepreneurial skills.

Thanks to Bradley's input, Georgetown University ran an eight-month pilot program, which targeted 50 kids and consisted of workshops on starting and running a business, field trips, and guest speakers. The program proved to be so successful that the university, parents, and community officials wanted to maintain it.

At first, Bradley envisioned running TEDI as a for-profit entity. But she realized that many of the people it would serve couldn't afford to pay for the services. Through the National Society for Fund-Raising Executives, she was put in touch with the Center for Community Change (CCC).

CCC provided TEDI space, agreed to be its fiscal agent, and gave me the schooling of my life in terms of what it would take to run a nonprofit organization. I learned how to put together a grant proposal compared to writing a business plan. I learned what you need to leverage with corporations and foundations to get funding. Even though I had a background in finance, I still had to learn about accounting procedures for nonprofits, which are a lot different from corporate accounting.

It took a year for the organization to get its 501.C3 status (tax structure for nonprofits). Despite the rigors of running the newfound undertaking, Bradley went on to get her MBA, as a graduate fellow, at American University. Many of TEDI's costs were offset by the CCC and American University student volunteers.

Bradley put together a nine-member board of directors, representing the academic community—including students—and corporate America. TEDI raised about $40,000 to $50,000 its first year, and twice that much its second year. At that point, the organization was able to move into a small office with a 10-member staff servicing 500 to 700 clients a year. TEDI expanded its services to four areas: elementary and high schools, public housing developments, detention facilities, churches, and other community groups.

Today, TEDI has branches and affiliates in some 16 cities and three countries—South Africa, Kenya, and Brazil. The branch offices service entire communities in such major cities as New York, Los Angeles, and Cleveland. Affiliates are existing organizations, such as the Boys and Girls Clubs, which have added TEDI's entrepreneurial training to their social format.

TEDI participants must start an actual entrepreneurial business or project in order to complete the year-long program. Students receive about $500 in seed money to get their business up and running.

We have had students that developed landscaping businesses, dog walking services, video production companies, coloring books, board games, computer software, pregnancy prevention programs, convenience stores, community newspapers, you name it.

In the last six years, TEDI has reached more than 15,000 young people. In 1996, Bradley was the national grand prizewinner of The Brick Award for Community Leadership, sponsored by the *Do Something* Organization, MTV, *Mademoiselle* magazine, and Blockbuster. TEDI received a $100,000 grant for its entrepreneurial efforts.

The 31-year-old has had no problem adopting for-profit management strategies in running TEDI. To make sure the program services its clients' needs, the organization conducts client surveys and market research. It puts its services to the test of its target market. TEDI's curriculum has three different tracks.

Track 1 is the training in finance, marketing, and organizational development. The students have to create a business plan as well as a life plan. Next, they go through a case-study book to help their critical thinking and analytical skills, and to provide them with an understanding of what happens in the real world.

Track 2 is leadership development in which the students have access to a database of mentors and micro-loans. There's also a youth-run advisory board called Youth VOICES (Victory on Issues Concerning Empowerment).

Track 3 is capacity building, which was recommended by a former student. This allows graduates to go back and teach the program to other young people.

Over the next year, TEDI will move in another direction. The organization will evolve more into a business development incubator. In general, business incubators are sponsored by private or public agencies and house a number of small start-up businesses at very low rents. Incubator tenants minimize their costs of operation by sharing many services, such as a receptionist, copy machines, fax machines, telephone services, and professional services.

For the first six years we were doing just training. But we have seen the emergence of other programs that offer the same thing. What is lacking is a place where the students can go to develop and grow their businesses once they receive the entrepreneurial training and graduate from these programs. By becoming an incubator, TEDI will better address the needs of its clients.

Bradley gave up her post as executive director of TEDI in 1997 to take a political appointment with the Office of Supervision at the United States Treasury Department. During the 15-month fellowship, she was responsible for theoretical and practical research in three areas: welfare reform, micro enterprise lending, and individual development accounts. Her long-term goal is to run her own community bank.

I realize that despite all of the training our students receive and the success they achieve, the banks don't want to loan money to them. They don't see these young people as having the capacity to run their own businesses.

For Bradley, being a woman, African-American, and only 22 at the time she started TEDI, has presented its own special set of challenges. Bradley, who grew up in a low-income, single-parent household, is grateful for the support of her mother, who worked three jobs to put her through college.

I also had to do battle with such stereotypes as the program was just going to create better drug dealers or that we were always begging for money. We had to convince them [funding sources] it was a win-win situation. We're not a social service organization, but an economic development organization. We are trying to help create businesses and economically self-sufficient people. Shifting those paradigms has been difficult.

Bradley plans to do a community stock option, where local residents would buy stock in their neighborhoods to create a pool of funds. In turn, a community board would make local grants or loans.

It is a way to get people to get off that welfare mentality— depending on the government. They can empower themselves and their communities. My job is to watch it [stock option], research it, document, and to help get it started.

CARRESE GULLO, PAST PRESIDENT OF THE NATIVE AMERICAN YOUTH COUNCIL

When New York City's Native American Youth Council was formed in 1992, Carrese Gullo, who was 18 at the time, was one of the first members. The goal was to encourage American Indian and Alaskan Indian youth between the ages of 14 and 24 to live healthy lifestyles and to be strong role models in their communities.

Gullo's involvement was cut short when she left to attend Native American arts college in New Mexico. But upon her return in 1994, she devoted most of her days and nights aiding the council in achieving its goals. She became vice president and then president in 1996. Assuming the role of leader came naturally; she helped the group organize and regain its focus.

To run a nonprofit, you need a core group of people who are going to be dedicated and work toward a goal. Sometimes people get sidetracked and lose interest. If you want to make sure some-

thing isn't going to fizzle out, you have to make sure that you have a community that is going to back and support you.

Although the Youth Council's membership has changed over the years, its core group has remained intact. The council meets once a week to discuss key issues and plan cultural events, including powwows—gatherings with singing, dancing, and arts and crafts.

The Youth Council is run with the help of the community. In fact, it is an extension of the American Indian Community House (AICH), which provides legal counsel, job training, alcohol and substance abuse counseling, and education and health care services.

In addition, AICH funds a performing arts program, which coordinates cultural activities and functions as a no fee booking agency for Native American actors, dancers, and models. And AICH's Gallery/Museum is the only Native American owned and operated art gallery in New York City.

The Youth Council works with members of AICH to render community service, whether it's providing food to the elders or helping out during art exhibitions or performing with the theater group. We provide a number of human and social services from running a clothing bank and food drive to providing HIV/AIDS education and group counseling for alcohol and substance abuse.

With a staff of over 30 people, AICH services more than 6,000 Native Americans each year, and has a current membership representing more than 75 different Native American nations. The Youth Council's activities are by no means strictly social. The group has taken political steps to educate the community at large on how to be culturally sensitive to Native Americans.

For example, we protested Crazy Horse Malt Liquor, which is named after a spiritual leader and warrior of the Lakota Nation. Unable to force the manufacturers to be culturally sensitive, the group targeted Arizona Iced Tea which is made by the manufacturer of Crazy Horse Malt Liquor, and is sold in neighborhoods

*where mostly people of color live. Until they take this product off
the market, we are protesting all of their products. Youth Council
members have gone to store owners and given them informa-
tional packages explaining why we are boycotting this product
and in turn why we will not buy from their store if they continue
to sell it.*

Indeed, she was able to convince a store across the street
from where she lives to stop selling Crazy Horse Malt Liquor
and to replace it with another product. Council members also
initiated a letter-writing campaign and picked local events to
plead their case.

The council is not alone in its efforts. It strives to interact
with other youth groups from different cultures, not just Native
Americans. However, one interrelated group the council is
associated with is the United Nations Indian Tribal Youth, Inc.
(UNITY), which comprises more than 1,000 youth councils
nationwide, all aiming to address social ills—poverty, unemployment, alcoholism, low self-image, education drop-out rate,
infant mortality rate, incarceration, poor health conditions,
inadequate housing, teen pregnancy, suicide, and discrimina-
tion.

While Gullo is no longer president of the Youth Council, at
age 23 she is the youngest of six department heads at AICH,
serving as director of communications. She is responsible for
maintaining AICH's archive of reference materials—a file of
about 500 different topics and current issues. Gullo also fields
questions from people who want to research their ancestry or
find a particular book by Native American writers or about
Native American subjects. She has even conducted tours for
groups visiting from other countries, including Japan and
Africa, and educated them about the Native American population in New York State.

Gullo's ties to her community have been advantageous in
other ways. More recently it has led her to start her own business, Native Sisters Harvest, a catering business that prepares

traditional and contemporary Native American dishes. AICH constantly contracted out to caterers for its numerous luncheons and cultural events. Gullo realized she could make money by preparing food for AICH and other groups or individuals in the community.

My partner and I both worked here at the center. We discovered we both liked cooking and she had done catering before. So, why not start here in our own backyard. We could tap into the center for resources and business.

Native Sisters prepares such cultural dishes as chili with deer meat, wild rice, summer squash, fried bread, ginger brew, cranberry cornbread, succotash, stuffing with wild rice, corn soup, etc. They also offer a variety of foods from the United States, Canada, and South America.

After a year of establishing her clientele through AICH, Gullo plans to incorporate the business in 1999, taking care of all legal areas—permits and insurance required to sell and prepare food in the Big Apple. Not only has AICH hired Native Sisters for their events, but the center has allowed them to use its kitchen and equipment—alleviating rent for a space and other overhead costs. Gullo and her partner pay only for the food and a small fee, mostly for cleanup.

Right now, we are very fortunate to have the support of the community and AICH. At some point we will go mainstream. There are people who want to see Native American businesses thrive. We would have a niche market, because there are no Native American caterers in New York. At the same time, we realize it takes a lot of money and a lot of time to build a successful catering business.

7

FINDING A FEW GOOD PROS: ACCOUNTANT, LAWYER, BANKER, ADVISOR, AND PUBLICIST

Great discoveries and achievements invariably involve the cooperation of many minds.

— *Unknown*

Many business owners attribute their success to surrounding themselves with smart people. You should build your business around a close-knit crew of people who complement each other's special talents as well as your own. Even if your business is a sole proprietorship, you will need a team of a counselors— namely a lawyer and an accountant. It's also important to have the input of employees, mentors, and a board of advisors to help with major business decisions.

Here's a rundown to help you structure such a support system.

Accountants: Accounting is a tool used to determine the financial health of your business. Remember, you are in business to make money. Accounting is an integral part of the business that you must pay close attention to from the start. Your accountant may even have connections and professional relationships that may be beneficial to you. You can divide accounting into three areas: bookkeeping, tax accounting, and financial accounting.

1. *Bookkeeping*. This involves the accurate tracking of money coming in and going out of the business (cash flow) and putting the transactions down on paper. You can hire a bookkeeper to manage record keeping or invest in a software program to prepare informal financial records (i.e., income statement, cash flow chart, and balance sheet). Popular accounting software: M.Y.O.B. (800-322-6962), Quickbooks (800-624-8742), Managing Your Money (800-288-6322), and Peachtree Accounting (800-247-3224). Most accounting programs keep bank account, credit card, and loan records; print checks; categorize expenses for tax purposes; and prepare monthly income and expense reports. Don't hire an accountant as a bookkeeper or to do all the financial recording. Not only is it more expensive that way, but it prevents you from staying on top of the day-to-day financial status of the business.

2. *Tax Accounting*. This area concerns how much money you have to pay in taxes. Here, the goal is to take steps to minimize your tax bill. Some tax reports are simple enough to do yourself, such as sales tax and employee withholding taxes—you will need a little knowledge of accounting procedures. When it comes to your annual income tax forms, you want to use an accountant who understands tax regulations and ways to save you money.

3. *Financial Accounting*. This area involves analyzing your company's financial performance and comparing current results with past accounting periods. You or a staff financial officer should oversee reporting and record keeping. You should use an accountant to prepare accurate financial statements for review by lending institutions or investors.

Accountant fees vary widely. Some of the large, national firms charge $50 to $100 per hour for their service. An independent bookkeeper may charge up to $25 an hour, depending on the region. You want to explore three types of accounting services:

- *Tax Preparers.* If you just want help with your taxes, you may be able to get by with a tax preparer. There are no professional requirements or testing standards for tax preparers. You might consider using a national tax preparation service, such as H&R Block, which has offices nationwide. Such tax preparation services are usually inexpensive, with an average fee of less than $100, and some agree to pay any penalties assessed due to an error on their part. Don't take a shoe box full of canceled checks, invoices, bank deposit slips, and bank statements to your tax preparer each year. You may have to pay extra to have that information input. For taxes, you need careful records of assets and depreciation, income and expense, capital gains and losses, inventory, and costs of goods sold. Look to preparation software: TurboTax (800-446-8848), TaxCut (800-228-6322), and Personal Tax Edge (800-223-6925).

- *Enrolled Agents.* These professionals have demonstrated competence in tax preparation by passing an extensive exam given by the U.S. Treasury Department, and they are authorized to represent taxpayers before the IRS. They usually cost more than a national tax-preparation service, but less than a CPA or tax attorney. Enrolled agents are full-time tax specialists, and they offer tax-planning advice. For more information or referrals, contact the National Association of Enrolled Agents (800-424-4339).

- *Certified Public Accountants (CPA).* CPAs are highly trained and must pass national exams and licensing requirements by the state board of accountancy. Be aware that not all CPAs are tax experts. You will want a CPA once you start looking for outside funding from investors. Whether you use a CPA or national firm depends on how large you expect your business to grow and what type of business you will operate. If you think your business will require large-scale financing or if you plan to go public with a stock offering, hire a CPA. Although more expensive, it will add credibility in the eyes of lending institutions, investors, and the IRS. For more information contact Independent Accountants International (305-670-0580) to access a CPA's standing, find out about his/her certification, educational background, and involvement in professional groups. Once you find a CPA, ask for an accurate assessment of how much certain services cost, and have him/her conduct an initial review of your business's finances. Ask for a proposal letter to find out what kind of work needs to be done for your company.

Make sure you feel comfortable with the person you hire. After all, he or she will be privy to the intimate details of your personal and financial life—how you make your money and where you spend it. Also, choose someone who has experience in your particular type of business. Ask for referrals from friends, associates, trade associations, or other professionals.

Lawyers: Calculate legal fees in your start-up costs and operating budgets. Your use of a lawyer will depend on the type of business you start. A small business lawyer can advise you on the advantages and disadvantages of setting up your business as a corporation or LLC, as well as on issues of credit, worker's compensation, and Social Security taxes. A well-connected attorney may even be able to help you secure potential investors and bankers.

Of course, this advice doesn't come cheaply. In a large metropolitan area, a general attorney can command $150 or more per hour and twice that amount for someone specializing in a particular area. However, it pays to ask. Sometimes fees are negotiable.

Bear in mind that a contract is legally binding whether or not an attorney draws it up. Consider writing your own contracts for simple transactions that are straight to the point. There are scores of books and software programs out there with fill-in-the-blanks legal forms and contracts. Even lawyers don't start from scratch every time they draft a document; they may use standard forms from their firm's files. The most widely recognized publisher of legal books is Nolo Press (800-992-6656), which publishes *Small Business Legal Forms*. A software program worth looking at is 301 Legal Forms and Agreements by E-Z Legal Forms (800-822-4566).

You may be able to get free or low-cost legal advice from a professional association in your field. The National Business Owners Association (202-737-6501) is a nonprofit organization that publishes the monthly *Business Owners' Legal Review*, covering pertinent legal issues.

Make sure you hire an attorney who considers you an important client, one worthy of his/her time and attention. You want someone you can trust and confide in. There are more than 700,000 lawyers nationwide from which to choose. Start by asking other professionals or business associates for recommendations.

Also, check your local library for the *Martindale-Hubble Law Directory*. This regional directory of attorneys provides a brief description of each lawyer and his/her area of expertise. Also, most state bar associations offer free referral services. You can get a copy of the booklet *The American Lawyer: When and How to Use One* from the American Bar Association, Information Services (312-988-5000).

In general, legal costs include fees and out-of-pocket expenses billed through your attorney's office, or that you incur on your own, such as filing fees, copying costs, phone bills, faxes, and the like. There are ways you can scale back costs:

- *Negotiate fees.* First you need to know how lawyers calculate their fees. Lawyers collect their money by the hour, by the project, or on a contingency basis (a percentage of any recovered money in a suit). Begin the negotiations by stressing the need to cut costs, not because you think the fees are too high or you don't value his/her services. Even if your lawyer won't reduce the going rate, maybe he or she will agree to set a limit on the overall amount charged per case. You would have to approve anything above that amount.

• *Know what you are paying for and carefully review all bills.* You may be asked to pay after services are rendered or to leave an advance payment (a retainer). Get an estimate of costs per case or project. Be sure to ask about expenses such as photocopies and faxes. Most attorneys charge by the page. Also, find out if your lawyer farms out work to paralegals, which will reduce your bills. Review all bills carefully before paying them. Mistakes do occur. Ask for itemization costs, not just "services rendered." Ask to be billed monthly so you can better monitor the money you're spending. Your bill should list the date of the service, the amount of time spent, the amount charged, expenses incurred, payment credits, and the total outstanding balance due. Make sure your bill lists the appropriate rates for associates, paralegals, or secretaries who worked on your case.

• *Be clear and concise.* You will get your money's worth by communicating your expectations clearly. When you first hire a lawyer, ask him/her to prepare an engagement letter that spells out what the firm will do and by when. Bear in mind time is money when you are talking to a lawyer. A lawyer may bill for his/her time in quarter-hour or six-minute units. If yours charges $200 an hour and bills in quarter-hour units, you'll be charged $50 every time he/she places a phone call or glances at a file on your behalf. So, be concise.

• *Be prepared.* The classic boy scout/girl scout motto applies whenever you visit your attorney. Have all important documents and information at your fingertips. Also, anything you do to make your lawyer's job easier saves you money.

There are two things you don't need a lawyer for—to get something notarized or to recover debts. Many banks, pharmacies, and stationery stores have notary publics on their staffs. And a collection agency can help you collect small debts.

When it comes to hiring a lawyer, you have three basic options:

1. *A private law firm.* One or more attorneys will handle your business's needs on an ongoing basis. The advantage is you can hire a firm with experience in handling issues specific to your industry. The disadvantage is that private lawyers are more expensive.

2. *A legal clinic.* Viewed as discount law firms, most clinics are listed in the Yellow Pages. They charge less, often offering fixed-priced services or a set fee for certain jobs, such as the incorporation of a business. And service is relatively speedy. The nation's first private legal clinic was Myers, Jacoby & Mosten. Today it's Jacoby & Myers, the national chain of high-volume law offices. The only real downside is that you can't expect specialized service.

3. *A prepaid legal plan.* These plans provide low-cost legal service for routine legal problems. In general, you pay a set fee for basic services, including telephone consultations, letter writing, and document review. Most prepaid legal plans require members to pay a small monthly fee to avoid paying stiff bills should a serious case arise. Plans for small businesses usually cost between $150 and $350 per year. Before you go this route, make sure you find a plan that suits your needs. The advantage of such plans is that you can use prepaid lawyers to review contracts and answer simple questions. Plus, the hourly rates for services rendered beyond the package are generally lower than those charged by private law firms. Obviously, the disadvantage is that you can't choose the lawyer assigned to you. For a list of

plans, contact the National Resource Center for Consumers of Legal Services (804-693-9330).

Bankers: In the initial stages of your business, you will need a bank to provide checking services, accept wire transfers, make federal tax deposits and credit card deposits, and render standard banking services. You will also need to deal with a bank for checking accounts, payroll tax deposits, credit card processing, and other administrative duties. It is important to start early on developing a good relationship with your bank.

Finding the right bank for your business can be tough. Here are six things to look for:

1. Does the bank have business-oriented programs? What business services does it provide (i.e., lock boxes, cash management, accounts receivable, money market funds, and record keeping).

2. How familiar is the bank with your type of business or industry?

3. Does the bank serve companies that match yours in size, operations, number of employees, etc.? (You may want to get recommendations from other businesses in the area or local trade associations and chambers of commerce).

4. What's the bank's reputation for small business lending? (You can check the bank's CRA rating— Community Reinvestment Act—which indicates its involvement in the community. Contact the Federal Reserve Board (202-454-3000) or the office of the Comptroller of the Currency (202-874-5000).

5. Can the bank meet your personal financial needs, providing insurance, mutual funds, and other investment vehicles?

6. Once your account holds more than $100,000, will the bank provide personalized services and assign you a private banker to manage your accounts and investments?

As your company grows, it needs cash to continue to thrive. A bank will be more inclined to grant you a secured loan or line of credit once you have established a track record. Just as you are cautious about loaning money to friends and relatives who never pay you back or are slow in paying you, banks are skittish about lending to new business owners.

Banks want their money (plus interest) back when it is supposed to be repaid, and start-ups are notorious for not paying back loans on time. Moreover, new businesses usually have fewer assets to use as collateral—loan defaults are expensive.

Your bank will review your record of frequent deposits. It will also document solid growth and financial performance. The bottom line is you'll have to convince the bank you are a solid customer and a good business risk.

You may want to start by establishing a small personal line of credit—$1,500—and then paying that off in 60 days. You could then increase that amount to $2,500 and pay it back in 90 days. From there, you can begin to request larger loan amounts.

Meet the bank officer responsible for your business account when you first open it and familiarize him/her with your business. Let the bank know what you expect from it in servicing your business—short-term and long-term requirements. Keep the officer updated on your business's progress, particularly new projects. Get to know other bank officers as well, just in case yours leaves. Keep your personal and business accounts in one bank.

If a loan officer isn't willing to sit down and talk with you, then that should signal a red flag. No matter what they tell you, banks have a lot of flexibility in what they can do for you. If a commercial loan officer is behind you and your business, you have a much better chance.

Advisors and Mentors: Corporations have a board of directors—a body of professionals, which helps develop policies and strategies, and provides direction to the fledging enterprise. This legal entity has some fiscal responsibility for your business and members are usually given ownership (shares) in return for their participation. In turn, they may be liable if the company is sued. More daunting, a board of directors can fire you from your own company—as was the case with Steve Jobs, co-founder of Apple Computer, who managed to bounce back.

On the other hand, a board of advisors is an informal group of people who counsels the business owner when important decisions must be made, but doesn't necessarily assume any financial and legal responsibility for the company. Typically, these are people who volunteer their services. So, while a business may not have a board of directors (based on its legal structure), it still can rely on the experience and expertise of a board of advisors.

A business advisory board can have as few as four to five people. An effective advisory committee might include members from professional and community groups, including an accountant, lawyer, financial planner, and associates from a local chamber of commerce and economic development center.

Obviously, the first place to start in building an advisory board is with people you already know and have developed a relationship with. Members don't have to be in the same industry. They can even be other young entrepreneurs. Some people choose their board based solely on individuals' reputations and affiliations, because it looks nice on the letterhead.

But it will be more advantageous to bring together a well-rounded group of individuals who can help you run your business and solve problems as they arise. This way your business benefits from the various opinions, backgrounds, and expertise of a strong mix of people. Equally important, an advisory board adds credibility to your business.

Most advisory boards operate as a roundtable discussion group, led by the business owner. Generally, members meet monthly or quarterly, and the cost for such counsel is the tab for a meal, although some board members have been known to receive 1 percent to 3 percent of net sales.

You can also take advantage of personal relationships with mentors. A mentor is a friend and colleague who can also offer business advice. You don't have 30 years to spend gaining expertise in a particular area, so why not learn from someone who's already experienced and well-connected in your industry? Mentors who have "been there and done that" will be delighted to impart their knowledge, help you with day-to-day decisions, and give you honest feedback.

Publicists: Before deciding whether you need a publicist, you need to understand the difference between marketing, advertising, and public relations. Too many businesses waste financial resources because they fail to make a clear distinction between the three in developing their budgets and strategic plans.

Marketing involves everything from creating a corporate image to attending trade shows to handing out coffee mugs imprinted with your logo. Advertising entails paying for space in a newspaper, magazine, or other print media, and buying air time on a radio or television station. Public relations involves getting your company mentioned in the media for free.

In the initial stages of your business, because of lack of funds, you will probably have to serve as your own publicist. You can learn some cost-effective ideas by reading the *Guerrilla Marketing* series of books by author and small business consultant Jay Conrad Levison (*Guerrilla Marketing Online* magazine: www.gmarketing.com). As your business becomes more successful, you may need to hire an outside public relations firm to put together a publicity campaign.

Whether a business is a two-person or 100-person shop, a public relations firm can save a company a lot of grief by handling major presentations and arranging special events. A good publicist can promote a positive image, neutralize the negative, and introduce your company's products or services to the right audience—clients and media.

When a publication writes a story about you or your company, that's free publicity. Needless to say, a publicist's services aren't free, they usually charge by the hour or the project. Depending on the firm's expertise, the hourly rate can vary between $50 and $250.

Many require a retainer or monthly rate anywhere between $2,000 to $5,000. However, public relations don't generally partake in any income generated from the publicity. To help control costs, try to get him/her to set limits on certain expenses, and to contact you before spending additional money.

To find a competent publicist, ask for referrals from trade groups and other businesses. Also, contact the Public Relations Society of America (212-995-2230) and check out the *Directory of Public Relations Agencies* (www.impulse-research.com). Draw up a written agreement that includes a cancellation clause for terminating the firm's services at any time.

Set a time frame for results. If after six months, nothing is happening in the way of increased sales or exposure, then it is time to hire a new publicist. Some publicists are willing to accept results-only payment—meaning, you only pay if their efforts render results.

Employees: Every business has at least one employee. If you are a one-person business, you're that one employee. When you hire an employee you are investing in a day's worth of work, and you should expect to receive an adequate return on your investment. Does the concept of teamwork ring a bell? In fact, if you think about the letters in team, they could stand for: *Together Everyone Achieves More when there's Total Effort from All Members.*

Before you even get started in your business, make a list of the different job descriptions you think your business may eventually need, along with a brief description of the responsibilities of each one. For example, which areas require key management positions, and what will each manager do? What other tasks need to be done? Do you need a messenger or someone on call to answer the phone? Will these positions be filled by staff members or outside vendors? For instance, will you hire an in-house messenger or will you use an outside courier service?

Moreover, you'll have to consider how you will compensate your staff—commission or base structure, or an hourly wage? A base salary is a fixed amount of money, whereas commission means the person only gets paid through a percentage of the total sale of your goods or services. These days, more companies are providing a small base salary plus a commission.

Ideally, you want people who work for you to have a sense of ownership. One of the best ways to do this is to share a percentage of the profits with the people who work for you. Many new thriving companies are offering employees equity ownership or nonvoting stock.

CRAIG REYNOLDS, OWNER OF REYNOLDS RACING

BMX (short for bicycle motocross) racing originated in California in the late 1960s. But it wasn't until the early '70s that it became a major craze, with dirt tracks popping up across America and young riders rushing out to get low-slung, knobby-wheeled bikes. By 1977, BMX racing was recognized by the American Bicycle Association, attracting over 100,000 riders.

It was in 1981 at the age of 10 that Craig Reynolds got his first taste of bicycle racing at a local park in Park Forest, Illinois. He loved it so much that he set his sights on becoming a professional racer. Indeed, Reynolds is today a AA-class, pro racer. The 26-year-old pro was ranked among the top 20 racers in the bicycle racing circuit in 1997. He is also the proprietor of Reynolds Racing, which sells BMX frames.

Subsequently, his business venture came about from his frustrations as a professional racer. It's common for pro racers to get salaries and performance bonuses from bike makers and other

Howard Simmons

CRAIG REYNOLDS

BMX-related manufacturers to ride, wear, and endorse their products. Top racers are known to earn as much as $120,000. Despite his winning status, Reynolds was only getting basic sponsorship money. In fact, he was getting paid less than some amateur racers.

After two years of riding for the same local bike manufacturer, Reynolds wanted to renegotiate his contract. But after his attempts to get a better deal fell through, he terminated his contract. With more than a decade of BMX racing experience under his belt, Reynolds decided to strike out on his own in 1992. At the time, he was a junior at Northern Illinois University, majoring in business management.

I got to a point where I didn't want to deal with another sponsor. Besides, every sponsor I ever rode for, I had to get a custom-made bike. Their bikes were either too short or their dimensions and angles were way off. So, I felt that it wouldn't be too much different to design my own bike and contract out the work to a welder. I already had some ideas in my head. I felt I was popular enough that people would buy the frames.

He was able to launch Reynolds Racing with an $8,000 loan from his parents and their blessings (his father is a stockbroker, and his mother is a paralegal). He found a local welding company to produce the bike frames to his specifications.

My parents were behind me 100 percent. In this business, most BMX racers don't have anywhere to go; they don't have an outlet after they finish racing. They may be able to go to work for one of the companies that sponsors them. But I will still have my own company when I'm through with racing.

In the beginning, Reynolds would give the welder his designs. They would then manufacture the frames and ship them directly to Reynolds who would unpack them, stack them, and put stickers on them. He sold his bike frames through local bicycle shops. He notes that a big selling point is that his bikes are made of chromoly, which is more durable than the more commonly used aluminum and therefore better suited to BMX racing.

I sent the bike shop owners flyers in the mail and I made a lot of phone calls. It was really important for me in the beginning to make sales calls, cold calls. It was scary at first. The frames were new and retailers weren't sure if they wanted to take on a new product. It took me about a year to get them to really buy on a regular basis.

Once the business started to take off, Reynolds decided to leave college. Running a business, going to school, and racing in the pro circuit all at the same time was just too much to handle. In its first two years, Reynolds Racing sold some 2,000 frames at $220 a pop. The company averaged profits of about $30,000 a year.

Reynolds concedes that he went into the business blindly. Looking back, he says one of the first things he should have done was to hire an accountant. Initially, he recorded all business transactions himself. It wasn't until tax time that he decided to see an accountant for the first time.

My accountant worked right next door to my mother's law firm, so she has known him for a while. As soon as I met him, we got along real well. But the first thing he asked me was why I hadn't come to him sooner. Fortunately, I had all of my information—sales, ID number, tax number, receipts, and so on—organized. It made it a lot easier for him.

Reynolds did make use of his computer and a leading accounting software package to help him keep track of his accounts receivable. Like many businesses, Reynolds Racing would fulfill an order but wouldn't get paid until 60 to 90 days out, since most of the bike shops had credit.

The software program I was using helped me to know where I was standing, not just for tax purposes but for managing my money, period. There were times when I knew I was missing money, but I didn't know where. It (software) would tell me that I was missing, say, $500 because Joe's Bike Shop still owed me from the last order.

Still, because he was a one-man shop, it was even more laborious for Reynolds to balance the books, design bikes, and race—sometimes all in one day. It wasn't long before Reynolds's racing performance and company sales began to lag.

I was in a catch-22 situation. I needed to be at the races to compete and do well. At the same time, I needed to be home to sell my product. I was working out of my parents' garage, filling orders, and shipping out the product. There just weren't enough hours in the day. I started to stress out. I couldn't sleep at night. So, I started looking for a distributor.

In 1996, Reynolds found a distributor to ease some of the load. It was because of past working and personal relationships that Reynolds settled on System Cycle Supply (SCS) in Dayton, Ohio, to distribute his bikes. Essentially, he would hand over the sales to SCS, allowing him to concentrate on his racing. The distribution deal also provides him with advertising support and access to SCS's database of more than 30,000 bike shops around the world. Despite his friendship with SCS's owners, Reynolds went through four months of serious negotiations. This is where his mother's personal contacts again came in handy.

My mom had someone from her firm look over the contract and advise me. SCS wanted to make sure that the product was going to sell well and that they would make money from the sales. My bikes still had to fit into their other lines. I gave them a small equity position in my company, because I needed them to invest money in the company to increase inventory of the bikes, sales, and distribution. But I have final say on how the bikes are made.

Reynolds's relationship is likened to distribution deals common in the music business, where a record company works with an independent record label. He is the creative force behind the bikes and SCS produces and sells the final product to bike shops throughout the United States and England. There are three main designs in the Reynolds line: the Puppy (small frame), Formula (midsize), and the XL (larger, super model).

Reynolds meets at least once or twice a month with SCS staff to discuss sales strategies and marketing plans for the bike frames. He receives a quarterly report from SCS, which he in turn sends to his accountant. He believes one of the reasons he is still in business is because he has an accountant handle his financial affairs.

Since partnering with a distributor, sales for Reynolds

Racing tripled to an estimated $100,000 in 1998. Reynolds also embarked on an advertising campaign, mostly print ads in trade publications. By continuing to race, Reynolds has his finger on the pulse of what's hot and what's not. He can see firsthand what his audience is riding and how changes in the sport affect their tastes.

Reynolds compares selling his product to buying a car, because a BMX frame is viewed as a high-ticket item. He explains that the frame is the main part and then there are smaller, cheaper components—handle bars, wheels, pedals, brakes, cranks, chains, and seat cushion—that are added to make up a complete bike.

My overall vision for the company is that I would like to see it grow to the point where I have a wide range of products. I want to have a complete bike line that can sit on the floor of a local bike shop or in a department store, like Kmart or Sears, as opposed to just having a bike frame hanging up. I'm not going to rush into anything until I know the line will sell. My bike frames are sold according to demand.

KEDAR MASSENBURG, FOUNDER OF KEDAR ENTERTAINMENT

All too familiar in the music business is the tale of the singer who sold millions of dollars worth of records only to end up flat broke, because he or she mismanaged funds. That's a fate that 33-year-old Kedar Massenburg is determined not to let happen.

Knowing the ins and outs of the business is a criterion he stresses with the family of artists on his three-year-old record label, Kedar Entertainment. He educates them about royalty payments. He also expects them to generate alternative streams of income, whether it's writing lyrics or producing songs. Kedar Entertainment has a half dozen artists, including Chico Debarge, whose famed Debarge family have sold a total of more than $860 million in records.

Massenburg has become one of the hottest young record

executives in the country, thanks in large part to a 26-year-old songstress from Houston named Erykah Badu. Her debut album, *Baduizm*, went multiplatinum and sold over five million albums, and the award-winning diva garnered two Grammys, one American Music Award, four Soul Train, and six Lady of Soul Awards in 1997.

Massenburg attributes Badu's success to her creative vision and his creative marketing strategy, which is a combination of the principles he learned in law school, short stints in corporate America, and modest beginnings as a manager for Stetsasonic, one of hip-hop's pioneering bands in the early '80s. The New York native grew up in the projects of Flatbush, Brooklyn, with his mother and older sister. Stetsasonic group member, Daddy-O, was a childhood friend.

Daddy-O used to write rhymes for my friend who was a rapper. I started the group with Daddy-O because I saw it as a stepping-stone that would open up other doors for me. If I see an opportunity, I will take it not only for what I can get out of it then and now, but for what it may bring me in the long run. I knew that managing Daddy-O as a producer (when he went solo) would help me to learn my way around a recording studio and it would eventually lead to my finding good acts. I believe in starting at the bottom and working your way up.

Massenburg didn't let his labor of love with music keep him from pursuing a college education, receiving a bachelor's degree in marketing from Central State University. He was hired by beverage giant PepsiCo and went from merchandiser to sales rep to district manager, where he handled chain store accounts and delivery truck routes throughout Flint, Michigan.

After spending two years as a district manager for PepsiCo, Massenburg put in time, a little over a year, as a territory manager for SmithKline Beecham Clinical Labs Pharmaceuticals in Detroit. By 1988, Massenburg had saved enough money to attend law school.

I was still working with Stetsasonic the whole time I was in col-

lege and while I was working at PepsiCo and Beecham. One of the reasons I wanted to be a lawyer was because I knew some of the most powerful people in music had a law background. Also, I realized that everything in this business is controlled by legal documents and contracts. There wasn't really a thing such as majoring in entertainment law at the time. So, I took courses in intellectual property, which teaches you about copyright and trademarks — how to protect intangible rights.

Massenburg graduated from the University of North Carolina Law School at Chapel Hill in 1991 and began managing Stetsasonic full-time. But after some infighting, Daddy-O left the group and partnered with Massenburg to start Okedoke Productions, which produced record remixes for such artists as Mary J. Blige, Red Hot Chili Peppers, the B-52's, and Chante Moore. The duo's track record garnered a short-lived production deal with Island Records.

But Massenburg wanted to focus on managing musical acts. The 26-year-old entrepreneur launched Kedar Management, using around $2,000 in personal savings to buy a computer, desk, fax machine, copier, file cabinet, and portable phone with an answering machine. He ran the business out of his apartment as a sole proprietor, but later incorporated for liability protection.

As a manager and A&R (artists and repertoire) rep, Massenburg hit the pavement scouting for talent much like a recruiter goes after a ballplayer. In addition to signing talent, Kedar Management financed musical artists' studio time, picked the right songs, paid for duplication tapes, and invested in photo shoots.

Acting as a liaison between the talent and the record company, Massenburg shopped his acts around to various labels. Once an artist was signed, Kedar Entertainment managed a budget and developed relationships with record executives, publicists, and booking agents.

There were several risk factors associated with the business,

namely Massenburg didn't always get a return on his investment. There were times when he dished out a lot of money on
an artist who never got signed by a record company. Still, by
1994 he had negotiated contracts to the tune of $1 million
gross. He saw his 20 percent cut soar to well above the six figure
mark.

As Massenburg made a name for himself, artists began to
inundate him with demo tapes. In 1995, a vocalist named
D'Angelo caught his attention, and Massenburg quickly inked
a record deal with EMI Records. Massenburg came up with a
marketing formula. He knew older generations would appreciate D'Angelo's sound, but to gain the acceptance of a younger
hip-hop community he created a stronger image.

*I put corn-rows in his hair and had him wear jeans and a
leather jacket. I knew no one would expect someone who sounded
like Marvin Gaye to look the way he did. It was important for me
that he looked like the average kid and to get the attention of
young people first. Another thing I did that worked was to create
a sampler of three of D'Angelo's songs, including "Brown Sugar."
I handed out about 10,000 copies throughout the community.*

Massenburg catapulted the producer/performer/songwriter's
debut album, *Brown Sugar*, to platinum sales, earning three
Grammy Award nominations. Massenburg's talent in discover-
ing and managing the career of D'Angelo (the two have since
parted ways) spurred Universal Music Group's CEO and chairman, Doug Morris, to offer the young executive a chance to
create and run his own record label.

*Once you beome hot, people seek you out to do your own label.
I was approached by many record companies. But I was prepared. I
had put together a business plan, a proposal. It outlined the acts I
had and what I wanted to get out of a distribution deal. It covered
how much I wanted in terms of money, points, advances, and royalties as well as publishing and merchandising rights. It also had
what I wanted as far as marketing commitments.*

Massenburg sought the counsel of mentors who were top

guns in the industry, including Sylvia Rhone, chairman and CEO of Warner Music Group's Elektra/EastWest. He handled the initial meetings himself but later brought in a lawyer to finalize the paperwork.

Even though I have a law background, it was important for me to hire someone with the right connections in this industry, who can get me in the right places at the right times. I picked Fred Davis (the son of Clive Davis, who is the president of Arista Records). I knew he could open certain doors for me. He handles all of my contracts, including the ones I have with each of my artists.

After a few weeks of negotiations, Massenburg signed a multimillion dollar distribution agreement with Universal. As part of the deal, he was appointed senior vice president of Universal. The music industry is dominated by six major record and distribution companies, which supply music retailers and wholesalers. In a typical sublabel deal, the major label advances the independent label money for start-up and overhead costs. The advance is recoupable against profits of each album.

Generally, the independent label gets 20 percent of total retail music sales—10 percent goes to the artist, 3 percent to the producer, and 7 percent to the company. Often, everything from the marketing budget to the release date of the album can be determined by the major label. But in Massenburg's case, Universal has adopted his marketing budget as the boilerplate for the entire company. Equally important, he has ownership of the masters, which means Kedar Entertainment has control over future reissues and sales of the music created during its partnership.

Massenburg notes that in the beginning he did all of the bookkeeping himself, but once the business started to generate a "decent" amount of money, it was important to hire an accountant. Still, Massenburg and his general manager keep count of every penny spent.

I am actually conservative. I don't believe in spending a lot of *money. For example, we only spent $150,000 on Erykah's video, whereas other artists have spent $1 million on their videos. [Meanwhile], they haven't even seen $1 million royalty checks. Your marketing dollars ought to be based on what you think an album is going to do in sales. We have a tight control on our marketing dollars and recording budgets.*

In addition to a record label and management company, Massenburg has a publishing arm. This way he gets a percentage of the songwriting business. Royalty sources can be broken down into performance (radio and music videos as well as live television and concert performances); mechanical (standard 6.95 cents per song the record company pays to a songwriter for sampling and recording his/her tune); synchronization (use of the song in motion picture scores, commercials, or television themes); and print (lyric sheet, hymnal, and music catalog sales). All of which explains why Massenburg handpicks artists who have vision and can write their own music.

As long as the person can write, you can go into the studio and work with them until you create the right sound. So, I look at the longevity of an artist. I want someone who is talented, who can perform with a live band, and who presents a distinct image.

Kedar Entertainment has 10 employees, including two people in its Los Angeles office. Massenburg is also working with the William Morris Agency to help him make the transition into movies and television. As he notes: Hollywood is always on top of what's hot in the music industry. Indeed, look at the careers of rappers Will Smith and Queen Latifah.

I want to have a multifaceted company that manages artists on all levels. I want to be known in the entertainment industry for artist development, which has become a lost art. I am concerned with developing careers for life, much like what Berry Gordy did with Motown.

8

HOME SWEET HOME OR MAIN STREET: YOUR BUSINESS LOCATION

Don't let adverse facts stand in the way of a good decision.
—*Colin Powell, former chairman, Joint Chiefs of Staff*

Your need to operate your business from somewhere, whether it's a small corner of your bedroom or office space in a commercial building. Choosing a location is a considerable business decision. A bad location can wreak havoc on any business. Many entrepreneurs have chosen a business address based on rent, only to buy the wrong space for the right price. They failed to realize a cheaper, out-of-the-way place could keep potential clients or customers at bay.

You may decide to operate your business from home like many shoestring start-ups who can't afford commercial space. This may be the best move to make in the early years of your business. Besides, several Fortune 500 companies started out in someone's basement or garage.

Whether or not you need a business site that is separate from your living quarters depends on how much business you can create from your location to cover expenses. You need to develop a budget and match it to the location that works for you. Assess your needs: How much space do you need? Do your clients come to you or do you have to go to them? Where does your target market live, shop, and work? Essentially, your business should be located where your customers want and expect to find you.

Should you lease, rent, or buy? Leasing ties you into a location for a longer period of time but provides you with rate stability. Renting provides you with the monthly option of moving elsewhere, but your rent can fluctuate at any time, and the landlord has the option of asking you to vacate. Buying provides tremendous stability, but with a large financial commitment on your part.

Take the time to scrutinize the facility you are looking to lease or purchase. Look for structural soundness and understand all costs. HVAC charges (heating, ventilation, and air conditioning) may be passed along to you. Some landlords charge separate maintenance fees based on the amount of square footage. Property taxes are often divided proportionally among tenants and are billed monthly. Some facilities also have tenant's association fees (community shopping malls often have an association comprised of the tenants to promote the area).

Should you need an office, but can't afford the cost of renting a space or buying office equipment, consider sharing or subleasing space. In this case, an existing business shares or subleases space to another business. Subleased space is often offered at a discount, usually $5 to $10 less than the going rate. On average, rental rates run between $6 to $65 per sq. ft. So, it could cost you about $8 per sq. ft. or $800 monthly for 1,200 sq. ft.

Another advantage of sharing space is that it also reduces your costs in outfitting your office, because it may already contain furniture. Moreover, you may have free access to a central receptionist, conference room, fax machine, copier, and other office amenities.

Another consideration in your quest for space is the type of operation you run. Is your business in service, retail, or manufacturing?

Service Location. Many professional services require an office that is suitable to receive clients. This site should fit the clientele's expectations as well as communicate confidence and knowledge. Basing your service business in a well-recognized location or building may increase name recognition and build trust. On the other hand, renting a nice location to present a better image of your business does not necessarily mean your business is going to generate more revenue.

Ask yourself several basic questions in choosing a site: Is the location easily accessible for potential clients or customers? Are any competitors close by? Will the location accommodate my business as it grows? You can search for office space on your own or you can work with a commercial real estate broker.

An even more economical option is to hatch your business in a small business incubator or executive suite. Both can help you cut your costs as you build your business.

- *Business Incubators* — These facilities are one-stop shops that provide affordable rents, flexible leases, clerical services, and shared office equipment on a pay-as-you-go basis, and allow new and growing firms to operate under one roof. Tenants also have access to a talent pool of professionals — accountants, lawyers, sales reps, and management consultants — who work pro bono or for reduced rates. Better still, many incubators have developed relationships with local bankers and venture capitalists, and they help their tenants become creditworthy and government-grant ready. There are more than 500 business incubators located throughout the United States and Canada. Many universities and colleges, government and nonprofit organizations, and private developers have created and subsidized incubators. Most cater to manufacturing, service, or high-tech companies, and are less likely to house retail businesses. The office space furnished by incubators is usually small, but utilities and the use of a conference room are usually included in the rent. Phones, secretarial support, and access to office equipment are available as well. These subsidized offices provide rents at a reduced rate, usually for a period between three to five years. Once a business is up, running, and profitable, it graduates from the program and moves into a commercial office space. In fact, a number of incubator alumni have appeared on the *Inc.* 500 list.

There are several considerations to take in to account before moving into an incubator:

1. *Space.* Does the incubator have enough square footage or room size to accommodate your business as it grows? A business may move three to five times within the incubator facility before getting a commercial space of its own. In other words, when you first move in, you may only need 100 sq. ft. to house a desk, computer, and telephone. But in three years, you might need to triple your office space to serve additional employees and an expanding client base.

2. *Focus.* If an incubator specializes in a particular industry (i.e., technology) and you are in a different field, you may not get all the benefits you need.

3. *Management.* What is the facility manager's business and entrepreneurial background? Does the manager have a hands-on business background and strong ties to local banks and business organizations?

4. *Success Ratio.* If the incubator is more than three years old, ask how many companies have graduated and how many have folded up shop.

5. *Word-of-mouth.* Does the incubator have strong ties with civic, church, and business leaders? Talk to other incubator tenants to learn how they feel about the services and benefits they are getting.

6. *Support Programs.* Your business will go through three stages: infancy, adolescence, and maturity. Can the incubator

provide support for each level? Does it hold seminars, workshops, or trade shows? Is there a networking peer group among tenants or other businesses in the community? Does it provide business plan review and preparation, marketing and sales support, and technical advice on product design and production?

7. *Capital.* Will the incubator assist you in securing financing or government contracts?

8. *Location.* Is the incubator in a good spot to attract the right customers? Do you have 24-hour access to the building? How secure is the facility?

9. *Advisory Board.* Ask for a list of board members; what level of experience do they have? Make sure the board understands your particular type of business and industry.

10. *Participation Agreement.* Does the incubator want a piece of your company?

• *Executive Suites*—As duly noted, business incubators provide below market rate office space, manufacturing space, shared overhead costs, support staff, and professional services. In comparison, executive suites mostly lease office space and offer secretarial, mail, and telephone services on a short-term basis. Occasionally, they will offer messenger services. Generally, you pay two-thirds less than you'd pay elsewhere for the same square footage. Moreover, many executive suites offer flexible arrangements. For instance, you can rent an office for a certain number of hours per week. This way, you can use the suite as your business address for mail, while still conducting most of your business from home. When choosing a suite, follow the same guidelines as you would when selecting regular office space with location and parking being the major factors to consider. Leasing flexibility is another important consideration. It is better to sign a month-to-month lease that has an escape clause, just in case your business experiences a cash-flow crunch.

Retail Location. In general, retail businesses require high-visibility foot traffic. If people can't find your business, they aren't going to buy from you. In fact, they may not even know you exist. Retail space is broken down into convenience, shopping, or specialty goods.

If you sell convenience goods (i.e., snack foods, soda, and toiletries), your customer mainly buys goods on impulse, which means the more people who pass by your location, the more sales you will generate. If you sell electronic goods (i.e., stereo, television, and fax machines), the consumer will do some research and price comparison before buying; here, convenience is important. Some specialty retailers (i.e., gourmet shops) have an advantage, because customers will go out of their way to buy their goods.

Here are a few location factors you need to think about:

1. *Competitors*—Are there a number of similar types of stores in the area? If so, how many? Visit those businesses to get an idea of the number of customers they are serving. How accessible is the site to a freeway or a highway? Will your customers be able to reach your business by way of car, public transit, or both?

2. *Foot Traffic*—This is a big deal for retailers. To make money, there needs to be plenty of it. Once you zero in on a location, compare walk-by and drive-by traffic. Foot traffic is needed and encouraged in high visibility locations, such as malls, downtown areas, and busy streets. One way to gauge foot traffic is to stand in front of the given location, and count and interview potential customers as they walk by. Select periods during the busiest hours of the day. You can check with the State Department of Transportation to get drive-by traffic statistics.

3. *Access* — Does the location provide easy, adequate parking, lighting, and access for customers? Is the building in compliance with the Americans with Disabilities Act, which requires access for physically challenged persons (i.e., signs posted in Braille and wheelchair ramps). Is the site safe and secure? You want customers to feel comfortable coming to your shop.

4. *History of Location* — What was the success or failure rate of the businesses that were previously at that location? Even if the businesses are different from your own, it is still a good idea to know why they failed or succeeded and the reason they relocated.

5. *Terms of the Lease* — Leases can be written to cover any period of time but usually will run from one to three years. The longer you are willing to lease, the lower the initial rent should be. The lease will include the type and amount of insurance that you must carry, operating hours, sign requirements, goods that will be sold or services rendered, and who's responsible for exterior maintenance of the facility. A lease is a legal document, a commitment between tenant and landlord. This commitment doesn't cease just because you decide to shut down your business prior to the lease termination date. Leases are usually very long, detailed, and written to protect the interest of the landlord. The time to negotiate the leasing terms is before you sign on the dotted line. Consider hiring a real estate broker; they can help you locate an ideal spot for your business as well as negotiate the contract. Also, hire an attorney to review the lease agreement (fees can run as high as $300 an hour).

When shopping for retail space, don't overlook kiosks or pushcarts — referred to as specialty retailing — which can be found in shopping malls, airports, train stations, bus terminals, and even college campuses. Several entrepreneurs have used these outlets as steppingstones to operating traditional retail stores.

Over the past decade, pushcarts and kiosks have grown enormously, populating three quarters of the nation's shopping malls, according to the latest statistics by the New York–based International Council of Shopping Centers. The pressure on malls and shopping centers to bring exciting, new products to their customers has not only turned specialty retailing into a $2 billion industry, but it has created a wealth of opportunities for enterprising individuals. No longer limited to newsstands, carts/kiosks sell a variety of products—from food to eyeglasses.

In 1994, following stints as a market researcher at Goldman Sachs, a large investment bank, and Zandl Group, a trend-tracking firm, Amy Nye launched AltiTUNES Partners LP. The 30-year-old entrepreneur has opened up 11 airport-based music kiosks in New York; Washington, D.C.; Orlando; Boston; and Memphis.

The idea first came to Nye as a 17-year-old traveling through Europe who purchased overpriced tapes for her Walkman from a poorly stocked store at London's Heathrow Airport. She wanted to be able to offer cheaper prices for CDs ($10.99). To bypass the expensive airport rent for a full-scale store, she conceived a 200-sq.-ft. kiosk that could hold up to 2,000 titles.

Nye's first kiosk opened in New York's LaGuardia Airport, after a tough sell to management based on some hands-on market research—she combed airport terminals with a clipboard and questionnaires—and information on the distribution and wholesale of CDs. Today, the $2 million, New York–based enterprise sells titles in various genres from alternative to gospel.

There is a slight variation between a pushcart and a kiosk:

- **Pushcarts**—These are the decorative, wheeled wooden vehicles you may have noticed along the corridors of most malls. They are less costly and risky to launch than full-fledged retail stores, while offering access to thousands of customers and a substantial earnings potential. You can license such a vehicle through specialty retailing programs that are sponsored by local shopping centers or other outlets. On average, it costs $150,000 in seed money to open a retail store in the mall, plus $7,000 a month for rent. A pushcart costs $3,000 to $8,000 in start-up capital and an extra $1,000 a month in rent.

• *Kiosks*—These are enclosed, semipermanent structures that require slightly more start-up capital. You know, the door-less and windowless McDonald's or Dunkin' Donuts at your local train station. The cost for a kiosk is between $10,000 to $18,000, with an average monthly rent of $3,000. Generally, mall traffic thickens in November and December, which can triple leasing costs. Then again, some carts and kiosks are known to gross more than $500,000 in a 10-week period during the holiday and peak seasons. To open a kiosk, you simply fill out a one- to two-page application, pay a fee and security deposit, and present a merchandising plan that the shopping mall views as profitable.

Before you take a stab at opening a kiosk/pushcart, ask the following questions:

1. *Can you offer salable products?* The key to success is research. Make sure you are offering a product that people want and can't get from any local five-and-dime store. A number of retail chains with deep pockets and brand-name merchandise are coming in and buying up carts/kiosks. In fact, a number of franchisors are selling kiosks to entrepreneurs.

2. *Is your inventory in good shape?* You must effectively manage your wares, which requires seasonal planning, profitable markups, minimal markdowns, cost-effective reorders, and well-maintained inventory. There may be royalty fees.

3. *Are you up to the challenge?* Are you up to putting in long hours and dealing with slow days? You have to be open for business as long as the mall is open. Are you willing to adhere to

strict guidelines or mall policies? You have to be aware of their rules, and be willing to play by them. Some malls require you to pay a penalty if you are late or leave your cart unstaffed at any time during the day. You may have to insure your venture against theft—between $300 and $1,200.

4. *Have you found the right spot?* Research a prospective site by doing a head count and interviewing other kiosk owners. Visit the site at different times during the day and evening. Is foot traffic high? Are shoppers carrying bags, indicating that they are buying and not just browsing? Keep in mind that the mall actually determines where you set up shop, be it a bustling area or one that's a dead end. A word to the wise: The mall may choose not to renew your license or they could move you to a less desirable location to make room for a new tenant.

5. *Are you ready to negotiate the lease?* Nothing is etched in stone. You can negotiate for a better location or leasing costs. For instance, if your pushcart is in a spot where there's low traffic, ask to pay cheaper rent than someone else in a more crowded area. You can always ask for a better deal when your lease is up. Shopping center leases usually run from six weeks to six months.

Bear in mind that people running specialty retail programs are entitled to their cut—usually 25 percent of your gross earnings after a certain level, normally $25,000 plus. Operating a cart/kiosk is like operating any other business; meaning, a poor business plan, product, or location could push your profits right out of the door. Seek out support and guidance from experts. The Washington, D.C.–based National Retail Federation (202-723-2849) offers educational seminars and puts out a directory of services. Cherry Hill, N.J.–based Sales Dynamic Inc. (609-482-7600) is a company that leases mall space but also sponsors seminars and trade shows, and publishes a quarterly magazine called the *Mall St. Journal* ($19.95). Never lose sight of the fact that you still have to effectively manage your cart/kiosk—from inventory control to cash-flow analysis—to keep the business running smoothly.

Manufacturing Location. Does your type of business require a warehouse, factory, or a processing facility? If you primarily ship, mail, or conduct work over the phone, it may not matter where your company is located as long as the site supports the daily operations of that business. You could rely on production houses for the actual manufacturing aspects and use your home for office-related tasks. In general, production facilities are chosen based on operational factors, including shipping, receiving, parking, and inventory space requirements.

DOING YOUR HOMEWORK

If you are starting a business where you are mainly visiting clients, you can use your home as your office. In fact, you can test your idea from home, while you reduce your overhead and financial risk.

Operating a business from home is the new trend for the twenty-first century brought about by factors such as corporate downsizing. There are more than 10 million home-based businesses nationwide. It has become increasingly easy to operate professionally from your home and communicate with the world thanks to modern technological advancements.

A personal computer, letterhead, and a separate telephone line are the required basics. For other equipment needs, you can use local business assistance centers that offer private post office boxes, copy and fax services, graphic design help, and mailing services.

Other obvious advantages of having a home office are flexible hours and tax deductible personal expenses, such as rent, utilities, and telephone costs. You are allowed to deduct the portion of your home used in conducting business and a percentage of your housing expenses—about 20 percent from your gross profits.

The downside is that many entrepreneurs fail to consider that running a business from home still requires strong management skills and discipline—it's easy for procrastination to set in and for the business owner to lose focus. There's a fine line between work and personal life.

Key areas of concern are compliance, taxes, and insurance. Most states have zoning ordinances or laws regarding home businesses, which vary depending on the type of business a resident owns and how it affects the community. For example, someone owning an exterminating company would have to show that he's storing pesticides in accordance with federal and state environmental laws. If it's a business such as a doctor's office or beauty salon, the entrepreneur has to prove the extra traffic can be safely accommodated without intruding on their neighbors.

Indeed, how your neighbors feel about your home-based business can be enough to close it down, especially if you're operating illegally. In many cases, the zoning office will investigate a home-based business when neighbors make enough complaints. It's the complaint process that leads to citations and fines—which can costs as much $500. Your local city hall can provide you with information on zoning or building codes in your area. There, you can also find out what permits you need to apply for and how much they will cost

While "there's no place like home" may sound attractive, especially if you're bypassing costs associated with more conventional office space, don't neglect the basic building blocks for a sound business. You'll still need to consider a business structure and the tax consequences and legal liabilities of being a sole proprietor or corporation. Moreover, you should view your business location as a part of customer service.

With respect to insurance, you need both property and liability insurance to safeguard your home business. A business owner's package covers everything from business equipment and property damage to bodily injury and loss of income resulting from damage to your personal being or home business. To find out more, contact the National Insurance Consumer Hot Line (800-942-4242) and National Association of Home-Based Businesses (800-414-2422).

Also worth looking into is the Independent Business Alliance (800-450-21BA), which provides products and services to small and home-based businesses. For an annual fee of $49, every IBA member can qualify for health insurance, commercial insurance, financing, marketing support, and discounts on travel, long-distance services, and computer and office equipment.

The American Association of Home-based Businesses (800-447-9710) offers many of the same discount services as the IBA, including long-distance and 800-number services, prepaid legal services, and management advice. The association sponsors national seminars and workshops on various business topics (an annual membership is $90 and includes a bimonthly newsletter).

Since most of your problems will be financial, operational, or both, you can lease space when you are confident about future business. Essentially, choosing a location may boil down to money. If you are financially strapped, you may consider starting at home until your business warrants moving out.

FRANK ALAMEDA, FOUNDER AND PRESIDENT OF FTD EAST SIDE SPORTS INC.

East Side Sports Inc. stands out in lower Manhattan, easily recognized by the 6-by-10-foot mural painted on the side of the building. But what makes the sporting goods store a neighborhood fixture is owner Frank Alameda and his commitment to the community.

FTD East Side Sports

FRANK ALAMEDA

Each year, Alameda sponsors local football and basketball tournaments where some 100 neighborhood youths, between the ages of 10 and 18 participate. It was Alameda's goodwill that impressed East Side Sports's landlord when Alameda inquired about the storefront in 1995.

The landlord was very interested with what I was doing for my community. He didn't want to rent the space to certain types of businesses. He didn't want to see another grocery store or convenience store come into the area. He also didn't want any manufacturing taking place from here. He wanted retail. [Just the same], he questioned how I was going to spend my money and if my business would succeed at this location. So, I still had to qualify for this space. But the landlord saw a future with me.

The rent for the corner store was $1,500 a month. It took about 10 months, from the time Alameda first read the FOR RENT sign posted on the building, until the first day of East Side Sports's grand opening. Alameda invested around $10,000 to renovate the store. He took on a lot of the work himself—as designer, builder, and contractor—to bring the costs down as much as he could.

What made the corner store an ideal spot for Alameda was the fact that it was near public transportation—buses frequently stopped to pick up and unload residents. It was close to recreational parks, so local teens and Little League teams regularly passed by the store.

This was a way for me to expand the retail side of my business, where I could sell sportswear and sporting goods. This store measures about 1,200 sq. ft. My first place was about 850 sq. ft.

By renting a larger space and having two locations, Alameda could do high-volume sales, and fulfill and deliver his customized orders more efficiently and quickly. He notes that his competitors (i.e., Foot Locker and Sports Authority) sell the same items as East Side Sports. But what distinguishes his business is that he provides custom-tailored clothing.

Alameda started his business in 1993 after learning that a 30-year-old neighborhood sporting goods store was going out of business. Alameda was attending Brooklyn College at the time, majoring in physical education. He wanted to buy the store, where he and his sports buddies were long-time patrons. But the paperwork process was so convoluted that Alameda had to pass up the deal.

Undaunted, his mother found a location—which was rent-controlled—at a price of $950 a month. He had a start-up budget of about $3,000 for selling T-shirts and baseball caps. He named the store East Side Sports.

While running a business is no easy task for anyone, it was even more trying for the 22-year-old only child. Alameda's mother died of cancer four months after he opened the store.

I was going to college full-time, starting a business full-time, and my mother was dying of cancer. I had no time to sleep. I had to fix and remodel the store myself because I had no capital to renovate the place. My family (uncles and cousins) helped me out a lot. They got involved with the business.

Even though Alameda didn't have a business plan when he first launched his enterprise, he took care of the necessary paperwork. He registered the business, set up his files and record-keeping systems, and got his tax identification number. He hired an accountant to help with his personal and business taxes.

It was the National Foundation of Teaching Entrepreneurship (NFTE) that gave Alameda an early indoctrination in business. For the past ten years, NFTE had been providing entrepreneurial education throughout the United States to inner-city youth, mostly Latinos and African-Americans.

I was working part-time at the Boys Club and they had all of these signs: BE YOUR OWN BOSS. At that time I didn't know I would go into business, but I took NFTE's courses anyway. This was before I went to college. Up until then, I had no knowledge of business concepts—cash flow, record keeping, or paying taxes. NFTE [proved to be] a big help down the road.

Alameda's ongoing relationships with the Boys and Girls Clubs and the Parks and Recreation Department were also invaluable. The two organizations placed orders with Alameda and referred other clients. Most of Alameda's customers are still young people—Little League and high school sports teams.

Alameda nixed the idea of becoming a physical education teacher and spent the first two years in business, selling retail sporting goods and fulfilling orders for custom-made work, which he subcontracted out. Once he was able to hire someone to do silk screening, he brought all the work in-house. He also purchased a used sewing machine, to do seam and special stitch-work on garments, as well as a heat press for lettering, team logos, and numbers.

I had just planned to do retail. But deals were coming in one after another. We started providing everything that a sports team needed—bats, gloves, balls, caps, and uniforms—you name it. But then I starting having problems with cash flow. We were laying out a lot of money to stock inventory. Sometimes, a lot of money goes out to fulfill orders way before the money comes in (people pay the balance when they pick up their orders). We had money to maintain the business, but it wasn't coming in fast enough.

East Side Sports's sales orders range from $6.50 to $1,900. Approximately 60 percent of Alameda's business is made-to-order uniforms and the remaining 40 percent is retail sales. Relying mostly on word-of-mouth and the Yellow Pages, East Side Sports managed to generate sales revenues around $150,000 in 1996. Local print ads helped boost sales to $250,00 in 1997.

Alameda invests every cent the store earns back into the business. He has a staff of five full-time and part-time employees and solid relationships with some 40 wholesale suppliers. For the first two years, Alameda wasn't able to secure bank financing—until the store had a track record. He now has credit with his suppliers and a $15,000 line of credit from Fleet Bank.

I wanted to raise enough money to get us to a point where we were stable. But it's tough to get the lines of credit you need to take your business to the next level. I had a hard time applying for bank loans because the only security I had was the store itself. I didn't have a house that I could put up for collateral.

In addition to needing about $25,000 total in expansion capital, Alameda is looking to get other businesses or sponsors to help offset the growing costs associated with his youth sports tournaments. He is hoping to snare some corporate sponsors. Alameda's commitment to youth extends to occasional presentations and speaking engagements on behalf of the NFTE.

Each day is an adventure for me. I am still going through the learning process. Sometimes I am completely exhausted when I get home. It's not easy. I'm trying every day to make my customers happy, my son happy, and my wife (of three years) happy.

As with many start-up business owners, Alameda barely takes a salary—just enough to support his family. Moreover, spending holidays and vacations with his wife is a treasured and scarce thing. Like any retail business, East Side Sports makes money by keeping its doors open.

I work from ten in the morning until late at night. I get up each day, dress my son, and take him to school. Then I come to the store and work the counters, go over the daily budget, pay bills, fill orders, and stock sporting goods that have come in. Then I go and check on my other site to make sure that we are completing our customized orders. I put in 12 hours or more into this business. It's like being married. It takes a lot of effort.

ANDRES LINK, PRESIDENT, AND RICHARD SWERDLOW, CEO OF EVERYTHING WIRELESS

Twenty-six year-old Andres Link was importing salmon from Chile, his native land, when he met Richard Swerdlow at a pick-up basketball game on a Miami playground in January 1993. A former loan officer at Chase Manhattan Bank with a degree in finance from Boston University, Link left corporate banking in 1992, while Swerdlow was on a six-month hiatus from practicing law. The two hit it off and formed a consulting firm to help South American clients negotiate business deals from franchise agreements to apparel licensing. It was by chance that Link and Swerdlow entered the wireless arena.

A cousin of mine in Chile owned an electronics store. He started asking me to send him cellular phone batteries. I would buy items from wholesalers here in the states and send them to him. The wireless business had taken off very quickly in Chile, because it would take you a year to get a land line in your house for a regular phone, whereas you could easily get your hands on a cellular phone. So, that was my introduction to the business.

Swerdlow Link Partners Inc., based in Hollywood, Florida, began doing business as Cellular Works. Swerdlow would serve as CEO and general counsel and Link would act as president and CFO. Taking $9,000 each in personal savings and a script for selling wireless communications products, they opened up a retail outlet—a 10-by-10 kiosk at Sawgrass Mills. The novel operation was one of six kiosks in the premier mall.

Cellular Works was banned from selling cellular phones, because the mall reserved that privilege for an anchor store that had an exclusive contract to sell phones. Undaunted, the duo shifted the focus of their business to selling cellular accessories such as batteries, antennas, and leather cases. Cellular Works found its niche by carrying such impulse items—products that people pick up as sort of an afterthought.

All the big retailers focused on activation. You know, sign up for this service and get a free phone. But nobody cared about servicing customers after the initial sale. We filled a void. If you purchased a cellular phone a year ago and you went back to the same store today to replace the battery, they would look at you as if you were crazy because they no longer support it. They have moved on to the latest model.One of the reasons having a kiosk worked for us was because we didn't have the breadth of merchandise required for a regular store.

Over the years, the duo have been moved a few times within the mall. Once, their sales dropped in half as a result of the new location. While Cellular Works generates repeat business, it's not like a regular store which can drive customers to its location through traditional advertising. Link stresses the importance of finding a location with good traffic that fits one's product demographics.

You don't want to balk at a higher rent if it's a good location and you don't want to take a location just because the rent is low. It's also important to get good long-term leases you can live with.

The worst thing that can happen to you, especially with a kiosk, is that you are locked into a one- or two-year lease and suddenly management tells you they are not renewing your lease or they are moving you to the other end of the mall. With cellular and wireless dealers on every corner (it seems), we can't afford to have mediocre locations. High visibility is key.

Link and Swerdlow had originally planned for Cellular Works to function as a secondary business to generate some cash while they continued to run the consulting firm. It wasn't until 1996, that the two thought of doing a business plan for their cellular enterprise. Today, Cellular Works has ballooned to three retail outlets, including one in Miami's International Airport, and 20,000 sq. ft. of office space and a showroom. There's also a consumer catalog, which is distributed nation-wide, and a Website.

In addition to cellular products, Link and Swerdlow now offer wireless phone service from AT&T, Sprint, and Primeco, and paging services from PageMart. Their 30-employee firm grossed sales revenues of $9 million in 1997 and an estimated $13 million in 1998, with cellular phone service accounting for 20 percent of those sales and accessories accounting for the other 80 percent.

Swerdlow and Link attribute their rapid success to aggressive direct marketing. On a slow day the company receives about 100 catalog orders. In the first three or four days after a mail-out, the numbers are well into the hundreds. Cellular Works has essentially evolved from a local retailer into a catalog company. After mailing 50,000 catalogs in 1995, 250,000 in 1996, and 500,000 in 1997, Cellular Works distributed over 1 million in 1998.

It got to the point where it was difficult to control the retail business, in part because mall developers dictate which locations you get. We needed a way to expand the business. As cellular phone users ourselves, Richard and I knew people weren't getting solicited through the mail to buy accessories. So, again we saw mail order as a niche. Plus, we could get a national presence a lot quicker this way than trying to open several retail locations.

They hired an outside design firm to handle the technical aspects. It cost them roughly $1.50 per book, which was extremely high, notes Link. They rented mailing lists and placed an advertisement in the in-flight magazine *Skymall* (available on most airlines). Link estimates that mail-order represents about 70 percent of the business, noting that retailing and cataloging are two entirely different businesses. The latter is statistically driven, based on name acquisition, analysis, and database marketing.

Not everyone in your customer records is the same. You have to segment your file where you have one group who buys once a year and spends $100 each and another group who buys three times a year and spends $500 each. So, you need to tailor your messages to individual groups. We will create a catalog, just for those people who requested a catalog but never purchased anything, with a cover that says, "We haven't heard from you in a long time, here's a $20 certificate to get you started." [On the other hand], for the people who bought from us more than three times a year, we will send them a different cover that says, "Thanks for your business and here's a $20 certificate to show our appreciation." It is all about relationship marketing.

The partners recently changed the business's name to Everything Wireless in order to more accurately reflect the wide selection of wireless communications products and services that they offer. The name change is a mere part of their continued formula for success: combining America's fastest-growing product category—wireless communications equipment—with a fast-growing distribution channel—at home shopping.

Our direct marketing business is really three distinct channels. One is the print catalog which goes directly to consumers. The second is our Internet site (www.everythingwireless.com) which is our electronics commerce platform. Third is our third-party fulfill-

ment. Meaning, we handle customer orders, questions, and con-
cerns for about seven to eight companies. Our largest client is
Duracell, which lists our toll-free number on the back of their
rechargeable products. We ship wireless products for them. These
days, many of the big manufacturers don't want to deal with the
end-user. That's a part of our infrastructure that we decided to
capitalize on.

LEE HUANG, FOUNDER OF YES (YOUTH + ENTREPRENEURSHIP = SUCCESS)

Local Philadelphia entrepreneurs are getting assistance in over-coming obstacles to business development through The West Philadelphia Enterprise Center (WPEC), a small business incubator and center. WPEC was founded in 1989 by the Wharton School of Business and provides support services, access to capital, and business assistance to start-up ventures.

A major WPEC program is YES (Youth + Entrepreneurship = Success), which will provide local youth with entrepreneurial skills, resources, and business opportunities. YES was con-ceived a year ago by 24-year-old Lee Huang, who first learned of WPEC as a senior at the University of Pennsylvania's Wharton School of Business.

Initially, he served as a volunteer, but came on board full-time as a financial manager upon graduating in 1995. Huang, whose official title is vice president of development and out-reach, was responsible for fundraising, grant proposal writing, overseeing the budget, and relationship building.

When I first went to Wharton, I just wanted to come out, make
a lot of money, and gain prestige. I grew up in west San Jose,
California, which is Silicon Valley. I had no intention of staying
on the East Coast. Toward the later part of my academic career I
decided to use my ambition and the business skills that I learned
and apply them to helping this community.

This was indeed an ambitious undertaking for the first-generation, Asian-American born in the United States (his parents are from Taiwan). West Philadelphia was seen as an economically depressed inner-city neighborhood. Huang saw WPEC as the solution to many of its challenges.

He worked closely with the incubator's tenants, assisting them particularly with their financial projections. He was also a key player in helping WPEC reach its goals, namely $3.9 million in financing in 1996.

That same year, Huang assumed a hybrid role of employee and business owner—he became an entrepreneur of sorts. He is running YES out of the WPEC building, much like a nonprofit entity but without the legal 501C.3 status.

It didn't make sense for YES to have its own legal identity. There was no need for both the parent company and its auxiliary to both have a nonprofit status. Still, I have to scrape for my resources. I have to raise the funds for this program and recruit employees (although some staff positions are intertwined with WPEC). It'll take about $100,000 a year to run YES.

YES is very much a bare bones program. Huang partnered with private companies to develop a four-year curriculum that was implemented in four high schools in the fall of 1997. Four more high schools are slated to execute the program in the fall of 1999. Students will learn about entrepreneurship in a classroom setting during the first two years. During the final two years, they will initiate and operate their own businesses out of WPEC's incubator facility.

Running it from within WPEC will be much more effective than had I tried to run this as an after-school program totally through the school system. I needed to work within a structure that was going to be the most productive for the kids. I already had a great relationship with several of the teachers going into this project. That made it easier for me to pitch the idea to the schools. I had also developed strong relationships with the principals of the four high schools. So I knew I could work from the top down, administratively speaking.

Ninth and tenth graders will go through various units related to business and entrepreneurship. Huang stresses that the students will be given the chance to run kiosks inside their respective schools—which will involve real money, real shares, and real profits. YES participants will have to determine themselves which items they intend to sell, based on market research.

YES consists of about five classes of 30 students at each school. There will be some 25 to 30 kiosks all together, which will be operated by teams. This allows the students to learn the basic skills of business management through hands-on experiences and classroom instruction.

During their sophomore year, the students will participate in a business plan competition. The winners will receive a cash award. The competition will be handled much like a venture capital interview. The goal is to enable students to run businesses outside of the school.

When the students hit the eleventh and twelfth grades, they will be running their businesses and we will provide them access to resources in the community, including accounting, technical assistance, coaches, computers, and library resources. We will directly assign them to a local business owner who will serve as a mentor or advisor. We are looking to provide at least $500 to $5,000 investment capital for their businesses. The money will come from grants, which will take care of the first eight years of the program.

YES will provide participants shared office space at WPEC's incubator facility. Teams of students will have access to the office after school during specified days of the week. This allows students to utilize resources at WPEC's newly renovated state-of-the-art building, which was the birthplace of Dick Clark's *American Bandstand.*

The facility houses the Microsoft/Compaq Computer Center and the Whitney M. Young Business Resource Library. In addition to event rooms, 24-hour copy, fax, and postal services, students will have entry to the Internet. Huang will mainly oversee the Internet component as it relates to YES participants.

Students get to learn about the history of the Internet and its relevance to business operations—e-mail, information, market research, and creating Websites as storefronts for their businesses. Entrepreneurship is something you learn about by being in the midst of it. So, we are going to give the kids as much of an opportunity to explore what it really takes to make decisions regarding business.

In conjunction with WPEC's Market Street Development Corp. and the City of Philadelphia Mural Arts Program, YES recruited local youth to learn about the history and power of public art, as well as design and paint murals. They worked on two murals per 10-week period in summer and fall of 1997 and spring of 1998.

YES is looking to co-develop a youth-operated ice cream parlor. The facility will also serve as a youth-run community center where teens can sit in on sessions to discuss social topics and have a safe place to eat and study. Huang is working with White Dog Cafe, a local restaurant, and ice cream giant Ben & Jerry's on structuring this project. Huang is very big on forming partnerships. He emphasizes that his strategic alliances are all win-win situations.

This isn't just about goodwill. We let our partners know there is a return on their investment. Relationship building is the name of the game when it comes to any type of business or venture. Partnering with other organizations is beneficial to me, especially because I have limited capital. It's key for me to leverage my program by combining assets and pooling talents with other groups. I don't want to try to do everything by myself, because it will only limit what resources are available to my kids.

Huang understands the challenges of moving from a business idea to a viable business—in that one needs connections, money, and resources. He knows all too well the failure rate of start-up businesses. Four out of five businesses fail within five years after they start, according to the Small Business

Administration. He believes his program can help minimize failures among would-be young entrepreneurs.

WPEC successfully hosted its first annual youth entrepreneurship "boot camp" in the summer of 1998. Youth between the ages of 12 and 19 attended five days of intensive training in business. The group also hosted its first annual Young Entrepreneur of the Year Awards. The participants heard from the presidents of eight local businesses and were exposed to five specific tools: give-back, networking, sales and marketing, technology, and company vision.

It is not really realistic for us to think that YES is going to spur all of these successful lifelong businesses. Hopefully, one or two of the students will achieve that level. But there is more to this program than physically running a business; it motivates kids to learn, to stay in school, and to go to college. A student may enter corporate America and then decide to travel the entrepreneurial road. Because of this program, they will have a greater level of experience and a better chance to succeed. That's something I can say I was a part of, and it is something that is going to take a long time to develop and nurture.

9

FRANCHISING:
A START-UP ALTERNATIVE

Learn from the mistakes of others. You won't live long
enough to make them all yourself.
— *Groucho Marx, comedic actor*

Have you ever gone inside of a Kinko's or Dunkin' Donuts and
said to yourself, "I could run one of these?" Through franchising you can do just that: purchase the rights to run a brand
name business and sell its products. One of the fastest growing
segments of American business, franchising is the partnership
between an independent entrepreneur—the franchisee—and a
large company—the franchisor. The franchisor sells the rights
to the company's name, trademarks, products, business procedures, marketing tools, advertising, and other components
unique to that particular business. The franchisee is backed by
the substantial knowledge, skills, experience, and financial
strength of the parent company.

Travel to any town in America and you're bound to find a
franchised business. Fast-food giants McDonald's and Burger
King automatically come to mind. However, there are about
600,000 franchises operating in the United States and generating nearly a total $1 trillion in sales. More than 8 million peo-
ple draw their paychecks from franchising. And they come from

every walk of life—from recent college grads to downsized corporate professionals.

The International Franchise Association (http://www.franchise1.com), a Washington, D.C.–based industry trade group, publishes the *Franchising Opportunities Guide*, which lists available franchises in over 70 industries. You can find franchises in virtually every business imaginable, including travel agencies, bookstores, day-care centers, computers, lawn care, electronic stores, florist shops, hotels, janitorial services, print shops, restaurants, security providers, and video rentals.

Another source is *Franchise Times*, which addresses the needs of prospective and existing franchisees. The Franchise Network (FRANNET; 619-490-1188), the nation's largest group of franchise consultants, matches prospective franchises with franchisors.

Franchising is not new. It's actually a business concept that has worked since the dawn of the nineteenth century—characterized simply as one party selling a product to another party who then sells it to a third person for a profit. Mike Powers, author of *How to Open a Franchise Business* (Avon Books), cites the first practitioner of product-trade name franchising was Singer Sewing Machine Co. which sold its sewing machines to agents who then resold them to the public. Singer set the stage for the three different classifications of franchises:

- *Distributor franchise*. A manufacturer sells you the right to stock and sell its product through a retail outlet. Auto dealerships, gasoline service stations, and clothing retail stores fall within this category. Chrysler, Ford, Honda, Toyota, and other major automobile manufacturers sell their cars through franchised dealerships. The dealers buy the cars from the parent company, mark up the price, and resell the cars to their customers. Home appliance franchises allow you to sell dishwashers, microwaves, refrigerators, and the like, while electronics outlets let you peddle televisions, VCRs, stereos, and other wares. The benefit of this type of franchise is that you have a defined market brand and you are only responsible for selling the product, not manufacturing it. But such retail outlets require a lot of upfront cash and are more vulnerable to changing market conditions—if consumers can't afford or don't have the urge to buy, your sales will suffer.

• *Manufacturing franchise.* Soft drink and beer distributors are primary examples. Here, the parent company, say Coca-Cola, grants you a license to create a product in accordance with its specifications. You bottle the finished product, package it, and distribute it to retail outlets. You have minimal contact with the buying public and little control over the product. For example, Coca-Cola changed its formula years ago promising a better taste. The new Coke flopped and many regional bottlers lost millions of dollars before Coke went back to its original formula.

• *Business format or chain-style franchises.* Every strip in America is lined with these outlets, like Burger King, Hertz, Midas, Century 21, and Holiday Inn. There are many business format franchises from which to choose, which are available at a wide range of prices. You get to use the franchisor's trademarks, slogans, and logos. You benefit from the franchisor's marketing efforts and new product development. A possible downside is that the parent company may require you to purchase products only from it. Also, you must adhere to strict rules and regulations regarding the operation of your franchise. For instance, as a McDonald's franchisee you must prepare food in accordance with the company's standards.

DOING DUE DILIGENCE

When considering whether to buy a franchise, look for one that has a product or service with long-term marketability. In general, franchises were established to serve a niche that wasn't being filled before or wasn't being adequately serviced. Look at the franchise from the customer's point of view in terms of company reputation, quality of product, and pricing.

Three key issues you should consider before seeking out the franchise of your dreams:

1.*Time.* Whether you intend to run a franchised or independent business, plan to put in long hours and a lot of energy. More than likely, you will be open six or in some cases seven days a week. What about holidays? You make money when the doors of the business are open. Owning a franchise also requires that you know a little bit about everything—banking, business, taxes, real estate, labor regulations, insurance, employee relations, and the like. It's critical that the franchise suits your lifestyle. Let's say you purchase a Starbuck's franchise. During the course of a day, you may have to buy supplies, deal with the building's landlord, pay insurance, handle the books, prepare tax forms, pay bills, schedule employee hours, and do payroll. Equally, you may have to pitch in and grind the coffee beans, make pastries, wait on customers, wash dishes, and clean floors before locking up.

2. *Financing.* Undercapitalization is the main reason most small businesses fail—and franchises are no different. When thinking about financing your franchise, your first source should be savings, family and friends, partners, or investors. You may be able to get financing from the franchisor, but expect very little. The big food chains are out of the reach of the typical franchisee hopeful. A McDonald's will cost anywhere up to $650,000. Some franchisors have start-up costs ranging from as little as $1,000 to $50,000. However, the average franchise costs about $150,000 to get up and running. To support yourself during your first start-up months, you should set aside enough money to sustain you for at least one year. Once you prepare your financial proposal and business plan—a must have—you will be able to

assess if your business can handle the monthly payments and still make a profit.

3. *Location.* Your overhead costs will depend on whether the franchise will operate out of a storefront or office building. Some franchises require a warehouse, factory, or a processing facility. A number of franchise companies are offering low-cost alternatives to traditional storefronts by selling kiosks—enclosed, semipermanent structures. Such nontraditional units are popping up at college campuses, supermarkets, malls, sports arenas, zoos, and theme parks. Running a kiosk could mean the difference between $50,000 and $500,000 in start-up costs. Think long-term in your planning. Most franchisors are looking to multi-units to grow faster and stronger. They want franchisees who are interested in owning several outlets and developing entire territories. Several franchisors own company units in main cities and franchise in secondary markets, selling to operators who can handle local customers.

CAVEAT EMPTOR: LET THE BUYER BEWARE

The first rule of thumb when buying a franchise is to protect yourself. Before you sign on the dotted line of the franchise agreement, ask yourself, How well do I know this franchisor? Knowing a particular franchise's systems will increase your chances of success. Here are some road rules to follow:

• *Develop a franchisor profile.* Evaluate the characteristics of that particular operation. Does the franchise suit your own personality traits? What kind of training or experience is required? Take into account the costs of the franchise. You can request marketing materials, media kits, and other information available on that franchise directly from the parent company.

- **Inspect the location.** Gather demographic data to determine if the neighborhood where you wish to set up shop supports the franchise you wish to own. How much foot traffic is there? How much competition will you face? Be forewarned that you may not be given the site you want—most franchisors have the right to approve the location. But many are assigning franchisees to specific territories, allowing them to choose the exact site.

- **Talk to franchisees.** Visit at least five different sites. There is no better reality check than visiting existing locations and talking to the owners, store managers, customers, and employees. They should be able to give you a clear understanding of what the day-to-day business operations entail. Observe traffic flow. This way you can see firsthand the volume and type of business that is being done. Note the quality of service and attitude of the employees. Drill the operators about the system and challenges of running the store.

- **Review the operating manual.** The franchise company's operating manual will serve as your guidepost for day-to-day operations. How comprehensive is the manual: Could you run your business from what you see in front of you? How comfortable do you feel with the home office staff? These are the folks you will be calling on for advice and ongoing assistance. It's important that you pay close attention upfront to the company and management background, start-up and ongoing costs, level of support, and provisions of the franchise agreement. If you get all your supplies from the franchisor, what will happen if the supplier is suddenly cut off—Does your franchisor have another? Are there any restrictions placed on you from obtaining products from suppliers and vendors of your choosing?

- **Scrutinize the franchise offering circular.** A significant amount of information can be found in the *Uniform Franchise Offering Circular*, a lengthy document with 15 different sections on the franchisor's operations. This is the most important document you'll come across in your quest for ownership. The Washington, D.C.–based Federal Trade Commission—an industry watchdog—requires all franchisors to disclose such information as costs, operations, construction, and violations or charges of fraud involving the parent company or executive officers. The *Circular* also should list current and former franchisees.

Watch out for a significant number of terminated, canceled, or nonrenewed franchises. If a franchisor has seen its share of owners come and go, this could mean that those locations weren't profitable or the franchisor didn't provide those franchisees with promised services. Some companies try to conceal the number of failed franchises by repurchasing these outlets and then listing them as company-owned units.

- *Consult a franchise attorney and accountant.* Carefully review the franchise agreement with a lawyer. Have an accountant go over financial projections. If there's anything you don't fully understand, refuse to sign. If a franchisor tries to coerce you into signing a leasehold agreement or accepts a deposit, the company can be held liable to criminal charges. Even if you're ready to commit after reading the *Circular,* you still have 10 business days to decide whether to sign the agreement. You also have the right to renegotiate the contract. Don't let the franchisor tell you otherwise. Also, the contract is penned for the franchisor's protection. Franchisors can take advantage of people who they know can't afford costly litigation. IFA's National Franchise Mediation Program provides alternatives to long and costly legal battles.

- *Determine total start-up and operating costs.* Make sure you fully grasp the cost of operating the franchise. Terms like "initial cost," "initial fee," and "royalties" should be made quite clear. Franchise fees and royalty fees (based on sales and payable every month, usually 4 percent to 6 percent of revenues) are the most widely known charges.

Hunt for hidden charges, such as costs for equipment, renovations, or a down payment on inventory. As a small business you'll be responsible for payroll tax, rent, and insurance. You also need to factor in advertising costs. Will you be required to participate in an advertising pool or to pay an additional fee for local advertising?

• **Watch out for inflated sales.** When a franchisor says you can expect to make an average $75,000 per year, get the number of companies included in that sample size. A particularly successful franchisee can slope the figures. A top tip: Get average sales of franchisees in your anticipated area, not just nationwide. Some franchisors provide gross sales, but these figures don't tell you much. Ask about net profits. Consider hiring an accountant to dig into the figures and calculate average sales for you. According to the FTC's free brochure, *A Consumer Guide to Buying a Franchise*, you should insist upon a written substantiation for any earnings and sales projections.

• **Contact trade associations.** The American Franchise Association in Chicago (AFA, 312-431-1467) provides referral services. Some franchisors have franchisee associations, which operate almost like unions. This is a great way to find out what other franchise owners think about the parent company and to get net sales information from their members. To find out if a franchisor has a solid reputation, contact the San Diego–based American Association of Franchisees and Dealers (AAFD; 619-235-2556). Under its new Fair Franchising Standards, franchisors will be offered accreditation of fair practice. Ask for a copy of AAFD's *Franchise Bill of Rights*. Also, in conjunction with the Association of Small Business Development Centers, the AAFD now sponsors training programs for existing and prospective franchisees.

• **Beware of encroachment.** Encroachment happens when franchisors establish new stores nearby existing ones—

say, around the corner or across the street. Their rationale: They need to achieve a significant market presence; prime retail space is scarce and if an area is a good market for one franchise, it's likely to be good for three or more franchises. Besides, franchisors make their money by selling new franchises and collecting royalties from existing ones. Encroachment is the subject of most franchisee-franchisor disputes, followed closely by claims of agreement violations and conflicts over contract renewals.

• *Devise an exit strategy.* Can you close shop for reasons other than fraudulent practices by the franchisor? What will happen to the lease and assets of your business if you negate your obligation? Should you decide to sell the business, you may be forced to sell it back to the franchisor who will pay only book value. Before you think about signing the franchise agreement, make sure there's a clause for letting you terminate your contract.

The franchise agreement usually gives the franchisor 30 different grounds to terminate the contract, while you have none. Generally, contracts last 10 to 20 years. If after considering these factors, you think you know a better way to run the business, then start your own company.

RUNNING THE DAY-TO-DAY OPERATIONS

An important factor in your decision to buy a franchise is: Will you be able to apply some previous experience to the franchise operation? Yes, you can expect training and support from the franchisor, but you are responsible for running the day-to-day operations of the franchise. If the franchise chain is small, you are more likely to receive hands-on assistance, whereas, a large chain will expect you to operate the franchise more independently.

On an average day, your responsibilities may entail ordering supplies, telephoning contractors, paying a few bills, and preparing sales reports for the corporate office. At the same time, you will have to train employees and wait on customers. Other duties include handling payroll, which means filing and paying payroll taxes (i.e., Social Security, Medicare, and federal and state withholding taxes). You will have to make bank deposits and keep track of bank accounts, income and expenses, projected sales, and other information. Since cash registers and ledgers are passé, you'll need to know how to work with modernized electronic systems.

Moreover, you will have to monitor customer buying habits to determine how much of a particular item you should order and how often. What happens when the air conditioner conks out? It's your job to fix it and anything else that goes awry during the course of a day.

Just how ready are you to "be the boss?" Working for yourself as a sole proprietor is one thing, managing other people's work is an entirely different ball game. Being the boss is not just managing employees, it's understanding how to manage customers as well.

• **Managing customers.** With so many choices today, customers demand the red-carpet treatment. Quality service is crucial in your business, if you want to keep customers from running to your competitors. What type of personal service will you provide to keep customers coming back? What value-added services will you provide?

Implement some customer service ground rules in order to maintain customer loyalty. Some people will be nice and friendly, others will be rude and irritating. Customers who don't get waited on in a decent amount of time are sure to have a gripe and they may even perceive your employees as disorganized—their perception is your reality. How will you (and your employees) handle disgruntled customers? You can't lose your temper. One nasty confrontation with a customer could cause other customers to frown upon your business and spread the word—negative news travels fast. If you aren't on top of customer problems or complaints, not only will they stop coming to your place of business but you can forget about getting referrals from them. You'll have to teach your staff the tactics of diplomacy.

- **Managing employees.** Starting out, you will have to wear several hats. But at some point you have to turn over the store into the capable hands of a general manager, who can open or close up the store, order supplies, and hire or fire employees. Before that eventual day, you will have the formidable task of hiring a responsible crew who can take on routine tasks. You'll also have to train employees to produce or provide goods in accordance with the standards of the franchisor (based on the training you get from the franchisor). Poorly trained employees could ruin your franchise.

You also have to make sure that your employees understand their job requirements and know what's expected of them. Supervising employees is a lot tougher than handling customers. In fact, you have to train your workers how to deal with customers. As the boss, you will have to set the tone for your workers. Meaning, that you have to show up every day and on time. You are the one who sets the policies for everyone else to follow—what people can and can't do in terms of breaks, behavior, dress, sick days, and so forth. What won't you tolerate from your employees? How will you enforce the rules—under what ground will you fire someone?

At the same time, you will have to discern when to reward as well as reprimand employees. How will you motivate them? Will you give merit raises, employee-of-the-month awards, bonuses? How will you get them to take pride in their work and the business itself? Remember the objective is to attract and retain good employees.

In the final analysis, franchising can be rewarding if you prepare for the highs and lows. By educating yourself, understanding the rewards and risks, and effectively communicating with your franchisor, you can achieve business success and financial independence as a franchise owner.

HOWARD LEV, PRESIDENT, HAREM FOOD CO. INC., D.B.A. (DOING BUSINESS AS) KRISPY KREME DOUGHNUTS

Howard Lev has managed to bring a little southern comfort, or rather Krispy Kreme Doughnuts, to New York City. An adored treat in the South for 60 years, the original glazed yeast-raised doughnuts were virtually unknown above the Mason-Dixon line until 1995 when 25-year-old Lev opened his first Manhattan Krispy Kreme franchise on Twenty-third Street and a second store in Harlem across from the Apollo Theater.

Every day people gather in cultlike fashion around the retro-green Formica tables and red-and-green neon HOT DOUGHNUTS NOW sign, waiting in reverence to get a taste of a fresh Krispy Kreme Doughnut. While Lev has had his problems—like resident neighbors complaining about the constant smell of sugar and frying oil—they have not been financial. His first store has grossed well over $1 million in revenues, and boasts such patrons as RuPaul, Rosie O'Donnell, and Sarah Jessica Parker. The second is expected to be equally profitable its first year.

A big part of Lev's success is that Krispy Kreme has a loyal following. Based in Winston-Salem, North Carolina, the $200 million chain has been around since 1937. There are more than 125 Krispy Kreme outlets in 17 states, churning out over 3 million doughnuts a day—at $3.49 a dozen—which are also sold at supermarkets and convenience stores. In addition to more than a dozen varieties of doughnuts, Krispy Kreme's line comprises six types of bagels, real fruit pies, and cinnamon buns. The company recently added a special blend of Arabica bean coffee to its staple.

We didn't know for sure that Krispy Kreme would be a hit here, but we definitely knew we were onto something when we started

Jules Allen

HOWARD LEV

surveying potential customers and they would recall childhood experiences about the doughnuts. We hung up our banner announcing the grand opening of the store, and people left voice messages saying "Thank you for bringing Krispy Kreme to New York." There are a lot of transplants here from the South, so people were already familiar with the product.

Lev was first introduced to Krispy Kreme doughnuts back in 1991 when he lived in Atlanta for a year, shortly after graduating from the University of Maryland. But the idea of owning a doughnut shop didn't occur to him until four years later, after his father tasted his first Krispy Kreme while visiting some friends in Mississippi. While the older Lev had no intention of giving up his 30-year-old shirt-manufacturing company, he approached his son about opening a Krispy Kreme franchise in New York.

My father knew I was looking for something else to do. I just didn't like selling shirts. We worked in an industry where you have 1,000 companies making the same white shirt to sell to several stores under different labels. We looked around and saw that there was only one brand-name company selling doughnuts in New York—Dunkin' Donuts. There was also a local chain, called Quick Donut.

In addition to comparing Krispy Kreme's product and program to that of Dunkin' Donuts, Lev looked at other types of food franchises, namely Ben & Jerry's and Häagen-Dazs. He got in touch with franchise lawyers and used their expertise to tell him what to look for and what to expect. After Lev's first meeting with Krispy Kreme officers (in May of 1995), he knew the two would be a good team. He was particularly impressed with the company's fund-raising program for nonprofit groups, which earn a 50 percent profit for every dozen doughnuts they sell at local events. Last year, these groups raised more than a total of $12 million. A company was formed to run the franchise, Harem Foods—named after Howard; his mother, Aura; his brothers, Russell and Eric; and father, Mel. Lev opened the first store in June of 1996.

We found that location by riding around and looking for empty storefronts. We would report back to Krispy Kreme and they provided us with market analysis on that specific neighborhood. We didn't know if the demographics of Northerners would equal those of Southerners. There was a doughnut/coffee shop on the corner of Eighth Avenue and Twenty-third Street. The guy wouldn't sell it to me, but there was a vacant store 50 feet up the block. Krispy Kreme ran the demographics; the report came back saying this was a great site to open the franchise.

Lev had to renovate the store, which operates much like a factory in that it houses an enormous contraption that makes one hundred and fifty dozen doughnuts an hour. In fact, the doughnut machine has historically been a Krispy Kreme selling point, because customers get to watch in full view every doughnut from the dough's formation into the traditional "nut" that travels along green wire mesh trays and falls into a tub of oil to its journey up and down a ramp where it's hosed down with a gusher of glaze.

Our start-up costs were $500,000 (including the franchise fee, cost of the machine and materials, and construction). We happened to see an ad in the newspaper for a bank that did franchise financing. It helped that my father had an existing business and lines of credit with other banks. The franchisor also stood behind us and helped us with the funds we needed.

The Levs, who are leasing both properties, went through a lengthy process with a lawyer and the landlord, each trying to get the best deal for himself. Lev's father, Mel, who was still working in the shirt business at the time, helped with the lease negotiations and contracts with vendors. His older brother, Russell, 32, now oversees production and the wholesale side of the business. It came in handy that their 28-year-old cousin, Jon Faber, had 10 years of food experience, including a stint in restaurants affiliated with the Marriott hotel chain. Faber came aboard as store manager.

Lev spent three months with Faber attending Doughnut University at Krispy Kreme headquarters. There they learned about the 60-year-old recipe for the yeast-risen doughnuts, which was created in New Orleans by French chef Joe LeBeau and has been enjoyed by such fans as the King, Elvis Presley, who ordered them by the box full. The training program focused mostly on the product side—equipment installation and maintenance, and the proper preparation and handling of the product.

Jon and I thought it was going to be a bunch of laughs making doughnuts. We spent our entire Labor Day weekend nursing this machine, trying to get it to run. Jon and I were (and still are) actively involved in the day-to-day operations. When I opened the first store, I might as well have put a cot in there, because all I was doing was going home to get some sleep and returning to the store bright and early the next morning. I should have had 10 different hats laying on the floor to put on for every different task I was doing at any given time.

Lev set his sights on Harlem for his next shop. He talked to real estate developers about the area, which was undergoing revitalization (mostly as a result of government empowerment zone funds). Once again, the site matched Krispy Kreme's market demographics. Lev was open for business in December of 1996.

Lev and Faber have invested seven figures as part of their plans for opening 30 Krispy Kreme franchises over the next six years—10 were scheduled for 1998. It was Lev's five-year business plan—which is updated quarterly—outlining his company's expansion goals that impressed Kripsy Kreme officers.

A general manager and two assistant managers are responsible for seeing to the needs of the store, which includes properly trained employees. An accountant and part-time bookkeeper handle the accounts payable and receivable for both stores.

My father let me see everything that went on in his business when I was growing up. I understood the importance of cash flow and keeping my receivables down, and taking care of my accounts payable. That was definitely an advantage to working in a family business.

Lev says a major challenge is keeping his 16-employee staff motivated. Everyone is a specialist. The production specialist mixes the dough from fifty-pound bags of Krispy Kreme Raised Doughnut mix; the processing specialist puts jelly into the jelly doughnuts and sugar onto the sugared doughnuts; and the people who sell them are the retail specialists. Lev spends most of his days working with architects and engineers on the next sites. But it really depends what day you catch him on. Some days he's in a Krispy-Kreme hat and T-shirt working the counter.

It's tough running a start-up company in the restaurant indus-
try—there are more openings and closings in this business than
anything else. Is it luck that people who work hard seem to do
well? I wasn't the A student; I wasn't the star athlete; I was the
one cracking jokes in the back of the class. But I always had a
hard-work ethic. If you want your business to be successful you
better be prepared to dedicate everything you have. The first eight
months my life was on hold. I have had to make some major sac-
rifices. But Jon, Russell, and I are dedicated and determined to
make this work.

SIDNEY WARREN AND CHUCK BAKER,
TCBY TREATS/MRS. FIELDS COOKIES FRANCHISES

It was the harsh reality of today's corporate environment—
where you can graduate cum laude and still end up working in
the mailroom or work years for a company with little career
advancement or job security to show for it—that led Sidney
Warren, 32, and Chuck Baker, 27, to quit their full-time jobs
five years ago to open up a TCBY Treats and Mrs. Fields
Cookies franchise. But it was also extensive corporate and professional training that helped the duo develop their business
building skills.

Baker had been an entrepreneur in high school and as a student at Georgetown University with ventures ranging from
computer maintenance to events planning. He went to work for
Procter & Gamble in 1991, where he was promoted from brand
assistant to assistant brand manager within a year. His position
grounded him in market research and strategic planning. His
job was to analyze data and find creative ways to get into the
eyes of the consumer so he could see who he was marketing to
and how he could better serve them. He was also afforded the
chance to put into practice the accounting and financial systems, formulas, and ratios he learned in college.

Baker and Warren, who attended Wright State University,

had toyed with several business ideas from opening a coffee shop to designing greeting cards to running a night club. Then in 1994, Warren, who had put in six years in advertising sales at the *Cincinnati Herald*, happened across a newspaper ad requesting a proposal for a franchise opportunity in the Greater Cincinnati/Northern Kentucky International Airport. It was part of a program for disadvantaged business enterprises (DBE) offered by Host Marriott, which was co-branding TCBY Treats/Mrs. Fields Cookies franchises. The deadline for the bid package was just a couple of weeks away and it specified 10-15 years of food and beverage experience, which neither Baker nor Warren had.

The first person they originally approached fell through. Undaunted, they recruited a neighbor of Baker's, Joey Nugent, to form the team. Nugent owned a casual-dining restaurant and brought to the table 17 years of experience.

Baker's position at P&G came in handy in writing the business plan, which was completed in nine days, and included all the right components—profit and loss statements, break-even analysis, market research, five-year financial projections, etc.

I had to write business plans and marketing plans for such brands as Folgers and Hawaiian Punch. I acquired the skill of learning how to write them very quickly. That's where the rubber hits the road in business, when you can think on paper.

Baker, Warren, and Nugent went through a grueling hour and a half interview with Host Marriott franchise department heads and airport board administrators. The trio had to discuss how they intended to implement the business plan in real terms. How were they going to manage the store? How were the finances going to be taken care of? How would they pay their bills? What inside marketing schemes did they have? What were their cash management systems?

What followed next was the initial franchise fee—$36,000. Warren's mother helped him get a small personal bank loan and the rest came from savings. Baker's share came from $7,000 in savings and credit card advancements. In addition to the fee, they had to secure a $30,000 cash guarantee from a bank in case they failed to pay their bills to the airport board and Host Marriott.

The guarantee was very difficult to secure, because banks don't normally like to loan money to people in the food and beverage industry since those types of businesses are more likely to go under than any other type. Joey became very instrumental in this area, because he already had a track record with local banks. So, we were able to lean on him to get the money.

The DBE program was unique in that the prime vendor, Host Marriott, financed the total build-out of the store—around $300,000. The franchisees would have to pay back the amount plus interest over the course of the lease. The site was already chosen for them. They would have to bear the responsibility of hiring personnel and managing the day-to-day operations of the store.

In May of 1994, three months after Warren saw the ad in the newspaper, they were open for business in the airport. Baker, who had already quit his job at P&G, served as president, Warren was vice president of operations in charge of maintaining systems put into place by Nugent, who served as mentor and advisor.

Baker put in 60 hours a week overseeing the day-to-day operations. He opened the store, supervised the employees, ordered the supplies, churned the yogurt, baked cookies, mopped the floors, paid the bills, and locked up each night. He had even attended a three-day training program with TCBY and five days with Mrs. Fields.

Warren came on six months later. From May to December of 1994, the store grossed roughly $400,000. Sales shot up to $830,000 in 1995, and the trio pulled down $1.2 million in sales in 1996. TCBY has a 10 percent charge up. Mrs. Fields has a 7 percent royalty and a 1 percent advertising fee.

Warren and Baker attempted to duplicate the success of their first store in another location—the Tower Place Mall in downtown Cincinnati—but this time without a third partner. They took out a $125,000 loan, secured with $25,000 in cash. The second store grossed $250,000 between May and December of 1996, and 1997 sales were estimated to be $500,000.

A successful tool the partners applied in the area of sales was to give a 10 percent discount to all airport employees and Delta personnel (and mall employees at the second store). This helped to build customer loyalty and to develop a sense of teamwork among everyone who worked at the airport. Given the high turnover in the food and beverage industry, Baker and Warren applied a management style of empowerment for their total staff of 35 (both stores).

Employees are an important aspect of the business. For us it costs more money to constantly train someone new to bake the cookies, make the brownies, and churn the yogurt, and provide good customer service. It makes more sense to give the people—if they earned it—periodical merit raises, bonuses at the end of the year, pats on the back, and in some cases, even help them find adequate day care. Employees can actually make or break your business, because they are on the front lines of the store. All you need are 15 bad complaints and you are losing business. You're not getting the cross-sales you should have.

Warren and Baker were quick to promote diligent employees to management positions. The dedicated general manager of the first store so impressed Warren and Baker that they are willing to make her regional manager if they acquire a third TCBY Treats/Mrs. Fields Cookies store, and to cut her in on a piece of the company ownership.

Moreover, the manager of their second store in the mall is a 20-year-old former welfare mom, with two children, who only has a GED. She was hired as part of a creative financing deal done with the city of Cincinnati, in which Warren and Baker could secure a low interest rate loan in exchange for creating a sort of "workfare" training program. The young woman, however, proved to be a major asset, working her way from store associate to store supervisor to assistant manager and now general manager.

The enterprising duo stresses the importance of having someone in place who will ensure the store is providing good customer service and maintaining quality brand standard (i.e., the cookie must be soft to the touch and baked fresh every 45 minutes, and the yogurt must have a certain consistency, not too much air).

Warren now oversees the business operations of both stores. Baker, who spent six months at Kellogg Business School before moving to Philadelphia in 1995, maintains ownership in the business. He does, however, continue to manage the cash-flow and accounting procedures. He used capital from the franchise business—around $65,000—to jump-start a record production and management company. It has grossed a little over $250,000 thus far. Notwithstanding, Baker isn't taking himself completely out of the franchise game. He and Warren will continue to scout for opportunities, hoping to develop into multiple unit franchise owners.

I've made money and I have lost money in my earlier ventures. But I had a professor at Kellogg who would say it's okay to make mistakes in business as long as they are smart mistakes. The way you grow your business is by understanding where you went wrong.

CHRISTOPHER MCCRAY, OWNER OF POTTSVILLE FORD DEALERSHIP

Growing up in Princeton, New Jersey, Christopher McCray wanted to be a professional football player. In fact, he won an athletic scholarship to the University of Massachusetts. But the sportsman was just as interested in UM's business school as its football program.

He didn't make the pros, but he did graduate in 1989 with a degree in financial management. He even considered pursuing his MBA. However, an uncle convinced McCray to get hands-on experience at the Heritage Lincoln Mercury car dealership, which he owned in Hackensack, New Jersey.

He told me I wouldn't be anyone special and that I would have to start working at the bottom. I could learn the business, save some money, and get a shot at owning my own dealership. Literally, my first week on the job he had me counting 100,000 car parts against an inventory list. Here I was sitting on the floor in some back room. I had been a big-time college athlete and I had this big degree from a good school. I got slapped into reality real quick. But it also taught me humility. My uncle worked me through every department from the ground up.

Today, McCray owns a Ford car dealership in Pottsville, Pennsylvania. The dealership generated more than $15 million in sales in 1996, its first year in business, selling more than 1,000 cars and trucks. Because of his longstanding reputation for "taking care of customer's needs," McCray has positioned himself as a major player in automotive sales.

But it didn't take the young entrepreneur a decade to get his own store, as his uncle had anticipated. About a year after working at Heritage Lincoln Mercury, Ford representatives took notice of a then 24-year-old McCray. He was recruited for a minority dealer training program. It was a grueling two-year program, with McCray alternating months between the Hackensack dealership and Ford's facilities for testing in Detroit.

You had to go through a 500-page manual in each of five department sessions—parts, service, financing, rentals, and new and used car sales. Each session lasted from eight to ten weeks. You were required to learn the manual inside out. You were given a verbal and written exam on it. And you were graded. If you passed you moved on to the next department session.

At age 26, McCray was one of the youngest trainees to complete the program in May of 1992. To prove to himself that his training had paid off, he went to work for a nonrelative at a Ford dealership in southern New Jersey. Within three years, he was promoted from finance manager to general store manager.

Again, Ford representatives became aware of his work. They offered him a dealership. There was, however, a slight catch.

Ford couldn't talk to me by law about getting my own dealership until I had a letter from my employer stating that it was okay with them. It was a risk for me because I was one of the head managers. The reason I got a lot of recognition from Ford in the first place was because my department was doing so well. We had won several sales awards. I asked for the letter from my boss. He said no problem, we support you 100 percent. Three days after giving me the letter, he fired me. All my money I had saved I needed to buy the dealership. So, I lived off of unemployment for three months.

McCray said goodbye to his $50,000 plus salary and used his personal savings to buy the Ford franchise. He scoured the east coast for a store. Ford showed him several different existing dealerships in New Jersey and Pennsylvania. After about five months, he had his own dealership.

I chose this location because I thought that it offered the best business opportunity. I felt I could make a major impact in this area. It was beginning to have economic revival. Other businesses were starting to move into the neighborhood. And the people living here are hardworking and family-oriented.

The facility—which is fairly new—sits on five acres. Still, McCray did about $50,000 worth of renovations. He also extended service department hours from six in the morning until eight at night, acknowledging that service and parts is a big business in automotive sales. He has beefed up his staff in this area to take care of the masses who come in with all models and makes of cars.

When it comes to staffing, McCray has had to make some tough decisions. Over the course of a year, he had to fire some 60 people. At the same time, he has had to replace workers. He recognizes that he is responsible for all his employees and their families. So, when he has to make decisions about his business, that's always in the back of his mind.

McCray says the key is to hire people with the right attitude, because he can always train them to do a particular job. This philosophy doesn't detract from the prerequisite of employing experienced mechanics.

You have to know your business inside out. You have to be able to show or train your employees—your sales staff—on what to do. You have to be an expert in your field, even if that means you have to start at the bottom. So, when you get a shot at owning a business, you know the right way to do it and people can't pull the wool over your eyes.

Pottsville Ford employs some 33 people, the majority of which are McCray's senior. But this hasn't presented a problem, he notes, because in the car business, people tend to judge you by what you know, not your age. McCray is quick to point out that he hires people with the same mentality he has—"the customer is always right, even when they are wrong."

People have so many other choices out there, if you don't keep the consumers you have, your competitor will go out there and scoop them up. My responsibility is to make a profit. I do that by taking care of my customers. You will get more referrals that way, which reduces your advertising costs. Word-of-mouth is a cheap but powerful medium. People hear about good things happening at a place and that's where they want to shop.

On average, about 200 people come into the store on a weekly basis for cars, parts, and services. The dealership has about ten different models in terms of new vehicles and just about every model in terms of used cars. Thanks to his sales, service, and marketing savvy, McCray woke up the sleepy Ford dealership, generating new and repeat business. Estimates for 1997 sales topped $17 million, with more than 1,200 cars and trucks sold.

Essentially, the way it works, McCray says, is that Ford offers its dealers all of its new vehicles for the current and incoming year. The dealer sits down with their representatives once a month and orders the cars, based on the different model lines and packages. The dealer chooses those cars that are more likely to sell, taking into account several factors, including color. From there it takes six to eight weeks for the cars to arrive. But the only way the dealer can make sound buying decisions is to know his or her customer.

You have to be at the dealership long enough each day to know your market (I am putting in about 70 hours a week). Whenever I am out I look at what cars I see on the street. Are they domestic or foreign? Are they luxury or compact? Are they mine or my competitors'? As a dealer, that's how you learn about your market. Once you know your market, you know what cars to order. Also, no two markets are alike. My market here is completely different than the market I served at the dealership in South Jersey. That market and the one here in Pennsylvania are completely different from my uncle's dealership in North Jersey.

As with most dealers, McCray's biggest challenge is the competition. There are six other Ford dealerships within a 15-mile radius. In terms of new vehicles the price is what it is, explains McCray, so now it comes down to who is going to do more for the customer.

We try to do follow-up and stay in touch with the customer through mail, telephone calls, and in person. I try to stay around the dealership, talking to people, shaking hands, and getting involved. We do all types of things to keep the customer coming back.

McCray plans to buy a second dealership in the next two years and a third one by the year 2000. His long-term goal is to build a five-dealership enterprise, with the continued backing and support of Ford Motor Co. He still follows the advice his father gave him as a boy: Anything good or worthwhile doesn't come easily or for free.

That's what my dad taught me. Whatever your field, be prepared to start at the bottom. And try to be the best at whatever you do. As soon as you become one of the best, people notice and doors start to open for you.

Opportunity Knocks

10

CYBERPRENEURS:
DOING BUSINESS ON THE NET

Every market has a key. And if you turn that key, you'll
undoubtedly capture that market.
— *Henry Parks, founder, Parks Sausage Company*

Over the last couple of years, the Internet has been transformed
from an online scientific and military information database to a
commercial juggernaut moving at rocket propulsion speed.
Thanks to low barriers to entry and the potential to reach millions of consumers around the world, small and large businesses alike have launched sites in cyberspace. Many hope to
boost sales of an existing business by expanding their market
online. Others are trying to make money by establishing full-
time cyber businesses.

For small businesses, the Internet has the potential to drastically increase market share and foster competition with large,
well-financed corporations in a way that was previously impossible. A small entrepreneurial venture can look as big as a
Fortune 500 company's Website.

A number of Internet companies, such as Earthlink
Network, and telecommunications giants, such as AT&T, are
offering tools that make it simple—and relatively cheap—for
small companies to create Websites. The benefits of the Web is
that it combines direct, interactive access to customers, unlim-

ited geographical reach, and unprecedented amounts of information.

Building a digital storefront to enhance sales or serve as a sole means for generating business is more viable than ever. Over the past year, it's gotten easier and cheaper to set up a Website that takes orders electronically. Moreover, Internet commerce has evolved into a fairly low-budget way for businesses without a distribution channel or retail location to sell their wares. For many, creating an online storefront requires a smaller investment than traditional retail outlets.

The online success of companies like Amazon.com and CDnow.com has breathed new life into an avenue of online commerce that was previously dominated by text-based offerings and lackluster sites. Many companies have gotten lost in the black hole of cyberspace, but only because they adopted the "everybody is doing it" mentality and piled onto the Web. After losing money, they jettisoned, shutting down their sites in frustration and proclaiming that the Web wasn't living up to all of the hype. The reality is that many of these businesses didn't totally understand what the new medium was all about and they failed to devise a clear online strategic plan to make the most of their virtual ventures.

The online shopping market will grow to $37.5 billion in 2002 and is on track to eclipse traditional catalog marketing within 10 years—creating a sales channel that no retailer can afford to ignore. Retailers specializing in a single product or service are expected to do especially well, dominating the medium. The unique capabilities of the Web are lower overhead, personalization, real-time promotion, contextual selling, and marketing alliances with other online entities. All of which will allow merchants to surpass off-line offerings by providing ease-of-use and more value in general.

More than 30 million households in North America have some kind of online access. The online population is expected to rise to more than 40 million households by the year 2000, according to Jupiter Communications, a New York–based new media research firm. In 1996, computer sales were notably out-selling televisions.

As of 1997, some 400,000 companies had online storefronts from retailers to investment banks. And commercial Websites started offering everything from flowers to high-tech electronic gadgets. At least 35 percent of large companies and 20 percent of medium-sized companies had a World Wide Web—WWW—site.

Depending on your type of business, target market, and resources, your company can make money by having a Website. The criteria for each company is different. The key to success online is planning, which includes doing a cost/benefit analysis. You must determine what you expect from your Website, and what you are willing to pay to achieve those results.

Building a Website is about more than slapping existing copy from a company brochure or traditional newsprint on a screen. The Web's true potential is as an interactive—and not a mass—medium for selling to a niche audience. Moreover, your company must have a tangible (product) or intangible (service) item that satisfies an unmet need. Your site must be designed and marketed in a manner that demonstrates how it meets that need.

The prosperity of any Website has to do with the quality of information, how interesting and engaging it is, how it is presented, and how it takes advantage of unique attributes associated with the medium. You have to have the right product, service, and price to meet market demands.

BUILDING A WEBSITE THAT GETS RESULTS

Your decision to build a Website should not be based on how easy it is to create, but on how efficient and effective you can make it. The actual design and costs associated with building an effective Website incorporates the five P's:

Purpose: What do you hope to gain by creating a presence on the Internet?

People: Who is your target market and are they online?

Process: How will you tailor the site to meet the unmet need(s) of your market?

Price: What are you willing to pay to reach your market—technical/manpower costs of designing, updating, and maintaining a site?

Publicity: How will you publicize your presence on the Internet?

Purpose. You need to determine one or more clearly attainable reasons for being online, whether it's sales, marketing, or customer service. Your Website should not be viewed as an aside or an extravagance, but as an integral part of your sales and marketing plan. After all, your sales and marketing plan is subject to identifying the most likely customers for your product or service, designing and packaging your product or service offering to best satisfy their needs, setting a price range for your product or service, choosing an overall advertising presentation to get customers to buy the product or service, selling your offerings to customers efficiently, sizing up your competition, and examining industry trends.

• *The Web as advertising channel.* Being online is like advertising your products and services in the world's largest directory. Most companies use the Web to increase visibility and to reach new customers. Even if your sole purpose is to increase awareness about your company to a wide range of people, your Website must pick up where traditional advertising leaves off. In general, radio, television, and print advertisements tell people that a product exists and tries to sell them on its benefits. Viewers or readers are often bombarded with ads designed to plant a message firmly in their minds. Your Website must be an interactive marketing tool that provides potential customers in-depth product information and links them to other sources. Your site should show that your product or service will improve their lifestyle. In general, advertising—if used poorly—can drain massive amounts of cash from a company with minimal financial return. You must make sure your site is visited by serious potential customers. There are a lot of cheaper ways to get the word out on your company.

• *The Web as a distribution channel.* There are different ways of getting your product or service into the hands of consumers, including direct sales, using employees to sell your offerings, retail stores, mail order, and independent sales or manufacturer representatives. The Web is also a distribution channel for selling your product or service. Electronic commerce—where the customer orders and pays electronically, and the product is delivered online or by mail—will ultimately become the new paradigm of doing business. By the year 2000 there will be 45 million to 75 million Web shoppers. Certain products lend themselves to online shopping, such as computers, software, gift items, books, music, cars, travel packages, stocks, mutual funds, consumer electronics, and homes. All of these are information-rich items in that people will take time to research or learn about them before buying them. Often people will go to friends, trade magazines, or attend product expos to make an informed decision. Products that don't require much thought are not likely to entice Web shoppers—you know, the thousands of grocery items you pass by in the aisles of supermarkets or drugstores. Who wants to spend time on the Web looking up the benefits of a particular toothpaste, dish detergent, soap, toilet paper, razor blades, or deodorant? Unlike television, where commercials on these items are forced upon you as you are watching your favorite television show, information is what sells products on the Web. Examine first whether your product is a good candidate for online sales. Could you better sell it by mail or phone order? You must furnish your site with facts, news, and advice on your products and services. Your site must distinguish itself by providing a broad selection, superior product expertise, below retail prices, and value-added services.

People—The Internet is ideal for reaching young, highly educated, affluent consumers, corporate customers, the government, and college students. Before you can offer your goods online, you have to thoroughly identify your target market. Are the demographics of the Web appropriate for your product or service? Simply put, is your target market using the Web? Even though a great many people are online, your Website must cater to a niche audience. What are the needs, attitudes, motivations, and perceptions of your market? If you hope to land any sales, you must learn about your customers' preferences, and then provide a service or product that satisfies those needs and builds consumer loyalty. The idea is not just to provide information, but to create an online community where people with similar interests can congregate and interact with each other on a regular basis. One way you can conduct market research or collect data on prospective customers is to develop an online survey or questionnaire. People will provide valuable information about themselves if you make the process truly interactive—contests, games, reviews, and recipes—and award prizes, gifts, or discounts in exchange.

Process—Either you or someone on your staff will have to be fully knowledgeable about Internet technology. In short, the Web is a segment on the Internet. Websites consist of electronic pages—of text and graphics, and sometimes video and sound—that are connected to one another within the same site or through other sites. A Webpage is a publicly available computer file stored on a computer (called a server) and attached to the

Internet for retrieval. By dialing into an Internet service provider (ISP), computer users from across town or around the globe can fetch a Webpage. Software on the server processes the requests to view or hear those files. Each site has an address or URL (uniform resource locator).

• *Constructing a Website.* You can construct as many Webpages as you so desire. You can set up your own Webserver (computer, software, and telecommunications services) or you can rent space on a company's server. You can choose an ISP or Web Presence Provider (WPP), preferably one that hosts merchant services.

Besides hosting your Website, an ISP may be able to help with Website design, provide software to set up an electronic catalog for order processing, or recommend vendors that process credit cards on the Internet.

If you are somewhat familiar with the Internet, for around $100 you can select from various off-the-shelf Web design programs, which contain templates and tools for building navigation bars and hyperlinks. Or you can hire a Webmaster (someone who builds Websites). But it will cost you—anywhere from $50-$150 an hour for custom work.

• *Creating Web content.* The front door of your site is your home page. It must be visually pleasing, inviting people to enter. What elements of the design and packaging of your site will enhance the attitudes of your target market? Which features and benefits will motivate them to buy? What do you want visitors to your site to do—join a mailing list, purchase a product, or request company information? These questions should not be taken lightly in designing your Website. Your content must grab your potential customers' attention and sustain it with something unique that causes them to return again and again. Because the Web allows for graphic presentations, it's easy to get caught up in the design. What you like may not sell a thing. Intense graphics and appeals to emotion are lost on many cybernauts. Text and graphics must work in tandem, with the focus on delivering comprehensive information about your products and services. For example, many computer company sites will contain basic product information and reviews for nontechnical consumers and another section with detailed analysis and upgrades for technophiles, which helps to cut down on mailings and toll-free phone calls from customers. Make sure your site offers value, is easy to navigate, and is reliable. How difficult it is to access information and purchase an item will affect a potential customer's decision to buy. Update your materials to get repeat customers, who are more likely to buy again and again. Take advantage of new technology to add new features, data, and resources. People want value, the best deal. They are not going to invest time and money into anything that doesn't convey this. For your site to work, it must be geographically engaging and easy to navigate. It must be informative, interesting, and interactive.

Price—The cost of building a Website can range anywhere from $1,000 to $100,000. Fortune 500 companies like Federal Express, General Motors, and Microsoft have spent $1 million or more to build their Websites. You can create a site with 10-30 megabytes of extra disk space, and an e-mail or a customer feedback form for free by signing up with such sites as Tripod. Costs will depend on how specific you want your site—say a retail site with photos, graphics, and audio or video components, or an interactive multimedia site with 200 plus pages. Then there are the costs associated with maintaining and troubleshooting the site. Maintaining and updating information on your Website is another cost—ranging anywhere from $30 to $500 a page, depending on how often (daily, weekly, or monthly) you update. Unless you can code your own Webpages, expect to pay for content changes. The life cycle of information will vary as it relates to your particular industry. However, if you intend to have repeat customers, you will have to keep your site reasonably fresh.

How committed and responsive are you to handling a 24-hour, 7-day-a-week business? If you plan to allow for consumers to ask questions about your products or services via e-mail, you must budget the proper amount of time to answer those queries. In some cases, you may have to devote an employee full-time to answering online questions and comments.

All of this is a part of your cost analysis. Your expectations for your Website should be in line with your budget. Be prepared to wait at least six months for results. Chances for achieving profitability, more than likely, will come from more than one avenue—selling advertising, sponsorship, or subscription fees, and inventing and charging for new value-added services.

- *Advertising/Sponsorship.* Large companies buy advertising on sites. The ads are usually icons or banners that appear at the top or bottom of a Webpage. Surfers click on these panels and up pops an ad or reference to the advertiser's own Website. You have to sell an audience. Companies are expected to spend $2.2 billion to advertise on the Web by the year 2000, according to Forester Research, Inc., a market research firm in Cambridge, Massachusetts. The most common advertising method is signing up companies as "sponsors." Larger firms will pay $50,000 or more to sponsor a site for one month. The price advertisers are willing to pay depends on whether they think the site will reach their desired market segment. Most Web advertisers are airlines, record companies, auto dealers, technology companies, and banks.

- *Subscription Fees.* A number of online companies have a membership service charging annual fees. A critical decision is what special services or features you will offer. The question is not so much, How much do you plan to charge? but What do you plan to charge for? Few companies have been able to attract a large audience and provide a high-quality, interactive experience to a core group of consumers. To get people to pay a subscription for some of your content, you are going to have to provide an incentive.

• *Value-added Services.* People are willing to pay for what they perceive as personalized, value-added services. One way you can convey value is to foster an online community, which can be achieved by hosting live chat sessions, creating a newsletter, and accepting viewer responses. Bo Peabody has done just that with Tripod.com, which has become the ultimate meeting place for hundreds of online community groups. The key says Peabody is to set up a mechanism to get responses from customers via a direct e-mail link or fill-out form; the more direct and immediate the better. Giving away product samples, coupons, rebates, and discounts are other ways of adding value.

Publicity—Even the best developed and most information-rich Websites can't guarantee visitors. You must take measures to draw traffic to your Website. Your URL should be printed on all company stationery, business cards, and marketing materials.

• *Search Engines.* A fast and easy way to publicize your site is to register with general-interest search engines and directories, such as Yahoo! (www.yahoo.com), AltaVista (www.altavista. com), Infoseek (www.infoseek.com), and Excite (www.excite.com). There are dozens of search engines and directories to help cybernauts find the kind of site they are looking for. Use key words and descriptions that make it easy to find you. Registering generally consists of typing in your Website's URL in the appropriate space and providing a brief description of your site. Announce-it (www.hilconet.com/announce/urls.hrml) will guide you through registering your site with numerous search engines and directories. You can also increase traffic on your Website by allying with other sites that offer complementary services or products. Here, you would provide a hypertext link (a line of text that will send the user directly to a specified page) to their site anywhere on the home page and they do the same for your site.

• *Newsgroups.* Joining mailing lists and newsgroups relevant to your particular industry is another way to publicize your presence on the Internet. A query to most search engines will give you a listing of mailing lists or newsgroups and their topics. They consist of text messages that can be responded to by any other member of the group. Don't post blatant commercial messages or advertisements. This isn't illegal, but it could be counterproductive. The idea is to establish your expertise and familiarize people with your products or services. A less intrusive way to publicize your site is to answer posted questions or comments in your field. Each response you post to a newsgroup contains your signature file, which consists of information about your products and services, your e-mail address, and URL. Members who find your comments useful will take the initiative to visit your Website. Moreover, most Internet service providers can aid your company in starting its own newsgroup or mailing list. This will give you even more latitude in promoting your services—again, don't misuse them as ads.

If a customer has a need for what you are offering, and you can provide a credible product or service that meets his or her need, within his or her budget, he or she will buy it. However, when it comes to the Internet, there is still the question of whether people will pay for what they want online. Security (the encryption and authentication that is required to conduct safe, valid transactions online) is often cited as a chief concern among business owners and consumers.

Internet security is improving. Acknowledging that most

people like to charge their purchases, the major credit card companies and Internet service providers, including Microsoft, Netscape, Visa, and Mastercard, have gone through great pains to secure electronic transactions. The word is catching on that entering a credit card number over the Internet is as safe as giving the number to a mail-order telephone agent or retail sales clerk—which most people do without ever giving it a second thought.

In addition, you can design your site with an alternative or backup scheme for orders—provide 800 numbers, allow users to fax or e-mail information, or have them establish a password in order to access an account.

The idea is to build trust among your potential customers. Relationship selling and superb customer service will make people feel more at ease with purchasing goods or services from your site. The key is to provide easy ordering, fulfillment, follow-up systems, and any other processes that will make their shopping experience as pleasant as possible.

CHRISTIE JONES, FOUNDER AND PRESIDENT OF PCORDER.COM

Christie Jones aims to change the way computers are purchased and sold. The 29-year-old president of pcOrder.com in Austin, Texas, is a prime example that Internet commerce can result in big business. Her emerging Internet-based company generated sales revenues of about $10 million in 1997.

pcOrder.com maintains and continuously updates a database on specifications and prices of more than 600,000 products from 1,000 different hardware and software manufacturers. Items range from memory boards and printer cables to video cards and spreadsheet software. A Web interface enables computer resellers and corporate buyers to automatically configure systems, compare pricing and availability, check on compatibility and other technical issues, and electronically place orders.

We want to be the largest electronic commerce system for the computer industry. Our goal is to grab market share quickly and get an entrenched market position, so that computer manufacturers and resellers will use us and not see a reason to create their own systems.

North American spending on computer sales reached $70 billion in 1998. In general, the big computer makers, such as IBM, Compaq, and Hewlett-Packard, move their merchandise through distributors and dealers. But they continue to lose significant ground to Dell Computer which sells directly to customers using electronic commerce.

Today, more than 15,000 resellers and corporate users access applications powered by pcOrder to buy and sell computers. Computer manufacturers can use pcOrder's software to set up their own Websites and to take orders directly from customers.

A major appeal of the company is increased sales productivity. Jones notes the average sales rep saves about 20 hours using pcOrder. Resellers have also seen value in reducing returns for PCs that were configured incorrectly.

With pcOrder, buyers can tap into all the product information they need to get answers as to how to configure their systems. What was happening was that the customer would order a system, get it, and it wouldn't work. This impacted customer satisfaction. Another problem was order-processing costs. Our clients feel that having sales orders placed electronically is ten times cheaper than placing calls using live telephone operators.

While major PC manufacturers and distributors are on board, only about 5,500 salespeople actually use pcOrder's software. Some 45,000 have yet to be convinced that ordering PCs over the Web beats doing business over the phones and faxes.

It's a tough sell. In fact, Jones spent several hundred thousand dollars on a direct-mail marketing campaign that flopped. She decided instead to use young, energetic, and eager sales reps to call on dealers directly.

Business is steadily picking up. In fall of 1998, pcOrder closed a deal—reported to be worth $30 million—with Santa

Anna, California–based Ingram Micro Inc., the world's largest computer distributor. Moreover, pcOrder filed to go public, hoping to raise $35 million.

It took about three years for pcOrder.com to get to where it is today. Jones had to take a number of steps to develop her Web-based company and solidify its market. She first wrote the business plan for pcOrder.com in 1993. The basic concept still holds true, but the actual details have changed tremendously.

The modifications had more to do with the business execution than the overall business operation. For instance, when I first wrote the business plan, I was trying to decide if the manufacturer was going to be the driver or corporate buyers or resellers. But after looking further into it, I realized that distributors and resellers would drive the company.

Jones's original business plan was to build her own Website and act as a sales agent for computer makers, taking a commission for each sale. However, distributors viewed pcOrder as more of a competitor. She pitched the idea to Ross Cooley, the 57-year-old computer industry deal maker who was running Compaq's North American operations at the time. Cooley persuaded Jones to revise her plan. Instead of setting up her own electronic storefront, pcOrder would provide storefronts for individual manufacturers and dealers. In turn, Jones convinced Cooley to come onboard in exchange for a 7 percent stake in the business. That was two years ago; Cooley now serves as chairman and CEO of pcOrder.

At the time she started her company, Jones was working at Trilogy Development Group, a software company she co-founded with six former classmates while still attending Stanford University. Jones initially approached Trilogy's board of directors, who were reluctant to invest money in pcOrder with Trilogy still in its infancy.

This basically meant I would have to bootstrap the business and develop a [financial] resource plan. But first I would have to try to find a customer base. We sent out marketing materials and copies of the business plan. It took about a year for resellers to sign on.

pcOrder started out as part of Trilogy—a sort of subsidiary. Trilogy had been the brainchild of Joseph Liemandt, an economics major, who dropped out of Stanford University, just months short of graduation in 1990, to launch the firm. Liemandt had held several part-time jobs at major computer companies where he noticed that shipments on customer orders often arrived late, or with missing or incompatible parts.

He studied sales configurations—how orders were processed. Much of it was handwritten using cumbersome inventory manuals and requiring lengthy consultations between sales reps and engineers. He responded by developing sales configuration software.

In 1994, Jones came up with the idea to use Trilogy's sophisticated software to custom-configure and sell computer systems to individuals, resellers, and small companies over the Internet. However, Liemandt wanted to continue selling software to big corporate accounts. But he was willing to let Jones test her idea. Jones cashed out of her Trilogy stock in order to get a bigger share of pcOrder and to finance the start-up.

Internet entrepreneurs have to be opportunistic and able to manage chaos. As with all start-ups, you're never right the first time. The fifth time, maybe. You have to be flexible and able to deal with changes every day.

Once pcOrder became a formalized operation in 1996, Jones spun the company off. At that point, Trilogy had grown into a 200-employee firm with estimated revenues of $70 million. Thanks to her boot-camp days at Trilogy, Jones learned two crucial things that she was later able to apply to building her own business.

One was the importance of managing your money and building up your expenses after revenues. In order to run a well-managed business you can't invest money and build up this huge cost infrastructure before you have real customers and sales revenues. Second was the importance of recruiting. At Trilogy we didn't put a full effort into hiring [for about four years]. We knew great people were required, but we didn't realize the magnitude of effort that was required to find those caliber employees.

A key player Jones recruited early on at pcOrder was programmer Carl Samos, who replaced Marc Andressen as lead developer of the National Center for Supercomputing Applications' Mosaic, the Internet browser project that spawned Netscape.

Jones describes pcOrder's organizational structure as organic. She currently is its president and is responsible for working with resellers and distributors, and coordinating internal operations. Chris Rofton, a former senior executive with Compaq, serves as chairman and CEO. Several key managers come from investment banking, technology, marketing, and other industries.

My goal right now is to create an environment where people come in here and feel like they are not bound by any corporate hierarchy. This [management philosophy] extends all the way down to the receptionist. In fact, our receptionist is doing recruitment now, because that's an area she felt we were still lacking in. Everyone here can take the initiative and create his or her own job description over time.

New sites on the World Wide Web have been cropping up at the rate of one per minute. However, many businesses are piling up on the Web without really understanding it.

The key is to provide real added value. In the computer industry, that works for us because people are more technology savvy and ready to embrace the Net. But the Internet is about more than technology, it's about customer service, creativity, marketing, and merchandising.

JASON OLIM, MATTHEW OLIM, FOUNDERS AND PRINCIPALS OF CDNOW, INC.

In just four years Jenkintown, Pennsylvania–based CDnow Inc. emerged as the hottest online music store and one of the first success models in Internet commerce. With over 300,000 music-related products, including CDs, cassettes, T-shirts, movies, and videos, CDnow's selection is ten times the inventory of a traditional brick-and-mortar retail store.

CDnow is the brainchild of Jason Olim, 29, the company's president and CEO. It was a botched request for a certain Miles Davis album that first planted the seed in Olim's head to start his own music store. The limited selection, uninformed sales staff, and inconvenience he encountered left him with a major headache and short $17.

This was back in 1989, when a friend loaned me Miles Davis's Kind of Blue. I liked it a lot and I wanted to buy another Miles Davis album. But I didn't know which one to get that would be similar to this one. When I asked the music store clerk, he just pointed and said Miles Davis is in the Jazz section under D. I ended up buying a Miles Davis album that was totally different from the sound I was looking for. I was extremely disappointed.

It was six years later, just before Valentine's Day, that the idea for CDnow began to blossom. While socializing with some friends at a local bar, Olim says it dawned on him that by taking the database of albums from record distributors who sell to retailers along with album reviews from various publications and merging the two together, he could build an online music store. Customers could look up hard-to-find albums, read reviews, learn about music, and shop.

The very next day, Olim began working on the concept. He talked to friends, soliciting their feedback and help. It seemed like a natural fit for the Brown University graduate, with a degree in computer science. He had spent two years at Soft•Switch, a company that designed e-mail software systems for multinational corporations. Now his passion for music and experience in technology, coupled with his entrepreneurial instinct, would help him realize his vision.

The following month, Olim was joined by his 24-year-old twin brother Matt, who was taking master's courses in neuroscience at the University of Pennsylvania. Intrigued by the idea, Matt made it his mission to develop the search engine interface—a programming device that enables users to find what they are looking for in a matter of seconds. He built a prototype in two weeks. Over the next six months, the Olims went to work on CDnow.

The brothers bootstrapped the business with a modest investment of $20,000—of which $8,000 came from their parents (their father is a private physician and their mother is a dietitian). In August 1994, CDnow was launched on the Internet, through a program called "telenet" that allows you to log into other Internet connected computers. In October of 1994, the Olim brothers launched CDnow as a Website.

At first, it was this big old clunky store. Back then the average modem was 9,600 baud. No one had a 28.8 baud modem. It wasn't out yet. We had too many graphics and they were big, which made the site very slow. (The site has evolved through many redesigns since then.)

The Olims were clueless as to whether the Website would work. It wasn't until they hired a market research firm in October of 1994 that they knew they had a real customer base. Through a series of telephone interviews and online market surveys, which posed 20 questions to people across the country who had visited CDnow's Telnet or Websites, the Olims were able to build their site around what their market wanted and needed.

Up until that point, we were operating in the dark. We started building this thing relatively blind based on my perception of the ideal music store. We began to learn more about our customers. Our market wasn't college students as we originally thought, but an older crowd (the average age is 30) who tended to like esoteric music. They didn't have the time to drive all over town to find a record store that carried the one particular album they wanted.

CDnow advertised in *Wired* magazine and posted information about the company on online news groups and bulletin boards. Olim's goal was to sell $300,000 worth of CDs that first year in business. That first month in business, he sold $387 worth of CDs and had a mere gross profit of $14. He attributed the low margin to pricing. In its second full year, CDnow sold $6.3 million worth of CDs, and $117.4 million in 1997.

The company grew quickly in size. Olim worked out of his parents' basement as sole proprietor until he incorporated the business in 1995 and moved into a commercial office. Between the summer of 1995 and fall of 1998, CDnow grew from six to almost 200 employees. And the company moved a third time into an over 25,000-sq.-ft. office space.

For Olim, the biggest challenge has been hiring a staff. One of his first hires was a human resources manager. Olim stresses the importance of surrounding yourself with competent and talented people who share a vision. In exchange for loyal service, he awards merit raises and bonuses. Plus, employees from receptionists to vice presidents have equity in the company. Olim has received most of his business training on-the-job. He handled the bookkeeping until he hired Arthur Anderson to do an audit in 1995.

My nose would twitch if we were off by thousands of dollars. When we wanted to have a professional audit [which is a prerequsite to raising money from investors], I hired a comptroller. She started bringing me receipts for $12 and asking what is this for? I was blown away. I didn't track small items. Here she was out there, cataloging every single receipt.

While Olim was not good at managing the accounts, he did learn the fundamentals of float (money collected from customers but not yet due to suppliers). In fact, he was able to expand CDnow by using his suppliers' money as working capital.

CDnow collected the credit card information when the customer placed an order with us. Once the vendor confirmed the item was shipped, we charged the customer's account. I remember looking at my account and seeing I was $30,000 in the hole, but I had $30,000 in cash. I called up a friend of mine who was getting his MBA at Stanford and mentioned this to him. He explained to me about "float" (the lag time between your customers paying you and when you pay your suppliers). So, at the beginning of a month, I would bill $100,000 in orders from my customers, but the vendors didn't bill for the orders until the end of the month [30 to 45 days net]. When I did pay, it may only have been $80,000 (because of vendor discounts).

CDnow has established different payment arrangements and

schedules with its suppliers. In fact, a chief point of negotiation is "how long can we hold onto your money before we have to pay you," Olim explains. This tactic enabled him and Matt to maintain majority ownership of the company and not to have to rely on equity investors—though their mom and dad own a piece of CDnow.

CDnow has developed relationships with five vendors with over $100 million in inventory between them. No CDnow employee ever needed to touch an order, which has helped keep overhead low. The customer orders through CDnow, who places the order with the vendor, who then ships the album directly to the customer.

It was tough getting suppliers in the beginning, because we had a very hard time convincing anyone to work with us (most people were still suspicious of the Internet as a sales channel). Finally, we found someone who was doing fulfillment orders for other companies, just not anyone who was selling over the Internet. But he had more vision than the others, at the time. After we got the first supplier, it was much easier to get the other four.

Unlike the average record store, where 80 percent of sales come from the top 1,000 music titles, CDnow's success is based on its deep catalog of hard-to-find items in various genres from jazz to classical to heavy metal. The customer enters an artist or album and up pops a discography page with biographies, ratings, similar artists, sound samples, videos, concert T-shirts, and reviews from major magazines, such as *Rolling Stone, College Music Journal*, and *Spin*.

CDnow appeals to 700,000 worldwide customers, with more than 6 million visits each month. Olim attributes CDnow's popularity to a comprehensive source of information, product selection, and convenience. For instance, the site has a text-only interface for slower modems. E-mailboxes are open and answered within 24 hours. And customers can preorder new albums up to a month before their official release.

Olim says he is very cautious about how he will grow CDnow, which did a private placement in 1997 to raise $10 million in expansion capital and $90 million in the public markets in 1998. To help CDnow thrive in the new millennium, Olim is banking on the advice of his senior experienced board members (one is from the music industry, two are in finance, and all have invested in the company).

CDnow already has expanded its consumer reach through aggressive advertising, including radio and TV commercials; strategic alliances, and merchandising links with such high traffic sites as Yahoo!, Lycos, Tripod, and Webcrawler. Olim is not afraid of change. He recently got rid of CDnow's news section—set up like a magazine—because customers didn't take to it. In its place are primers on a given style or genre of music.

People use the Internet in a very goal-directed way. We allow people to browse or to go right in and buy something. We don't just sell CDs, we market them to people. We help them discover music. We have a team of data miners whose job is to go through our customer base to find out who likes what. At the end of the day this is a business about helping people who want to learn about music. We want to give people the best experience they have ever had.

Staking a Claim on the Internet: Amazon.com CEO Jeff Bezos

Hordes of business prospectors are trying desperately to stake their claim on the World Wide Web. Claiming itself as the "Earth's Biggest Bookstore" is Amazon.com. Indeed, the online bookstore has some 3 million titles, including hard-to-find, out-of-print books as well as CDs, videos, computer games, and audio tapes.

Named after the world's largest river, Amazon.com is likewise many times bigger than the largest brick and mortar store, which typically stocks up to 175,000 different titles at any given time. It is the premier bookseller on AOL, Excite, Yahoo! and AltaVista.

Amazon.com has 3 million customers in more than 160 countries. The 614-employee firm has sold more than $147 million worth of books and other products a year.

Amazon.com CEO and 33-year-old founder Jeffrey P. Bezos's premise for the Web-based bookstore was that its main attraction would be selection. Indeed, his concept paid off royally, with Amazon.com generating $30 million in revenue in its first two years (plus the company went public on the stock market in 1997). By comparison, the average bookstore generates $5 million annually.

It was back in 1994 when Jeff Bezos, a 30-year-old Wall Street investment whiz, became intrigued with the Web and online commerce. Initially, he contemplated some 20 products that he could sell online from music to magazines. He settled on books, packing his bags and moving with his wife to Seattle, because of its proximity to high-tech talent and a major book distributor. He wrote a business plan, rounded up seed capital, and wrote the software for Amazon.com.

Bezos sold his first book in July 1995. He started out of his garage wrapping orders and delivering them to the post office in the family car. Without any advertising in its first year, Amazon.com attracted enormous attention via word-of-mouth. Initially, Bezos projected a 10-times impact from word-of-mouth—meaning that one satisfied customer's experience would influence ten other people. However, the site had 100-times impact and sales grew an average 34 percent the first year in business.

Customers can search for books by author, title, subject, or keyword. The way the cyber storefront operates, Amazon requests books from a distributor or publisher, which delivers them to the company's warehouse. The order is packed and shipped. On average, customers receive the books two to five days after ordering them, or they can pay extra to speed up the delivery by the next day.

About 90 percent of customers pay by credit card online; the others fax or phone the order in.

Amazon.com offers 10 percent to 40 percent discounts on books. Besides the margins it makes on each book, Amazon charges $1 per book and $3 per order service charge.

Bezos was bent on making the site as fun and enjoyable as real bookstores. Only instead of doing it with café mochas and couches, he did it with both customer-to-customer and customer-to-author interaction. His staff of booksellers try to encourage impulse buys by giving their top picks of intriguing, obscure, and funny new books in 45 categories. There's also Amazon's miles of aisles, which display the hottest titles. The site draws on snippets of reviews from other publications. And customers get to voice their opinions through shorter reviews, creating an online community of literary aficionados.

Amazon.com continues to rank as one of the world's best Websites, because of its huge inventory, convenience, price, and reliable service—available 24 hours, seven days a week.

Bezos has developed an extensive customer database. Customers specify their reading preferences in certain genres or subjects. And in return they receive regular e-mail notifications when books from their favorite authors come out as well as recommendations on new titles.

Amazon.com pioneered the concept of syndicated selling on the Internet in 1996 with its Associates Program. The number of Associates has climbed from 5,000 since the program's inception to more than 100,000 participants today. Associates range from large and small businesses to nonprofits, authors, publishers, and personal homepages. Among Amazon.com's Associates are AOL, Yahoo!, Netscape, iVillage, Kemper Funds, and Adobe.

The Associates Program allows Website owners to participate in hassle-free electronic commerce by recommending books on their sites and referring visitors to Amazon.com. In return, participants earn referral fees up to 15 percent of the sales they generate. Amazon.com handles the secure online ordering, customer service, and shipping (plus it sends out weekly e-mail reports).

By making a dent in the book market, competition has heated up for Amazon.com, with the nation's largest bookseller, Barnes & Noble, opening an online bookstore— although more as a promotional vehicle for its conventional stores. To stay ahead of the competition, Bezos has expanded the number of titles the company stocks and improved delivery time by working closely with its partners to build the Amazon.com brand name. He has also implemented a national television advertising campaign.

In the fall of 1998, Amazon.com acquired two Internet companies to enrich its e-commerce experience for customers. PlanteAll, based in Cambridge, Massachusetts, provides a unique Web address book and calendar. Jungle Corp., based in Sunnyvale, California, is the leading provider of a virtual database technology (based on award-winning doctoral research by the company's founders at Stanford University) that helps shoppers find millions of products on the Internet.

11

TRENDSETTERS AND JETSETTERS: DEVELOPING BUSINESS OVERSEAS

Luck is what happens when preparation meets opportunity.
—*Unknown*

In your search for business opportunities look through global spectacles—see the world as a huge marketplace. Several of the young entrepreneurs featured in this book introduced their products or services to international markets just after a year in business, including Hard Candy, the cosmetics company, and Nantucket Nectars, makers of bottled fruit juices.

By doing business overseas, you get your products in the hands of worldwide customers. Global trade is no longer the bastion of large corporations. Businesses of all sizes—from graphic design to investment banking—now sell goods and offer services abroad.

Thanks to affordable information technology, telecommunications, and other high-tech systems, the geographic borders of the world are blurring. Even a home-based business can use a telephone and fax service to contact foreign-based firms quickly and efficiently, and take orders from points on the other side of the globe. By the year 2000, nearly 50 percent of all U.S. businesses with sales of $2 million or more will be engaged in some form of international trade, according to federal trade officials.

Typically, global trade is used as a growth strategy. Existing businesses with well established products or services in domestic markets decide to boost sales by offering these same goods abroad. Still, as a new business you need to practice forward thinking—meaning think long-term. You may even see an opportunity off the bat to sell your goods to foreign consumers—a small but more stable customer base.

Global trade offers both financial risks and rewards to budding entrepreneurs. The upside to going global are market niche, a diversified stream of revenues, and faster sales growth. The downside is political instability, currency fluctuation, and slow foreign payments.

Doing business overseas isn't elementary. It requires strategic thinking and planning as well as a long-term commitment to making it work. It may take a couple of years to establish a loyal following of foreign customers. Before you attempt to establish an overseas presence, you must develop a market strategy; assess financing options; learn about the duties, trade regulations, and tax requirements of the overseas country; and understand its cultural nuances and customs.

SEEK OUT AND EXPLORE WORLD MARKETS

There are two primary ways you can explore and enter the world marketplace—exporting or importing. The former refers to the sale of goods, services, or technology produced by a company in one country to customers living in a different country. For example, an American company manufactures goods that are shipped to France or Germany. Importing is just the reverse: the purchase of goods, services, or technology by a company in one country from businesses stationed in another country. In this case, an American company purchases goods that are manufactured in Italy or India.

Granted, these definitions can get a bit sticky. For instance, when McDonald's sets up franchise restaurants in Russia, it is exporting. But Coca-Cola isn't exporting when it opens a plant in South Africa. This is because when an American company has a manufacturing plant, distribution center, retail outlet, or office in a foreign location, these facilities are referred to as foreign direct investments.

Historically, companies imported merchandise to reduce labor costs or peddle items not made in the United States. The appeal of importing to most small companies is that they can buy quality products or materials at less cost from foreign suppliers. Most importers work directly with a customs broker or trade representative in the respective country, or its consulate or embassy.

Over the last decade, more small U.S. companies have entered the world market by exporting products—seeking out new markets for their wares. Most hire an export management company to handle foreign sales activities, contract negotiations, and all shipping matters—customs, clearances, shipping papers, packaging, freight forwarding, and so on. This alleviates some pressures on the small business owner in dealing with local customs and language barriers.

The intricacies of selling overseas cannot be covered in a few pages. Two books I highly recommend are: *The World Markets Desk Book: A Region-by-Region Survey of Global Trade Opportunities* (McGraw Hill) and *Exporting and Importing and Beyond: How To Go Global With Your Small Business* (Adams Media), both by business guru and CPA Lawrence W. Tuller.

Key questions you need to answer before embarking on your global venture:

1. Is the product or service needed in another country?

2. How will you finance your international operation and what resources are available?

3. What steps can you take to insure your international customers will pay for your goods on time and in full?

4. Will you need to learn another language or can you rely on translators? (Debate the pros and cons of doing either or both.)

5. How will you overcome differing cultural customs which could affect your company, product, or way of doing business?

What's important is to find a market where your product or service is needed. Remember the entrepreneurial mantra: *No matter how great a product or service is, if no one is interested in buying what I have to sell, I don't have a business.* The general sentiment among experts is that new products that have not been tested and accepted first by customers in domestic markets will not do well in foreign markets.

Which countries make the most sense to target will obviously depend on what industry you're in and what the market analysis of a particular country shows. Your wares may do well in London but not Paris, or flourish in Southeast Asia but not Australia.

The Big Emerging Markets (BEMs), as identified by the International Trade Administration, is a compilation of a small core of developing countries that will account for more than three-quarters of all world trade growth in the next two decades, surpassing Japan and Europe. Included on that list are Mexico, Argentina, Brazil, the Chinese Economic Area (People's Republic of China, Taiwan, and Hong Kong), India, Indonesia, South Korea, Poland, Turkey, and South Africa.

The major industries that are most promising to global-minded entrepreneurs include information technologies (Web development, computer equipment and software, and telecommunications services and cellular phones), health (medical and dental supplies, pharmaceuticals, and healthcare services), transportation (aerospace technology, road and rail projects and development, upgrade and expansion of bridges, airports, railways, and transit systems), automotive (motor vehicles and parts), consumer goods (those that are difficult to obtain overseas), marketing and business consulting, financial management, and fashion.

Some companies use the funnel approach, which means they consider all countries as potential customers and then identify the best potential markets using demographic and economic reports, U.S. Census statistics, domestic and foreign government regulations, political and currency stability assessments, trade barriers, and special assistance programs.

As a newcomer, direct your efforts to one or two (no more than five) different countries. Review these foreign markets from the past three to five years. Has market growth been consistent from year to year? Pay attention to world events that influence the international marketplace.

To get started in evaluating a potential foreign market, examine these four areas:

1. **Economic Statistics and Demographics.** As you learned in Chapter 2, in order to identify your target market you need to look at demographics—population size, makeup, and income; geographics—country and regional differences; and psychographics—lifestyle, religion, and cultural nuances. Also, take into account literacy rates, life expectancy, education level, national and indigenous languages, and religion. Economic statistics will tell you about production, distribution, and consumption of goods in a particular country—who's buying what and why. Demographic, social, and economic data can be obtained from The Center for International Research, a computer database service maintained by the Bureau of the Census and the Statistical Yearbook available through the United Nations. STAT-USA (http://www.stat-usa.gov) tracks trade and economic information on trends around the world and provides

daily reports and background data provided from the State Department and the CIA's *World Factbook*. Industry sector analyses, alert reports, and country commercial guides are all available from the Department of Commerce (DOC) and provide economic information and market trends for each country. The DOC (http://www.ita.doc.gov) provides a wealth of services, resources, and data to U.S. businesses looking to go global. Its Trade Promotion Coordinating Committee is a one-stop shop for information on government programs, including overseas trade fairs and trade missions. You can search through the DOC's National Trade Data Bank (NTDB), a federal database on all products and services exported out of the United States and import data for 137 countries abroad. It can sort and rank by product or country and contains more than 10,000 documents, including *The Basic Guide to Exporting; The Industrial Outlook* that contains industry-specific data; and *The World Fact Book* that contains country-specific statistics and other information. The NTBD database is released monthly on CD-ROM (for use on any IBM-compatible computer). You can access files containing information on sales leads, exchange rates, foreign trade data, industry statistics, and much more through the Electronic Bulletin Board (202-482-1986). The International Trade Administration (ITA) maintains a bank of market information, resources, and programs through the Commercial Management System (CIMS), which provides a customized report (for a minimal case-by-case charge) about any country's business and economic climates, import restrictions, tariff and nontariff barriers, competition, and distribution practices. ITA also puts out a biweekly magazine, *Business America*, which gives trade leads, export tips, economic analysis, and individual country marketing reports.

2. **Competitive Data.** What companies are competing in your market? What are their market shares and growth plans? The NTBD's *Foreign Traders Index* identifies foreign

businesses looking to import U.S. products. The ITA publishes *Market Share Reports* (commodity series), which compares the competitive status of U.S. and foreign exporters by commodity and provides statistical trends and market shares. ITA's *Overseas Business Reports* gives market information on specific countries.

3. **Trade Policies and Barriers.** While most of the world talks about free trade, not every country practices it. Familiarize yourself with foreign trade barriers, such as tariffs (import duties) or U.S. barriers, such as export controls. Information kits produced by the Overseas Private Investment Corp. (http://www.opic.gov) may be helpful in learning about the U.S.'s and other countries' trade policies.

4. **Pricing.** Evaluate all variables that may affect the price range for your product or service. If your price is too high, your goods won't sell. If the price is too low, you will lose money. It's important to examine your competitors' price structures. Unless your product or service is totally new to the market, you may have no choice but to offer your goods at a price that matches the competition. For most consumer products, per capita income is a good gauge of a market's ability to pay. Currency valuations also alter the affordability of goods. In U.S. markets, pricing is traditionally based on the cost to produce, sell, distribute, service, and finance the product; market demand; and competition for the same or similar products. This holds true for pricing overseas products. But there are also incremental costs that apply to exporting or importing goods, including credit checks, international postage, telephone rates, translation costs, currency exchange rates, customs charges, sales commissions, and other costs involving foreign representatives, consultants, and freight forwarders.

GETTING PROFESSIONAL HELP

Once you've done your homework, chosen your market, and developed a few contacts overseas, you can get some professional help to navigate your way through the unfamiliar terrain of trade finance, international law, documentation, and local customs.

New exporters can get a free consultation with an international attorney via the Export Legal Assistance Network (ELAN), which is staffed by lawyers from the International Law Council of the Federal Bar Association. You can get the name of a regional ELAN member by contacting the local district office of the Small Business Administration (http://www.sba.gov) or the SBA's Answer Desk (800 8-ASK-SBA). Moreover, the SBA's Office of International Trade offers export counseling, matchmaker events (trade delegations), reports and publications on the fundamentals of exporting, and trade data reports from the Export Information System (XIS).

The Commerce Department's U.S. and Foreign Commercial Service (US&FCS) has 67 offices in the United States and 126 offices in foreign locations, which provide counseling services, market research, and matches domestic companies with foreign buyers.

Also, the International Trade Administration (ITA) assists U.S. exporters in locating, gaining access to, and developing foreign markets nearly anywhere in the world. The ITA provides World Trader Data Reports, which are customized reports that contain business and background information on foreign companies.

In addition, the ITA sponsors matchmaker programs, trade missions, foreign buyer programs (trade shows), and trade fairs (larger in size than trade shows). Matchmaker trade delegations are designed to introduce U.S. exporters to prospective foreign sales representatives or joint venture partners. Trade missions are bands of U.S. executives that travel together to one or more countries. Many small businesses assert that trade shows are among the most valuable ways for a company to gain market intelligence, establish contacts, and swap global war stories with like-minded entrepreneurs. Trade shows and fairs are attended by foreign buyers; here you get to display your wares without having to travel overseas.

Federal and state governments, even in most major cities, have an international desk or affiliation, and in some cases, offices abroad that you can call on. Check with your state's economic development office. Many states now have their own international trade offices with field officers located around the world that provide information on special assistance programs.

The Export-Import Bank of the United Sates (Eximbank: http://www.exim.gov) provides financing and insurance assistance to U.S. exporters. It sponsors Export Assistance Centers (EAC), which are one-stop resource centers where you can get expert advice, foreign market research, and access to export financing. There are some 19 EACs throughout the country, which staff commercial service officers to assist in your research and provide on-site counseling free of charge. Foreign commercial service officers overseas are also a source of information on a particular product or distributors in a given country, which can be funneled back to EAC offices in the States. Also available are customized services ranging from $100 for profiles on an international company and trading partners to $5,000 for a comprehensive market analysis report. EACs are hyperlinked to ITA's Website (http://www.ita.doc.gov).

The Internet offers an easy portal into the many export programs available from the federal government, nonprofit organizations, and the private sector. Through these Websites you can study the basics of exporting, learn how to apply for loan guarantees, and find links to trade resources. Check out the Agency for International Development (http:www.usaid.gov), U.S. Trade and Development Agency (http://www.tda.gov), and Council of Economic Advisors (http://www.whitehouse.gov/wh/eop/cea).

Don't overlook trade associations—part of their mission is to help their members join the world economy—as well as colleges and universities with course offerings on doing business abroad or exchange programs.

SELLING YOUR PRODUCT OVERSEAS

Once you have created a market strategy that includes objectives, networking activities, financial planning, and scheduling, you need to figure out how you will distribute your product. Will you sell direct through sales reps or distributors, or indirect using purchasing agents or export management companies?

Indirect exporting allows you to sell your product via a middleman, such as a broker, export management firm, or trading company. Many U.S. and foreign corporations, general contractors, foreign trading companies, international distributors, and retailers purchase goods for export. The buyer assumes all the risk and handles all the details of exporting. Purchasing agents travel throughout the United States to find consumer products or services for foreign buyers.

Export management companies and U.S. export trading companies offer a fast, low-cost way for small businesses to enter the global marketplace. The entrepreneur engages the services of these intermediary firms to find non–U.S. markets and buyers for its products. The disadvantage for the business owner is less control over sales, customer relations, and smaller profit margins.

Direct exporting lets you sell directly to foreign consumers using company sales people or foreign sales reps. Both methods are good options for getting into the international market. But selling direct is more ambitious since you will handle every aspect of the process personally.

Through ITA's Trade Opportunities Program, exporters can obtain current sales leads of foreign customers seeking to buy their products or services, and a current listing of foreign sales agents seeking to represent U.S. exporters. You can also find qualified foreign sales reps through ITA's agent/distributor service.

Once you have identified potential representatives or distributors, you should write to each. You'll want to obtain the following information:

1. *Company history.* Get background information on the company and its principal officers.

2. *Personnel and other resources.* How many salespeople do they employ? How is the sales staff compensated? How is sales performance measured? Can the firm accommodate your account without making changes? Does it have adequate warehouse facilities?

3. *Sales territory.* What area of the country does the firm cover and is it consistent with the coverage you desire? Does it have branch offices in the territory you seek to export to or import from?

4. *Sales record.* Has sales growth been consistent over the past five years? What is the sales volume per person? What are its sales objectives? What methods are used to introduce new products into a sales territory? What media are used to promote sales?

5. *Typical customer profiles.* Ask for names and addresses of U.S. firms represented as well as trade and bank references.

When you contact potential representatives or distributors, provide information on your company. Just as you are seeking information on them, foreign representatives are interested in your company and product information—history, resources, personnel, and all other pertinent matters. You'll need to hire legal counsel to handle the foreign sales agreement, which spells out the responsibilities and your relationship with the sales reps or distributor.

With importing you are relying on shippers, freight carriers, or other outside sources to handle the process of getting goods from foreign shores to domestic doors. You or someone in your organization will have to monitor the transaction to make sure goods aren't lost, damaged, or delivered late, and that everyone involved does his/her part.

There are several administrators involved in the shipping of foreign goods to the United States, including shipping agents who notify your company of the day and time goods will be delivered. When the goods arrive, a customs broker obtains customs releases and necessary clearances, checks bills of lading and delivery orders, and makes payments (i.e., duties and clearance fees). U.S. Customs officials verify compliance with customs regulations and collect duties (all goods with a value of more than $1,000 go through a formal entry process). Terminal operators verify the accuracy of the delivery orders and arrange for your company to pick up the merchandise.

Shipping across the ocean is cheaper and more commonly used for transporting large cargo, while air freight carriers are used for smaller deliveries. The drawbacks of ocean shipping are high insurance, the risk of damaged goods, and the amount of travel time.

International air freight offers quick, reliable service. However, shipping containers must be small enough to fit into a 747 airplane—the largest commercial aircraft in use today. Plus, the goods must be relatively insensitive to low pressure and wide variations in temperature and they must be high enough in price to justify the greater freight costs.

If you are importing goods from another country into the United States, you need to familiarize yourself with the trade regulations of that foreign country as well as U.S. Customs and state requirements governing foreign products. If you don't know the right procedures, it will cost you money and time in receiving your goods. Contact U.S. Customs to obtain information on how to import your products, a list of goods that are considered detrimental to U.S. citizens, plus the names of authorized shipping agents and customs brokers.

FINANCING YOUR BUSINESS OVERSEAS

It is virtually impossible to export or import goods without using banks. Money (or guarantees) flows from the central bank agency through a commercial bank to either the exporter or the foreign buyer. Collections from foreign customers flow through commercial banks. Export credit or guarantees from central bank agencies (i.e., Eximbank) utilize commercial banks as supporting parties to the transaction.

For exporting from the United States, it makes sense to use a U.S. bank. Importers normally work through a foreign branch of a multinational U.S. bank, such as Chase Manhattan Bank, Citibank, or Bank of America. Major international banks maintain branches worldwide.

The most important consideration for choosing a commercial bank is its expertise in handling international transactions. The size of the bank isn't as important as its international expertise and relationship with overseas banks. Most banks maintain loose associations with other banks in other countries and maintain credit balances with other financial institutions.

Even if you don't use a commercial bank to finance overseas transactions, you need one to handle collections, payments, and money transfers. Collections from foreign customers and payments of foreign invoices are seldom done with checks. Bank notes, bills of exchange, or drafts (formal promise to pay) are commonly used for international payment. Most companies like using wire transfers—no money actually changes hands. If you received a check from a company, say, in London, your bank would charge you extra fees to exchange the money into

U.S. currency. It's important when dealing with another country to understand its currency and exchange rates, shipping costs, and customs fees.

Letters of credit, documents issued by a bank guaranteeing the payment of a customer's drafts up to a stated amount for a specified time period, are used frequently for financing import/export transactions. It substitutes the bank's credit for the buyer's credit and eliminates the seller's risk. Be sure to ask for an irrevocable letter of credit (the issuer can't change the terms).

LEARNING A COUNTRY'S CUSTOMS AND CULTURES

It is important to learn the intricacies of the culture of a foreign country to avoid embarrassing situations. Clothes, expressions, posture, and actions are important considerations when conducting business abroad. Research the political, religious, and cultural heritage of the country you want to do business with. A lack of sensitivity to your client's customs can stop a deal in its tracks. Outside of America, you are the foreigner.

Awareness of accepted business practices is paramount. Because cultures vary there is no single code in which to conduct business. Certain business practices, however, transcend cultural barriers. Here are a few tips on handling business etiquette and protocol:

1. *Never force the meeting place.* Try to schedule meetings in a formal setting such as an office. However, there are times when the other party may want to meet in a hotel lobby, airport lounge, restaurant, or private club. Local protocol may dictate an informal surrounding. Be careful not to get too relaxed. Informality breeds mistakes.

2. *Answer requests promptly and keep your promises.* The biggest complaint from foreign importers about U.S. suppliers is failure to ship as promised. That first order is crucial—it will shape a buyer's image of your firm as dependable or undependable.

3. *Be polite, courteous, and friendly.* Good manners, polite conversation, and courteous actions go a long way in business dealings. Don't reinforce the stereotype of the brash, "ugly" American. If your host offers you food or beverages that you have never heard of before or don't particularly like, it is good manners to sample a small portion. Some international firms think the brief U.S. business letter lacks courtesy. In general, form letters are unsatisfactory. Personally sign all letters.

4. *Avoid idiomatic phrases.* Stay away from slang and unfamiliar phrases. Clarify the meaning of words that could cause confusion. On the other hand, you may have to decipher the meaning of colloquialisms native to that foreign country.

5. *Be aware of different business styles.* In nearly every country, giving a business gift to visiting business people is customary. Generally, the host business person expects something in return. Simple, inexpensive gifts are in order. Also, in some countries, offering an incentive is a part of getting your product into the hands of consumers.

6. *Attend social outings.* Accept invitations by the other party to go to dinner, the theater, or sporting events. It may be customary to do business during such outings.

7. *Familiarize yourself with foreign phrases.* Communication is crucial. Most international firms communicate in English, the international language for doing business. But it behooves you to become familiar with the language of the host country. People usually do business with people they know or get to know, and feel they can trust with their ideas, time, and money.

8. *Be prepared.* Always carry a letter explaining who you are and who to contact in the host country and the United States just in case of an emergency. If you get in a bind, know how to contact the local American embassy or consulate.

Opportunities abound for small business owners abroad. But it takes creativity, ingenuity, and that pioneering spirit to tackle the wide world of importing and exporting. Equally important, it requires building the right network of foreign and domestic contacts, and gathering the appropriate market research.

DANIEL LUBETZKY, PRESIDENT OF THE PEACEWORKS, INC.

In 1993, Daniel Lubetzky set out to Israel on an economic scholarship to research the Israeli-Arab conflict and the potential for economic joint ventures. The Stanford Law School graduate envisioned businesses that would unite Jews and Arabs. Most people found the idea noble but unrealistic.

To prove them wrong, Lubetzky created the Middle East Trading and Investment Co., a consulting firm that would help develop joint ventures between the adversarial neighbors. To some degree, the doubters were right.

No one was interested in consulting. People in the Middle East don't like consultants. Their attitude is, "Don't tell me how to do it." My business obviously wasn't going to fly. So, I decided to go back to the States and become an attorney.

Shortly before his departure, Lubetzky came across a flavorful sun-dried tomato spread that happened to be made by an Israeli company and most of its raw materials were grown by Palestinians. He didn't even know what a sun-dried tomato was, but he knew he liked the way it tasted. He reasoned others would too.

Lubetzky traced the spread to a manufacturing company on the verge of collapse because of distribution problems. He convinced the Israeli owner that he could help him penetrate the American market—something the company had unsuccessfully tried for five years. In March of 1994, the then 25-year-old attorney took $10,000 of his personal savings to create New York–based The PeaceWorks, Inc., which would serve as the exclusive marketing and distribution partner in this venture.

John Bentham

DANIEL LUBETZKY

We are not owners of the manufacturing company, but trad-
ing partners. The joint venture we established provides us with an
exclusive importing right and the possibility to invest in the
future in the processing company. We drew up an agreement stip-
ulating that [Olivia] would purchase all of its materials from
Arabs and Palestinians. We examine the products they send us
and determine if people in the American consumer market will
buy them, based on market research—pricing, quality, taste,
competitors, and so forth.

He spent the next three months traveling back and forth
between the two countries working on quality control, packag-

ing, labeling, and other fine points. He got most of his market information by spending hours talking to distributors, suppliers, and retail store owners, who were impressed with his zeal. To determine which U.S. outlets the spread would sell best in, Lubetzky experimented with the flavor to meet the so-called American palate. He also changed the packaging to a cleaner, neater look. Most of all, he coined the catchy term spraté—a multipurpose sauce, spread, and paté.

PeaceWorks's first line of condiments was Moshe and Ali's World Famous Gourmet Foods. The zesty spreads have labels featuring two lovable cartoon characters (one Jewish and the other Arab). The company started out with nine products—three of which became big hits. Lubetzky learned early on that it makes better business sense to focus on a few good products that sell well as opposed to a large line of items.

Only go with winners. You may sell 10 products to a store, but only nine do well—they sell out. The product that stays on the shelf is the one the store owner is going to remember and will get upset that it didn't move. That store may not want to carry any of your products. We didn't know upfront which three flavors were winners. It's better to start out slow and then build your product line once you have a loyal following. All of our products sold, but the spratés were moving two cases a month and other sauces were selling every two months. Four products were real slow movers.

Being overly creative brought its share of problems as well. PeaceWorks's Israeli trading partner developed a powder using dried olives that you could sprinkle on food. But people had never heard of it before and they weren't sure how to use it.

If the product doesn't fit people's lifestyles, they aren't going to buy it. You have to understand what people want and then give it to them. Also, our product was very tasty, but we were initially talking to the consumer only about PeaceWorks (trying to sell a concept and not a product). People only cared about that as a secondary feature. They were more concerned that our product tasted good, the price was right, and the product was of high quality.

PeaceWorks started emphasizing features which appealed to consumer tastes and trends—all its products were kosher/halal, natural, and vegetarian (containing no animal or dairy products). Lubetzky also discovered when he tried to sell directly to consumers out of a retail booth in the World Trade Center that consumers were much more likely to purchase a product if it is affiliated with an established company. The booth didn't work. He didn't even cover his cost to set up the booth.

The peace worker's next formidable task was finding an outlet to sell his products. It was practically impossible for a start-up to land a national distributor. Lubetzky was left with trying to sell directly to department stores, natural foods stores, supermarket chains, or independent specialty stores. Each one of those venues had different players, distribution channels, and methods, margins, and payment terms. The specialty stores bit first.

By the end of 1994, PeaceWorks started selling its spratés to 30 independent stores nationwide, including New York–based Zabar's, the well-known food and housewares store. The company averaged about 10 cases per store. In total, the company sold about 400 cases of the spread. During the first couple of years, all sales climbed to more than $1 million. Profits went right back into the business.

To get into the stores, we had to compete against larger, very sophisticated companies. We had to be persuasive, persistent, and creative in terms of getting our products shelf space. We were able to show the chain stores that we had a loyal following through sales from the independent stores and the vocal consumer satisfaction.

Today, PeaceWorks imports millions of jars of spraté into the country and boasts a large distribution network of over 50 distributors and 5,000 stores, including major supermarket chains. Lubetzky also has a freestanding rack and display at such department stores as Macy's in New York.

About 90 percent of the company's sales are generated in the

United States, the rest includes Canada, Mexico, Europe, and South America. The company has expanded its line of spraté to 15 flavors, such as Sundried Tomato, Olive, Garlic & Dill (fat-free), Mediterranean Pepper, Ginger, Basil Pesto, Mint Pesto, Cilantro Pesto, Garlic Slivers in Olive Oil & Wine, and Pure Fire.

PeaceWorks also has gone global by introducing a line of spraté made with Chipotle peppers (smoked jalapeño peppers) from the war-torn Mexican state of Chipotle (through Azteca Trading Co. Salsas). Another recent addition are Wafas (premium hazelnut chocolate candy bars), from which 10 percent of the profits are donated to a nonprofit summer camp called Seeds of Peace.

Once run out of a basement room, PeaceWorks now operates out of a large second-floor office and has 10 employees in the New York office alone. In spite of his success, Lubetzky finds little time to rest on his laurels. He recently established an advisory board with 11 representatives from various industries—banking, food, international relations, and academic fields—including Ben Cohen of Ben & Jerry's ice cream chain.

Lubetzky encourages upstart companies to keep their overhead low. PeaceWorks has been able to keep costs down by outsourcing the responsibility of managing its warehouses, which are located in New York, New Jersey, and California. He believes too much outsourcing though is counterproductive for business. The objective is to take advantage of what your special talents are and build on other people's talents as well.

One thing that has worked well for us is our preferred vendor program. We guarantee the products, if they commit to trying four cases of each item in our line (about $2,000 worth of product) and placing them on store shelves. We have about 500 vendors in the program. Only two percent haven't worked out. We instill trust and the sense of a long term relationship. If the stores give us a chance we give them our best.

Lubetzky's long-term goals are to raise investment capital

and to take the company public. He hopes to repeat Moshe and Ali's success by building similar enterprises in Mexico and South Africa. He remains confident that his condiments will spread the message of global harmony. He allocates at least 5 percent of PeaceWorks's profits back into the community by donating to nonprofit organizations that foster tolerance and co-existence.

The second oldest of four children, Lubetzky was born in Mexico City and grew up in San Antonio, Texas. He credits part of the company's success to his family's support. His father, a Holocaust survivor and self-made entrepreneur, steered him to a competent customs broker, who handles all importing duties. He also found his son a bank that was willing to give lines of credit to the fledgling business, with guarantees from family members.

My family thought I was crazy; they wanted me to be a lawyer and settle down. They supported me, but they were concerned. Starting a business is like riding a roller coaster, sometimes you get great highs and other times you are really down. Sometimes you have issues in terms of managing people, other times it's managing the business's growth. Business in general is not for the faint of heart. But the satisfaction is unmatched.

TRACY MELTON, PRESIDENT OF MELTON INTERNATIONAL TACKLE

A new breed of students are roaming the campuses of America's colleges and universities—budding entrepreneurs. The numbers tell the story. There are more than 500 formal academic entrepreneurial programs today, compared to just a handful less than 10 years ago.

Thirty-year-old Tracy Melton got his entrepreneurial indoctrination at the University of Southern California. Over the course of his studies, Melton completed two business plans. One led to a good grade, the other helped jump-start a thriving enterprise, Melton International Tackle. The Anaheim,

California–based mail-order and retail company sells big-game fishing tackle and accessories. Melton's 100-plus-page catalog of more than 3,000 top-of-the-line, custom-made products has generated over $1.5 million in revenues.

Melton used the fishing lure business of a friend and professional charter boat captain in Hawaii as the basis for the business plan he did at USC. It was a natural fit since this was Melton's favorite pastime. He took fishing vacations five times a year. In fact, he spent the night of his college graduation en route to a fishing tournament in Hawaii.

What he learned by doing the plan was that the market was a lot bigger than he had ever imagined—it included international and domestic customers alike. People were fishing all over the world and paying top dollar to do so. In fact, foreign customers were more inclined to pay top dollar for hard-to-find fishing equipment.

Melton saw that there was a particularly great deal of interest in custom-made items, among both foreign and domestic consumers. He compiled a list of all the unique fishing gear that people had heard about, or had limited exposure to, but were not commercially available—they were not sold through traditional retail outlets.

But that in and of itself wasn't enough to induce Melton to start a business. It was a casual meeting during a family outing that sparked the then 23-year-old Melton's interest in launching a mail-order business in 1993.

My boat captain friend introduced me to one of his vendors from Australia who had a flourishing mail-order fishing tackle business. We hit it off real big; he liked my enthusiasm for fishing. He told me that there wasn't a decent catalog business in the States and if I wanted, he would show me how to start one. I had been working in my dad's machine shop business (for about six months since graduation). My dad believes that you will always be more successful at something you enjoy doing. So, he told me to see how much it would cost to do it and he would help me out as much as he could.

Creative work, paper, postage, and other production costs could run upwards of $6,000 a page. This was one of the reasons Melton took on the brunt of the work himself, contracting out only the photography. He chose the products, assisted on photo shoots, designed layouts, wrote the copy, and mailed the catalogs to prospective customers. He hired a couple of part-time employees, including his mother.

Melton's start-up costs included mainly office equipment and furniture. The biggest expenses were inventory and postage (around 50 cents per catalog). Melton was able to launch the business with about $30,000 worth of fishing products. Today, he has $300,000 worth of inventory and a 14-employee staff working out of a 2,500-sq.-ft. multitenant industrial park. It costs $125,000 to distribute and produce the annual catalog (including $75,000 a year in postage).

Melton faces stiff competition from about half a dozen mail-order fishing catalogs. His age hasn't presented a problem, though he believes some people in the industry have an issue with him being assertive and aggressive. But he has no problem stirring the waters. His primary concerns are finding the right kinds of products and providing hands-on customer service.

My products are very specific; they're not something you would find at a typical all-purpose department store. Unlike most big mail-order places, we don't have a mail-order fulfillment center. We take our own orders. So, it's very common for people to get me on the telephone. This works to our advantage because when people call up, they get someone who fishes. My staff asks a lot of questions and makes suggestions. Our customers know we will bend over backwards for them. The big companies just can't offer that kind of personal service.

It comes as no surprise that Melton distributes his catalogs (in English) overseas given his Australian mentor and the findings of his original college research. Indeed, Melton International Tackle does a bulk of its business with foreign customers, particularly a large European and Asian clientele. Some of Melton's foreign customers are interested in him setting up shop (retail) in their native lands, especially in Japan where big game fishing is popular. Fishermen from all over frequent the eastern Pacific islands and the coastal waters of California. The right tackle and techniques can make their trip more rewarding and enjoyable.

Big-game fishing (e.g., marlin, swordfish, yellowfin tuna, sea bass, and dolphin) is done mostly on the east coast and gulf coast. People like traveling to destinations that have tropical settings — like the Caribbean waters of the Bahamas. I started doing business overseas from day one. There was a lot of interest in our catalogs. Plus foreign customers are more inclined to spend a lot of money on high caliber equipment than people in the States.

It does make Melton's job more demanding to maintain his own inventory and fulfill both domestic and international customer orders. When a customer calls, Melton and his staff of fishing experts just can't pull a couple of items off the shelf and ship them out. He has to place the orders directly to his vendors, which total around 100 manufacturers. The products are then shipped to Melton, who in turn ships the items to customers, who pay for the delivery costs. This allows for customers to enjoy "have it your way" service.

Melton deals primarily with standard air freight carriers, such as Federal Express and UPS, to fulfill orders. FedEx offers door-to-door service to most areas of the world. And UPS offers competitive arrangements. Melton also relies on freight forwarders, which are shipping and transport agencies that act as the primary coordinators among exporting companies, shippers, bankers, customs officials, and other parties. They prepare all documentation necessary for shipping goods, insuring cargo, and collecting payments from a customer.

About 95 percent of all Melton International Tackle's orders involve some form of customization or tweaking — whether it's putting fishing line on a reel or skirting up lures in specific colors. The reward is tons of repeat customers.

I have customers who spend in a year what some people would *love to earn a year—around $30,000 and $40,000—just on fishing equipment. It is definitely an elitist high-end sport in that it is limited to the upper economic type. You have people who charter a boat for $1,500 to $2,000 for one day, to go catch marlin in certain parts of the world. We get calls from guys on their boats using their cell phones. They take our catalog along with them.*

In 1998, Melton International moved into a 4,000-sq.-ft. warehouse space to accommodate the mail-order end of the business and a new retail showroom that would offer the same products featured in the catalog. Melton spent roughly a quarter of a million dollars to build a mock-up of a 45-foot sailboat, allowing customers to literally see and touch the products.

People kept coming into our warehouse asking about our products, so we felt we could better serve them by having a showroom. Besides, business was growing; we needed to expand. We wanted to show (our existing customers and potential customers) what a properly set up boat should look like from the inside. Our customers get to play with our products much like a child would play in a toy store. The showroom emulates the kind of boats our clients indeed own.

For instance, the retail showroom features such items as a $9,000 chair designed specifically for fly fishing and fiberglass replicas of 1,000-pound marlin and other big game, including swordfish and tuna. Melton eventually expects the store to generate a bigger percentage of his company's sales revenue. His biggest concern right now is staffing the store with knowledgeable sales reps.

We have to have the right kind of people service our customers who come into the store. It's not just a matter of running up an order, our staff people have to know how to answer questions about our products and at the same time keep the phones from ringing off the hook. All of our sales people fish, as do many of our other employees.

Melton runs advertisements in various fishing trade publications to solicit customers. He also does some direct marketing.

When it comes to the catalogs, he continues to write most of the copy, because he knows which features appeal to his audience.

You have to write descriptive stories about the product in a way that appeals to your customer base. I am selling myself as much as anything else. When someone reads the description of a product in the catalog, it should be able to take that guy away from his home, office, wherever he is reading it, get inside of his mind, and make him visualize using that product. I think this is a big part of why we are successful. We use a lot of adjectives and jargon associated with fishing. My time is better spent doing things other than writing stories about the products. But then, it's not something that you can just teach anyone who walks in off the street (now tell me in 50 words why I should buy this product). The writing comes more from inner knowledge.

In the short term, Melton International Tackle plans to expand the mail-order business by putting out additional catalogs. Melton's long-term plans are to open up franchised retail outlets worldwide, in part because of the high demand.

The ambitious entrepreneur, who puts in anywhere between 70 to 100 hours a week, knows firsthand the significance of running a business you enjoy and are knowledgeable about.

You know what they say: Knowledge is power. I'm going to run my business on the bet that I know more than any of my customers about the products they want to buy. I can use that knowledge to my advantage—whether it's knowing the right words to say when describing a product—like stainless steel, lifetime guarantee, or hand-crafted. I know what sets me off. You [would-be entrepreneurs] will be more happy doing something that you love than just running a business that pays the bills.

IV

As You Get Bigger

As You Got Bigger

12

THE MARKET: MAINTAINING THE COMPETITIVE EDGE

> Even if you're on the right track, you'll get run over if you just sit there. —*Will Rogers, actor*

Let's say you manage to come up with a new or improved product. As soon as you enter the market, someone will react. Maybe not right away, but inevitably another business will pit its services and products against yours. More than likely, you will enter an arena with existing industry players, which means you are taking away their customers. Feeling threatened, your competitors will fight back to maintain their market share.

To protect your market niche, you must formulate a tight offensive plan—a strategy to compete, which includes staying on top of industry trends and current events, and understanding the mode of operation of indirect and direct competitors. Remember: Indirect competitors are companies who sell products or services similar to yours but are not solely dependent on these products. For instance, a Barnes & Noble selling CDs would be an indirect competitor to a local record store. On the other hand, that same Barnes & Noble would be a direct competitor to a local bookstore, since both businesses exist to sell similar products in the same market.

Each year thousands of companies go belly up, many of which lacked a focused strategic plan. You need to find a way to be better than the competition and to know your market better than anyone else. Those companies that succeed do so by focusing on specialized niche markets and developing a competitive advantage.

Answer the following questions:

1. Does the product truly fill a niche?

2. Does it offer value?

3. Is it a superior version of existing products?

4. Does the product leverage what you do well?

5. Can you actually manufacture and deliver it? (Don't put a new product on the shelves unless you're prepared to handle the demand.)

Analysis of your company, customers, and competitors should be an ongoing part of your marketing plan. Refer to your business plan—which should be updated quarterly or annually—and review your strategic and tactical plans for your product, target market, distribution, promotion, pricing, packaging, and value-added services (See Chapter 3).

SIZING UP YOUR CUSTOMERS AND THE COMPETITION

There are four areas you need to look at to maintain that competitive advantage:

- *Competition*—Who are your competitors and how do you stack up against them?

- *Customer Satisfaction*—How happy are customers with your product/service?

- *Distribution*—How efficient is the delivery of your product/service to customers?

- *Specialization*—How well does your product/service meet a unique customer need?

Competition: Study and learn from your competition—what are they doing well and what are they doing poorly? Buy their products, review their marketing materials and product catalogs, subscribe to their newsletters, and visit their Websites. Look at how they position their products and services. Discover the reasons why people buy from your company as well as each of your competitors, using surveys, focus groups, e-mail, and other forms of customer feedback.

Some of the reasons people will buy are:

1. *Solution.* The product solves a problem like no other product.

2. *Features/benefits.* Customers consider one feature or benefit particularly important.

3. *Performance/Quality.* Customers buy those products they feel work best and are well-built.

4. *Image.* The product reinforces the image a customer has of himself/herself (i.e., a Jaguar is considered a high-status car).

5. *Price.* Some customers buy the lowest-priced product, while others pay a premium for perceived value.

6. *Relationship.* Some customers only buy from certain businesses, either because of tradition, they like the owners, or they like the way the company does business.

7. *Service/warranty.* Customers like the company's return policies, backup service, warranty periods, and exchange procedures.

8. *Selection.* Customers have their pick of a number of products that are well stocked in a store or from a broad product line.

9. *Location.* Consumers find certain stores or businesses are more convenient to buy from.

10. *Emotion.* Consumers buy a product because it makes them feel good, allows them to impress other people, or is a way to show love or appreciation.

Customer Satisfaction: Most businesses fail or succeed based on their relationship with customers. Outside of profitability, productivity, and market share, customer satisfaction is the real measure of your business's performance. In a market where your product is equal to your competitors' in quality, customer satisfaction will make all the difference.

Customers perceive poor service as either not getting what they want from a company or they sense that the company doesn't care about them. Unfortunately, you may never know how customers really feel about your business. Only one in five customers with problems ever says anything about it. While some irate customers might explode in your face, silent, unhappy customers with slow-burning fuses will quietly disappear.

Loyal customers are the key to a thriving business. In fact, repeat customers generally provide 95 percent of a company's revenues. Keeping your customers satisfied means keeping your business in the money. So, it's important that you identify your best customers or clients. Look at how long they have been with you, how much they spend during the year, how much support service they require, and how much money they are likely to spend with you in the near future. Also, figure out how much it actually costs you to serve them.

Albeit, trying to provide service to customers who are forever dissatisfied, unreasonably demanding, and rude toward your staff isn't worth it. But spending money on evaluating and improving customer service is a smart move, given the cost of keeping a customer is 20 percent of the cost of getting a new one. It is critical to your business to resolve customer problems quickly and efficiently, knowing that your window of opportunity is only 15 seconds. That's the time frame during which a small issue can escalate into a major crisis and result in your losing customers.

What do you do when your company makes a mistake? First, own up to it. Second, make up for it. If you don't have a customer service department, assign someone to specifically address customers' concerns. Set guidelines for what is and is not acceptable. For instance, allowing a customer to stand in line or wait on the telephone for 15 minutes before a sales rep ever acknowledges his or her presence is unacceptable.

In order to keep your customers satisfied, you must train your employees to be both product- and customer-driven. And, you must formally measure the effectiveness of your company's customer service, which means soliciting feedback. Conduct a customer-satisfaction survey using telephone polls, focus groups, product sampling, or questionnaires. Among the things you want to find out are: What do they like about your products or services? What don't they like? Do they buy from your competitors, if so, which ones? How do they feel about your prices? How helpful are your employees? Are they regular customers: Why or why not?

Your goal is to find out what they think of your business, so you have a better idea about how to improve it. In time everything changes, including customers' demands. You need to do ongoing market research to find out what your customers really want, so that you can give it to them. Set up a computerized database of customer profiles and demographics. This way you can keep track of customers' buying habits and preferences—what they buy, how much, and how often.

Don't wait until a problem arises. Stay in touch with your customers through phone calls, letters, newsletters, note cards, or anything else that lets them know you value their patronage. This will also help you determine whether customers will pay a premium for special services or features (e.g., the airlines provide first-class and coach service and charge accordingly). Brand-loyal consumers who were once interested in mainly getting the best quality for the lowest price have shown they are willing to pay a premium for perceived value.

Industry experts contend that most business failures occur because companies don't conduct proper customer and market research. Customers like to believe that your goal is to help them, not merely to take their money. They want you to care about their welfare, and to truly go out of your way to satisfy their needs. Adding a toll-free telephone number or posting a Website may not be enough. You must relate to their problems.

A prime example is Nike, which was unheard of 25 years ago. Adidas and Puma were the sports shoes everyone was wearing. But those shoes didn't really give runners what they were looking for and the two companies weren't interested in the feedback they received from an Oregon runner named Bill Bowerman. So, Bowerman went out and started his own company, called Nike. He knew which features to include because he knew what his fellow runners wanted.

Distribution: How difficult is it to purchase your product or service? When people feel inconvenienced, they don't see the product as satisfying their needs. They won't waste any time and money to acquire it. Review which channel of distribution works best: mail-order, wholesale, retail, independent sales reps, chain stores, specialty stores, etc.

You can gain a competitive edge through distribution. Take L'eggs for example, the maker of pantyhose that are packaged in egg-shaped containers. Part of L'eggs success was due to the product—pantyhose were much more practical than stockings for women who wore short skirts. Another part of its success was due to packaging—the egg-shaped container was far different from the undistinguished flat packages of stockings and other pantyhose brands. Moreover, L'eggs provided point-of-purchase displays and shelf racks for its egg-shaped containers. And it sold its products through mass merchandisers rather than the lingerie departments of women's clothing stores or women's departments of large department stores.

Also, examine how you package or present your product or service. Packaging is about more than appearance: It conveys the products' features and benefits—all of which will influence whether someone will buy your product and how much they are willing to pay for it.

In evaluating your company's distribution strategy ask the following questions: Are there any ways I can improve the quality of my sales force? Are there any unique ways, or places, I can use to more effectively sell the product? How can I add to or modify my product line to maintain market share? What can I do differently in the way of promotions—advertising, special events, and publicity—to draw attention to my product or service and raise credibility?

Needless to say, you need to be able to afford your distribution strategy. Look at the costs of the measures you chose and their ability to increase sales. You need enough money to carry out each strategy and still preserve capital to run the business. To save on costs, employ tactics like:

1. Co-sponsoring events—seminars, classes, contests, demonstrations, and the like; participate in co-op advertising programs.

2. Partnering or forming strategic alliances with similar but noncompeting businesses.

Specialization: You can't be everything to everybody. But even if you concentrate on a tiny segment of an overall market, you can do quite well as long as you serve that niche more efficiently than your competitors. Besides, you may not have the money needed to provide a variety of products or handle heavy volumes. Superstores are large companies with deep pockets, so they can provide customers a wide selection of offerings.

Examine your product features and support services, and look for ways in which you can develop a specialized niche. Position your product or service in the minds of your customers and develop a unique sales approach. There are a number of ways you can position your company in the way of product benefits, technical support, personalized service, or proprietary features (i.e., trademarks, patents, copyrights, and unique manufacturing capabilities).

SERVICE ABOVE AND BEYOND

Obviously growth becomes an important issue once your business is established. Diversifying allows your company to penetrate a different market. However, don't make the mistake of venturing beyond your niche until you have mastered it.

To grow their businesses, many entrepreneurs create offshoot ventures—you know, a restaurant adds a home-delivery service, a financial planner sells money management books, or a magazine publisher creates a television show. This enables those entrepreneurs to reach more customers and increase sales.

But branching out is risky business. Before adding a sideline venture, analyze your company's strengths and weaknesses in the marketplace. As with any new venture, you must first examine if adding an offshoot business will help increase profits. Set revenue goals and profit projections. Also, your primary business should show a pattern of solid growth before you develop a sideline venture. Take into consideration the cost of new equipment, employees, and other expenses. Devise a financial strategy: Will you finance your ancillary business from the company's cash coffers? Or will you have to seek additional funds from outside sources?

A potential hazard of starting a sideline business is neglect-

The Art of Target Niche Marketing

The outplacement industry enjoyed a lucrative environment beginning in the 1980s thanks to downsizings by large corporate giants. For years to follow, big companies retained outplacement firms to assist displaced employees with their job search.

Lately, however, individuals who are gainfully employed—from mid-career executives to young professionals—are looking to private career coaches to help them with their career search before any company can downsize them. Guaranteed employment is no longer common in today's corporate structure. Thus, employees must be ready to develop their skills and hone their self-marketing strategies in this competitive job market, particularly while they are still employed.

Hence, private career coaches and image consultants have reached a new level of demand. In fact, the industry has the potential to grow even more rapidly over the next 10 years as leading technologies create jobs for the 21st century. Those consultants who are destined to succeed are the ones who position themselves to help individuals manage their careers, not just to find a new job.

Seeing a void in the market for younger job seekers, Jane Hyun founded Crossroads Associates Inc., a New York–based company that provides career management advice to college students, recent graduates, and professionals. Hyun, who holds a bachelor's degree in economics and international studies from Cornell University, spent over seven years at JP Morgan, the Wall Street financial services firm. She left her post as vice president of human resources to venture out on her own.

Crossroads Associates provides a wide range of techniques, including self-assessment exercises, resumé review, interviewing skills, salary negotiations, and networking techniques. The 30-year-old Korean-American businesswoman also helps sophisticated job hunters better understand new methods that companies are employing such as behavior-based and case study interviewing. Moreover, Hyun provides specific coaching and ongoing consultation to Asian-Americans regarding interpersonal and diversity issues in the workplace. Whenever possible, clients are referred to other sources of information such as recruiters and search firms.

Long before the birth of Crossroads, countless numbers of family members and friends (including parents on behalf of their college-aged children) approached Hyun and requested her assistance with interview prep and resumé critique because of her unique perspective from the other side of the interview table.

Also, as she puts it: "Job seekers need to get smarter about how to approach their careers. After college, young professionals often lack the resources they need. Headhunters/executive recruiters can identify job opportunities but they are business people who are hired by the manager of a given company, and not the job seeker."

Hyun came up with a hands-on strategy for soliciting clients, including ad-hoc marketing via media sources (e.g., newspapers and radio engagements). Word-of-mouth marketing and referrals also proved crucial. However, Hyun also makes sure to distribute business cards, brochures, press releases, and a self-published newsletter whenever the opportunity presents itself. She has built up her business by utilizing her network of local alumni associations, career/networking groups, nonprofit organizations, and a variety of Asian-American groups with large numbers of young professionals.

Indeed, she has presented at least 20 career seminars to over 1,000 individuals since the inception of the business. To further target her niche and establish herself as an expert, Hyun regularly contributes articles about career management, such as "Get the Salary You Deserve" and "Interviewing Skills for Asian-Americans," for local and cultural publications, such as the *Korean Times.*

Hyun does a lot of one-on-one coaching with her clients. Says Hyun: "When they meet me for the first time, I spend a good amount of time identifying their needs. Some people come to me when they are undergoing a major career change. Others are going on a lot of interviews, but still, they aren't getting a lot of job offers. Still others may have been in one company for their entire careers and want a resumé assessment before going on a job search." Regardless of the need, Hyun's personal approach has attracted many repeat customers, many of whom have successfully found the jobs they were seeking.

Today, Hyun has on average some 50 clients a year and maintains a very steady growth in revenues. In the next few years, she plans to increase her marketing efforts to reach a broader client base. She also works part-time for Deloitte & Touche Resources Connection as a recruitment manager. Resources is an affiliate of the Big 5 firm, which identifies interim project assignments for accounting and finance professionals.

"Working for Resources allows me to maintain a close pulse on the hiring trends in corporate America," explains Hyun. In turn, "this allows me to be more effective with my own clients."

ing your core business. You don't want to lose the momentum you have with your primary enterprise because it is competing with your secondary business. The two should complement and feed into each other.

Your best bet is to follow a steady pattern of growth and develop your market in stages:

1. Increase sales of your present product or service by using promotions and advertising to convince customers to buy more.

2. Enter new markets within a geographic region (i.e., city, state, or country).

3. Create new and related products or services you can offer your existing customers to keep them coming back.

As you develop your company's strategy for growth, keep in mind that customers will continue to do business with you as long as you can deliver a quality product at a great price; don't promote something you can't deliver; thank them for their business; deal with them fairly and respectfully; ask if there is anything you can do to make their life easier; and finally, go out of your way to find out about their ever changing needs.

KARL KANI, KARL KANI INFINITY

For the past ten years, Karl Kani has gained a strong foothold in the urban sportswear market. And right now, it seems that he has an infinite space in retail stores throughout the world. His company, Karl Kani Infinity, Inc. sold more than $65 million worth of clothes in 1997. His fashions are available in more than 400 retail shops nationwide and his footwear is a hot seller in over 14 countries, including Belgium, France, Japan, Switzerland, and South Africa. In addition to a Los Angeles headquarters, Kani has a 4,600-sq.-ft. showroom in New York's fashion district, Chicago, and Atlanta.

Initially, Kani's core business was jeans and active wear, followed by children's wear and footwear (namely sneakers and hiking boots). But since 1996, the company has been steadily gearing up for a larger share of the apparel industry by adding more product lines: outerwear, sweaters, Kani Endurance, dress

Karl Kani Infinity

KARL KANI

clothing Black Label (couture line), and women's KK^2 fashions (though some designs have a unisex appeal), men's underwear, and a full line of clothing in foreign markets. And in the works are infant and baby clothing and Kani fragrances. The young clothier competes with established names in young men's apparel like Polo, Tommy Hilfiger, Guess, and Nautica. With the introduction of his couture line, the 30-year-old Kani is posturing for brand-name recognition in the same vein as Armani and Hugo Boss.

We have been going after customers that we don't normally sell to. We want Karl Kani to be a household family name. We are building up our marketing and advertising to make people more familiar with the brand, which in turn will boost sales. We are building up our TV ads and print ads in magazines. We are doing major billboard ads.

Product placement is also a big part of the company's marketing plan. Kani wear has been placed on actors of popular soap operas, primetime dramas, motion pictures, and music videos. Moreover, professional athletes are sporting Kani gear on the basketball court. With the growing popularity of women's basketball, Kani is actively pursing WNBA players to endorse his Kani Sports line.

Karl Kani has come a long way from making jeans to running a full service clothing company. Born Carl Williams, he designed his first garment when he was 16; it was a denim outfit—jeans and a top. Growing up in Brooklyn, Williams was street-smart and fashion-conscious like many other urban youths.

Never having received any formal training, he began sketching his ideas and buying materials from a local fabric shop. He took his designs to a local tailor (who his father regularly used), who in turn created the patterns and sewed the garments. His one-of-a-kind outfits caught the eye of neighborhood teens. Soon he had a small homespun garment business.

I had about six different designs, mainly a T-shirt, pants, velour sweat suits with leather trim, baseball jerseys, and nylon sweat suits. At the time, I really saw it as a way to make some extra pocket money. I wasn't trying to start a business.

But by age 19 Williams was ready to make a go of it as a professional couturier. He penned a trade name for his designer label—Karl Kani (pronounced like can I)—which played off the notion "Can I" really do this? After extensively researching the business, Kani found that New York was not the most cost-effective place to manufacture clothing. Following the lead of established brands like Guess, which made much of its clothing in L.A., Kani headed west.

All I had was $1,000 and a bag of dreams. I went down to the garment district in L.A., put out an ad, and hired some sewers. For about a year and a half, I was working and living out of the store. (It served as a studio, home, and sales office.) But then the store got robbed, so I moved to a loft apartment. It had an upstairs (where we did most of the sewing) and a downstairs (where we packaged the clothes and I slept).

Kani generated sales through mail order (at $2 per catalog). He placed an ad with an 800 number in a trade rag that was popular among teens. He soon developed a small but ever-growing following. But business started to slow down in the South Central shop in 1990, when Kani decided to partner with Carl Jones and T.J. Walker, founders of Threads 4 Life, d/b/a Cross Colours, the hip-hop clothier known for its knee-length baggy shorts and hooded sweats.

At that point, I was making around $320,000 a year in sales. I had thought about moving back to New York a couple of times. It was hard trying to make it without adequate financing. I had tried to get money from banks, but they basically told me I didn't have enough experience in the business, even though I had put together a formal business plan. I tried the investor route, but no one seemed to share the vision I had for my product.

Threads 4 Life bought Kani's company and placed it under its corporate umbrella. Kani's trademark style of baggy jeans and oversized casual knits found a wide audience, and helped Cross Colours rise to prominence. Sales ballooned from $15 million in 1991 to $89 million in 1992. And in 1993, Kani's designs accounted for 65 percent of Cross Colours' $97 million in sales.

But Kani soon became disillusioned with the Cross Colours deal. For one, he didn't have any control over his line. Unlike when he was the boss, he now had to get his ideas approved by someone else. Second, the two clothing lines appealed to similar markets and started to look similar in design and in fabrics used. Kani also ran into serious problems with counterfeiters.

The police don't recognize counterfeiting as a major crime—it's a misdemeanor. But it is serious in that it hurts business and it deceives the customer. In 1992 and 1993 we spent $1 million trying to crack down on these people, filing lawsuits, shutting them down.

In 1993, success began to wane for Cross Colours. The fast-growing urban clothing manufacturer and designer was unable to supply the goods to meet high market demand. Disgruntled retailers had invested heavily in merchandise that was never delivered. This added to a host of management issues, mostly undercapitalization and overextended credit. Threads 4 Life was forced to license its Cross Colours brand name and to forgo all in-house production. In less than a year's time, Threads 4 Life had to shut down operations for good.

Seizing on the opportunity to strike out on his own again, Kani negotiated the return of his trademarked name and bought out his contract. In November 1993, he launched Karl Kani Infinity Inc. armed with $500,000 from profits earned from his stake in the company and various licensing deals (he also received financial support from outside investors).

I learned from the Cross Colours experience that it was better not to try to make so much money right away, but to look long-term and grow the business slowly. You may get $3 million worth of orders one month. You then go out and buy a lot of fabric. But if you are a day late, the store turns around and cancels the order. Now you are operating at a loss. Poor planning can ruin your business. The key to surviving in this business is to be on time.

Kani asserts that it is very hard to be an expert at designing, marketing, manufacturing, and distribution, not to mention costly. He also stresses the importance and challenges of providing quality goods at the right price for retailers and customers.

Most designers license their trade name, allowing them to

concentrate on the creative end. In a typical licensing deal, the designer creates the fashions, while the licensee manufactures, sells, and distributes the clothing under the designer's brand name, usually paying the designer a 6 percent royalty and guaranteeing a minimum amount of sales. Often the licensee is given the right to create various other products under the designer's name.

Kani's licensing deals are more like partnerships. In fact, the company maintains a general office at one of four current licensees, Siegfried & Darzifal, which makes all of Kani's jeans and most of his knit active wear. The other licensees are Saxony, which makes leather goods; and Modish, which manufactures Endurance line. Kani wants to control who he sells to, how he sells, how much he sells, and when he sells his clothes. Because he oversees sales, he receives a royalty that is around 8 percent to 14 percent.

It's important that you enter relationships with the right companies [those that are sound fiscally and managerially]. Some [licensees] think they own your name and they can do whatever they want with it. You have to let them know that you are giving them permission to put your name on their products and that they have to abide by your rules and standards.

Kani puts a great deal of emphasis on having the right people in place. A key executive is Derek Tucker, president, who has 20 plus years of industry experience (i.e., past president of Oaktree, one of the nation's largest men's clothing retail chains). Kani and his 28-employee staff are involved in the day-to-day operations of the business, including manufacturing, shipping, and receiving, store purchase terms, ordering goods from overseas, and customer service.

Kani personally attends trade shows to meet with buyers. His savvy manufacturing and marketing tactics have heightened his clout with buyers at large retail chains, such as Nordstrom's, Maison Blanche, and Macy's. Other national accounts include Champs, Footlocker, and Foot Action. In some stores, Kani clothes occupy their own exclusive department—a distinction enjoyed by such renowned designers as Tommy Hilfiger and Calvin Klein.

Kani continues to face stiff competition in the lucrative young men's market, which is deluged with smaller designers and labels like FUBU and Mecca. Even Russell Simmons, CEO of Rush Communications (Def Comedy Jam) has a clothing line called Phat Farm. To grow and thrive in the industry, Kani must continue to serve his core clientele, yet seek out new markets. He hopes to open a retail shop by the year 2000. For now, the hard part is predicting what the consumer will want next—a designer can't do too much of any one style.

It's important for me to keep an open mind and to listen to what my customers have to say. We conduct seminars. We send out teams of marketers to the neighborhoods to survey people. We use grassroots promoters to go to the clubs to show people the product and to get their input. A lot of companies go out of business because they lose touch with their customers.

Kani's Big & Tall line, launched in 1996, came to him after numerous conversations with NBA stars, who complained that they could not fit into much of his merchandise. His customer base of five years ago are now professionals in the business world. This in part led him to secure an Italian manufacturer to develop his couture line, which includes slacks, shirts, blazers, and other garments made of gabardine, worsted wool, cashmere, silk, and linen.

Instilling a broader image of Kani clothing won't be easy. Once a designer cuts his teeth in one area, it is hard to break into other segments. But Kani is up to the challenge. He doesn't mind taking risks, as long as he's the one controlling his destiny.

Any time you start a business you have to realize that there are going to be some rough roads ahead. But you just have to prepare yourself and stay focused. That's what separates people who make it from those who don't, being able to get through the rough times.

SCOTT SAMET, DOUGLAS CHU, FOUNDERS OF TASTE OF NATURE AND TABACON CIGAR CO.

Raisinettes, Goobers, Milk Duds, Skittles, and M&M's, to name a few of the candy items that could satisfy any sweet tooth, can be found at practically any movie theater concession stand. Responding to the taste buds of healthier movie goers is Taste of Nature, Inc. The Beverly Hills, California—based company supplies such snacks as yogurt covered pretzels, dried fruits, and trail mixes to some 500 movie theaters in 45 states.

Taste of Nature was conceived by Scott Samet, 28, and Douglas Chu, 29, just short of their two-year training program at Bankers Trust in 1992. The two buddies met during their senior year of undergraduate studies at Wharton University.

All the big investment banks and Wall Street houses have a financial analyst program. Basically you get thrown into the fire for two years, dealing with corporate finance, mergers and acquisitions, leveraged buyouts, and corporate restructurings. Typically at the end of the program, people leave Bankers Trust and go to graduate school to get their MBAs, or they go to work for another firm. Instead, Doug and I chose to start our own business.

The partners (Samet was 23 at the time and Chu 24) started the business using some of their bonus money from BT, about $15,000 (they had to live off their personal savings for nine months). While the two knew they wanted to be entrepreneurs, they didn't sit around and try to think up a business idea. Samet describes the process as more like stumbling on an idea and going for it—pursuing it as a viable business.

We went to movies very often. And there is a certain amount of health consciousness out here in L.A. We both realized that there weren't any healthy snacks being served for the moviegoers who wanted them. Basically, the theaters were serving popcorn, candy, hot dogs, and nachos. The healthy niche was ignored. We

started going around to different health food stores and analyz-
ing prepackaged goods. We learned who were the manufacturers
of all prepackaged as well as bulk health snacks.

After talking to a theater chain head, the duo realized that
prepackaged snacks was not the optimum method for selling
health snacks. The plastic bags made too much noise when you
opened them—much like the rustling sound of a bag of potato
chips. This would have created a disturbance in the movie theater. Samet and Chu brainstormed with one concession stand
manager on a way to sell health snacks in bulk.

They ended up ordering snack bins, which were acrylic displays with four storage compartments. Employees would scoop
up healthy items and place them in paper bags—much like a
French fry bag—imprinted with the Taste of Nature logo.

We had to do two things, find suppliers of the bins and design
them. A consultant from the Metropolitan Theater Corporation
here in L.A. sat down with us and highlighted the important
points of a successful concession program. We combined that
with a general understanding of designing and making acrylic
fixtures to come up with the display bins. It took about eight to
10 weeks to get the stands in place.

While Samet and Chu didn't do a business plan starting out,
they did make some elaborate presentations about the benefits
of having healthy snack bins. The crux of their sales pitch was
that the healthy items would not cannibalize the current concession items, but would add incremental sales—those moviegoers who were unhappy with the current offerings.

The only cost to the theater owners was to purchase health
snack items exclusively through Taste of Nature. Samet and
Chu paid for all of the up-front costs in developing the displays.
Chu notes they even had to redesign the bins.

We had to design smaller display bins, which were more eco-
nomical and effective because they were easier to move around
and you didn't have to fill it up as much. So, that meant that the
products would stay fresher. The smaller displays also helped us

to get better shelf space—in the front of the concession counter rather than in the back.

The enterprising duo did a lot of cold calling—knocking on theater doors and telephoning movie managers throughout Los Angeles. They regularly attended trade shows to solicit suppliers and test their products. By the end of 1993, Taste of Nature's products were featured attractions at roughly 1,000 screens or 200 plus movie theaters (given an average of five screens per theater at that point in time).

This industry is very consolidated; the largest 20-theater circuits control more than 80 percent of all the movie screens. So, our sales calls were very concentrated. The number of people we needed to contact was less than 30. Concession decisions are generally made at the corporate headquarters and they decide for the whole circuit. We worked with national concession distributors to deliver the product.

After two years in the business, Taste of Nature expanded its product mix by offering the more traditional bulk candy items to movie theaters nationwide. But the journey into the land of jaw breakers and gummy bears took the business in yet another direction—cigars. In 1995, Samet and Chu started the Tabacon Cigar Company and the Monthly Cigar Club.

There are a lot of tie-ins between candy and tobacco. The majority of candy and tobacco distributors are one and the same. Doug and I had enjoyed cigars for years. We realized it was a boom that was gaining popularity. We were intrigued by the mail-order business. We wanted to create a Monthly Cigar Club modeled after beer-of-the-month and wine-of-the-month clubs.

For Samet and Chu, the Monthly Cigar Club was a good way to test the waters and learn what cigar smokers wanted. More important, they could bypass the costs of leasing space and stocking inventory by pursuing the mail-order aspect. Samet and Chu gave a great deal of thought as to how they would promote the cigar club. Would they advertise through television, radio, newspapers, or magazines? Would they use direct mail or word of mouth? What was the club going to offer members in the way of products and premiums?

We decided that each month we would offer the customer four different premium, hand-rolled cigars along with a newsletter that talked about the cigars and offered discounts on cigar accessories (such as humidors, lighters, and cutters), all at below retail prices. It was an informative way for the customer to save money. We also offered exclusive club specials on cigars. By not having a store on Rodeo Drive, we were able to keep our costs low and have a lower markup on each box. It was cheaper to order through us than walking into a local store. We have good insight into the industry because we ourselves are cigar customers. We have positioned ourselves as industry experts on cigars, products, news, and information related to the tobacco industry. Scott and I are real industry gurus.

Samet and Chu were able to successfully guide the operation of both businesses. Taste of Nature generated $1.5 million in sales revenues in 1996, and Tabacon (which means big tobacco in Spanish) saw 1996 revenues reach $1.1 million. The cigar company has experienced faster growth, exceeding $4 million in sales in 1998.

Sales are generated through a direct sales force, a brokerage network, and distributors—all three of which have designated territories. Much of the company's revenue stream is fueled by the "Gillette" method of sales and marketing—"give them the razor and force them to buy the blades." In Tabacon's case, countertop humidors (which are used to store cigars) are placed in various retail outlets, including bars, hotels, liquor stores, and nightclubs. The retailer doesn't pay for the humidor, but he or she has to buy cigars exclusively from Tabacon.

This has allowed the company to secure excellent shelf space, and Samet and Chu get to display point-of-sales materials describing each cigar. They support sales by advertising in several national consumer and trade publications, helping bolster brand-name recognition and demand.

It has been trial and error with respect to the humidors. [For instance], coming up with the right counter size and the best way to display the cigars. The difference between a humidor and a cigar box is that the former regulates the humidity levels of the environment so that the cigars stay moist and don't dry out. We had started working with a lot of catalog companies, sourcing cigar products for them and retail stores. We established all of these contacts in the industry who helped us with the next step— to come up with our own special cigar brands.

Tabacon has experienced exceptional growth with respect to its five premium, proprietary brands of cigars: Rosa Blanca (Nicaragua), Del Vale (Honduras), Don Jivan (Dominican), Nivelacuso (Dominican), and Tabacon (Honduras). Samet and Chu have developed proprietary blends of tobaccos in the form of cigars. They are the exclusive importers and distributors of two of the cigars. The other three cigar brands are their own proprietary creations—they contract out to have those exact blends made for them, and they then import the cigars into the United States.

The Monthly Cigar Club caters to an upscale cigar and accessory mail-order client niche. And while Tabacon's five premium cigar blends are sold through the catalog divisions of such ritzy stores as Neiman-Marcus, Saks Fifth Avenue, Bloomingdale's, and Brookstone, the company also serves smaller shops and boutiques. International expansion is next on the horizon with a distributor in Asia gearing up to sell all five brands.

We will continue to expand on the premium brands that we offer as our growth strategy goes forward. The way to build value in a company is not to have generic items. Through a lot of taste tests, we found some great blends. So, why not create our own brands. Why rely on selling other people's brands. Just the same, Taste of Nature is also a brand name in and of itself. We will continue to expand and grow that brand as well.

In 1998, Samet and Chu launched Cookie Dough Bites,

milk chocolate coated cookie dough candy, which has become
one of the most popular candy items in movie history, ranking
ahead of all Hershey, Mars, and Nestlé items in the candy case.
Only Red Vines (or Twizzlers on the east coast) usually rank
higher. Large circuits, such as Regal Cinemas, have placed
Cookie Dough Bites in each of its approximately 260 theaters
nationwide. United Artists recently agreed to a circuit-wide roll-
out as well. The duo also launched Brownie Dough Bites
(fudge brownie dough coated in milk chocolate). Blockbuster is
lauching both items in 3,400 corporate-owned video stores and
700 franchisee-owned outlets nationwide. And Tosco Corp. has
committed to place both items in its product assortment for all
of their 2,500 Circle K and gas station convenience stores.

ALONZO L. WASHINGTON, PROPRIETOR OF OMEGA 7, INC.

In a place not far away lives a real action hero. Community
activist turned comic book creator, Alonzo L. Washington is the
founder of Omega 7, Inc., a six-year-old independent company
based in Kansas City, Kansas. In 1998, the 30-year-old entrepreneur launched his six-inch action figure, Omega Man—a
superhero who fights crime and drugs. Payless shoe stores
recently approached Omega 7 about developing a line of
Omega Man children tennis shoes.

Washington is the first independent publisher to produce an
African-American action figure based on a comic book character. Before the first toy rolled off the assembly line, Washington
distributed flyers and press releases to drum up interest and pre-
orders for Omega Man. The toy (retailing for $9.99) is sold in
comic book stores, cultural shops, and via mail order.

Omega Man warped into 10 different Toys "R" Us warehouse locations from California to New York. In fact, Omega
Man sold out in the first hour of his debut at the Toys "R" Us
store in Washington's hometown. Kaybee Toys also has
accepted Omega 7 as vendor. The new action figure helped

Omega 7, Inc. climb to $1.5 million in total sales for 1998 from over half a million dollars the previous year. Omega Man has even garnered cross-cultural appeal.

The way the action figure came about was a factory in Hong Kong read one of my comics and they sent me a fax about manufacturing the toys. That was around November of 1996. I started looking into all of the costs involved and what it would take to make the toys. I sent a proposal and marketing tape to several retailers. But Toys "R" Us was the only one who showed any interest. I began building molds and prototypes of the toy. It took about six months before I had what I wanted. I brought in a patent attorney to protect my ideas and to negotiate the deal.

Omega 7 bears all the production costs—at least $60,000—of the action figure. Then there are the costs associated with importing the product. Some 15,000 toys have been shipped from Hong Kong to America and then delivered to various outlets. In the first six months of the toy's debut, some 10,000 Omega Man dolls were sold. There is no middleman, such as Kenner or Mattel, which means that Washington doesn't have to worry about sharing his profits.

Since he was ten, Washington has made his own toys using model clay and paint sets from hobby shops. He's been reading and collecting comic books since he was eight. Because he could never find any positive role models who were African-American, he started drawing his own characters and creating stories. Soon, the young Washington's classmates in grade school began asking for the crude comic books and he was able to sell them at 25 cents each.

He continued to draw over the years, but by the time he was 18 years old, he was entrenched in the role as a community reformer. He went to the local grade schools and high schools, speaking against gang violence and drugs. He was the head of a community organization. He even produced a public affairs program on cable television in hopes of bringing positive images to inner-city youth.

As part of his crusade to introduce them to African-American role models, Washington created a comic book in 1992, called *Original Man*. Contrary to many of his colleagues, Washington wanted to deal with real issues and not fantasy. But what started out as a one-time project turned into a profitable business venture, because of the overwhelming demand.

Washington began researching the comic book publishing business. He contacted mainstream publishers about his idea but they were not receptive. Accustomed to adopting a grass-roots approach to "get the job done," the then 24-year-old Washington began self-promoting *Original Man* on posters and flyers. He sent literature to cultural shops, which began placing orders before he had actually published the first issue.

Washington received 1,000 advance orders and used the money as a down payment to print 5,000 of *Original Man*. However, total production costs, which included color separations, paper, ink, boxes, and shipping fees cost an additional $5,000. To help pay the balance, Washington took a box load of the comic book to a local bookstore to autograph the limited editions. He managed to sell 2,000 copies at $2 apiece. Even more impressive, he took orders for another 13,000 copies. Washington walked away with $30,000 in sales for the first issue.

Before I even printed my first book, I copyrighted the characters. But after the book signing went so well, I decided to incorporate and make this a real business. I got a business license and business address, which was mainly a P.O. Box. I worked out of my home. I got the necessary materials to begin doing mail order. I put together a press kit.

Washington did about five more issues of *Original Man*. From that point on, he began developing other superheroes. To date, he has six titles: *Mighty Ace, Dark Force, Original Man, Omega Man, Original Boy,* and *The Omega 7.* Many of his titles are spinoffs from his prior comic books. While Washington writes all of the story lines, he does hire some freelance artists to draw the characters. Omega 7's comics showcase black male and female action heroes stomping out crime and violence and campaigning against racism and crusading for cures to deadly diseases.

Washington's business continues to thrive in an industry that is full of uncertainty. While 1993 was a boom year for the comics industry, 1994 saw many smaller publishers and retailers go bust. Several battles raged among the survivors, with a host of small publishers fighting over a 20 percent share of the $1 billion industry dominated by six comic book companies: Marvel, DC, Image, Dark Horse, Malibu, and Valiant.

Moreover, independents have always had a hard time getting their comic books into mainstream stores, newsstands, and major retail chains. They mostly rely on small bookstores and expositions to sell their books. For the most part, retailers won't even look at a publisher's titles unless they are listed in the catalogs of major distributors.

Since the first year, Washington's books have been picked up by major distributors, namely Diamond Comic Distributors, Inc. and United Brothers and Sisters Communications System, Inc. His comics are sold throughout the United States and abroad—as far away as Japan and Africa. Diamond, the world's largest distributor of American comics, represents more than 4,000 retailers. But there was a time when Washington refused to give distributors his books. He held out for about a year, demonstrating that he could deliver the books to his audience himself.

A big part of my success is that I do great PR. I know how to promote my ideas. I had a marketing plan starting out that was not based on the mainstream comic book market. This meant that I would have to move product through mail order, schools, and cultural shops (which is a totally different business than dealing with distributors). I also focused on getting picked up by the local press. I concentrated on building a following, which is why it was important for me to do a lot of book signings at the cultural shops and black expos.

By pitching his books at cultural shops, on the radio, and in newspapers, Washington sold more than 100,000 copies of all titles, ranging in price between $2 to $4, during those first three years in business. Washington also promotes his characters on such merchandise as clocks, T-shirts, mugs, baseball caps, and trading cards.

There have always been a few black superheroes dating back to the late 60's and early 70's. *Spawn*, *Steel*, and *Blade* are prominent examples of black comic book characters to make it to the silver screen. But most ethnic characters range from the culturally out of touch to the blatantly stereotypical.

I have always been visible in my community. I still have a second business, which is public speaking. I get paid honorariums to talk to high school kids and even college students. I started out by being active in the community. It also helps that I have a niche (in part, the urban, hip-hop generation). I am not selling to the average comic book buyer. I'm selling to people (black and white) who want to read a comic book that deals with real issues, whether they are the L.A. riots or the Million Man March. My books are truly different and unique.

Washington runs a small home-based operation. His mother, Millie, a divorced preschool teacher, helps with the company's day-to-day operations. Dana Washington, an HIV counselor, is vice president and head of promotions for her husband's comic book company. She has even dressed up as Original Woman on occasion when speaking at local public schools about health, drugs, and other pertinent issues. The couple have five sons, Antonio, 11; Akeem, 5; Kamaal, 4; Malcolm, 3; Khalid, 2; and a daughter, Alana, 6 months, who are the ideal test market for Omega 7's toys and comics.

Washington is working on releasing three other action figures. He has been approached by VISA to do a print ad. Independent publishers hardly ever make it to the level of a DC Comics, which generates billions of dollars from television animation and syndication, movies (particularly the Batman films), product licensing (ranging from trading cars to cereal), promotional tie-ins, and trademark deals. But there are definitely more exciting adventures awaiting Alonzo Washington.

I hope to do an animated series. But it's a fight when you deal with Hollywood. I've already been approached by the studios to do television and film. But a lot of times they want to change the story and turn it into a comedy. Or they want the character to be an ex-con or athlete. Those are the same negative images I'm trying to erase with my comic books.

13

RUNNING THE BUSINESS: HITS AND MISSES

> When life knocks you down, try to fall on your back,
> because if you can look up, you can get up.
> —*Les Brown, motivational speaker*

As a business owner you have to pay attention to details, the day-to-day management of the business. Of course, you can't do everything by yourself, though starting out it may feel that way. But you need to stay on top of a number of growing pains that often plague new businesses.

According to the Small Business Administration, roughly half of all start-ups go out of business within four years, mostly due to ineffective planning, insufficient capital, too much debt, and poor record keeping and cash-flow management. Also, too many entrepreneurs fail to have a contingency plan to address such issues as insurance (i.e., disability, property, and liability insurance) and taxes (i.e., sales and Social Security taxes).

Another trouble spot for many entrepreneurs is pricing. An entrepreneur can run his/her business into the ground by doing a poor job at pricing a product or service. Running a business—whether you provide a service or product—requires that you know how not to price your goods or services too high (people won't pay) or too low (you don't make any money).

Your company's balance sheet and income statement are good indicators of where you stand. If you have significant cash on hand, show a profit, make payments promptly, and have repeat customers, you're in business. Always keep in mind that it's possible for a profitable, fast-growing business to run out of cash and be forced into bankruptcy. Your business success will be based on profitability, not volume of sales. You don't want to increase market share at the expense of declining profits. In fact, some companies have been forced to close shop because they were unable to supply the goods to meet high demand.

Like most business owners, you want your business to grow. But expanding too quickly without having the right infrastructure in place could be the sign of death for your business. Many companies have failed because they strayed away from their core products or services; or they added ancillary products without mastering their niche.

Many businesses incur tremendous losses by expanding outside of their market without doing the proper research. Take for instance, a retail store owner who opens a second or third outlet, yet fails to provide proper training to the new staff.

Or the same store owner ventures out in other geographic locations without understanding the different buying habits of those areas. In both scenarios, the upshot is poor customer service, dwindling sales, and a cash shortfall.

If you want your business to survive, you need to educate yourself early in the process on how to manage through lean and hard times. And yes, there will be hard times. As long as you are committed to staying in business you will face challenges.

Here are some tips on handling at least three problem areas common to new businesses:

1. **Credit Management:** You need to implement strategies for extending credit to customers, stretching your bill payments, and collecting receivables (money due you).

2. **Cash-Flow Analysis:** You need to perform a cash needs assessment on a monthly basis, and to develop a living budget to make sure money is on hand when you need it.

3. **Inventory Control:** Supplies, raw materials, works in progress, and finished products are all considered inventory. Inventory control involves how much to order and when to order it.

MANAGING CREDIT

There are basically three ways you can get paid for your services: cash, check, or credit card. In an ideal situation, you provide a product or service and your customer or client promptly pays up. In reality, business owners generally have to wait 30 days, 60 days, or 90 days—and sometimes never—to get paid. Since you need your money to pay your bills on time, you have to set up some internal systems for addressing how you get paid and when you collect those payments. Consider the following:

- *Cash.* A familiar business adage: "In God We Trust, All Others Pay Cash," or, "Cash Is King." Paying by cash is a quick and easy transaction, whereas checks need to clear a bank and credit card charges have to be recorded and posted by financial institutions.

With cash, you deposit the money in your account and you know it's there when you need it. However, a downside to getting paid in cash is that you need to be meticulous with your record keeping. There is always some paper trail with checks and credit cards. In cash businesses, like bars and restaurants, unscrupulous characters are more inclined to steal from you. Once you are beat out of your money, that's it. Also, from a tax standpoint, you have to make sure you declare your money as income.

- *Checks.* According to bank experts, businesses lose around $10 billion a year from check fraud. And why not? There are a number of things that can go wrong: The customer or client may have insufficient funds to cover the amount of the purchase; the account may be closed; the person endorsing a business check isn't authorized; or the customer can put a stop payment on a check after receiving the goods.

Nonetheless, there are ways you can protect yourself against bad checks. You can refuse to accept personal checks and insist on certified checks, cashier's checks, or money orders. If you are in the service business or dealing with large accounts, have the client's bank wire-transfer the money into your account. You may establish a policy where no work is performed or goods provided until a check clears. Also, notify customers you will charge a processing fee for bounced checks; most places charge $10 to $20. You can ask for personal information on the check, but know the law.

One way to spot bad checks is to look at the federal routing number and check it against the city and state of the financial institution. Located on the bottom corner, the financial institution's transit and routing number has nine digits and always has the stop symbol at the beginning and end. Personal check numbers almost never go above four digits, and appear at the top of the check and to the right of the transit and routing number. Keep your eyes open especially during the weekend; studies show that's when most fraudulent checks are passed.

Many businesses use check verification and guarantee services (i.e., companies providing insurance for bad checks). TeleCheck (713-522-0990) charges 50 cents per check but will refund you for any check that turns out not to be good. The business owner verifies the customer's check through one of these services by phoning in information using the person's driver's license or other identification, or swiping the check through an electronic terminal, which then reads the check. Others are ETC (425-483-2500) and Equifax (404-885-8000).

• *Credit*. These days, nearly every kind of business relies heavily on credit. Even some street vendors now accept credit cards. There are basically five credit cards you can accept: VISA, MasterCard, Diner's Club, American Express, and Discover. Paying by credit is a simple process. A customer gives a card, the business owner swipes it through a machine (or electronic terminal), punches in the amount and expiration date, and presses enter. He/she gets the okay and writes down the approval code on the sales receipt. The customer walks away happy, goods in hand. And the business owner has gotten paid for a job well done.

However, there's a cost to credit card processing. For starters, you need a machine to process the card. You can buy one yourself, or like most business owners, you can rent one from a credit card processing company, which charges an application fee (somewhere between $65 and $100) as well as a fee for programming and installing the machine (around $35 to $50) for VISA, MasterCard, and Diner's Club transactions. American Express has its own processing network called the Electronic Draft Capture, as does the Discover Card. That's not all: Credit card processing companies deduct a percentage of the amount from each and every purchase. The rest of the money then goes into your bank account. Also, your bank may charge you a transaction fee for each deposit.

Just as a customer can put a stop payment on a check, someone can contest a credit card charge, costing you money, because you will have to fight the claim with that customer or client's credit card company. It's important that you implement a credit collection policy and procedure, such as how to handle credit card transactions over the telephone.

To ward off problems, you can offer credit only to preferred repeat customers. Or you can have prospective customers or clients complete a credit application or information sheet, then run a check with a credit reporting agency. Consider charging interest if a credit payment isn't paid within a certain time limit.

ANALYZING YOUR CASH FLOW

Each month, you will need cash to pay your employees, your suppliers, and your bills. If the money isn't there you are in big trouble; you could end up losing valued workers, contracts, and a roof over your head. The best way to stay on top of your finances is to prepare a monthly cash-flow analysis statement, based on your inflow of cash (i.e., cash sales, receivables, and investment income) and the outflow of cash (i.e., operating expenses, merchandise, payroll, overhead, marketing and sales, and taxes). By comparing the sources of money against the uses of money, the cash flow statement will indicate if you have a cash surplus or shortfall for that month.

The cash flow statement doesn't reveal profit or loss. It shows cash on hand. Basically, it tells you how quickly money is going out of the business and how promptly it is being collected. If you are in a cash business, like a restaurant or a hair salon, you are paid immediately after you provide a certain service; in this case, either a meal or a new hairdo. Even if you own a retail shop, you will get paid up front, be it cash or credit card.

Whenever you extend credit, or provide goods or services that haven't been yet paid for, this means your customers or clients are using your company's money interest-free. Meanwhile, you have expenses and payables. Ideally, you want payment terms with suppliers so that you pay them later, but collection procedures with your customers so that they pay you earlier.

If you set up payment terms where customers settle their bills in 15 days, while you arrange with your suppliers to settle your account in 45 days, then you are in good shape. On the other hand, if you have to pay your bills in 30 days, but clients pay you in 60 days, you are likely to be short on cash and will have to look elsewhere for funding. If you always have to borrow money to do business, the cost of money will become extremely expensive.

You can improve your cashflow by monitoring how you collect your accounts receivable, turn your inventory, and pay your bills. Consider giving customers or clients an incentive for bills paid early—a 2 percent discount—or you can attach a late fee to encourage them to pay on time. You may even try to get customers to pay in advance—before you even ship out the product.

Also, don't be afraid to negotiate arrangements with your suppliers and vendors to give you broad payment terms—90 days out—when you place an order instead of the customary 45 to 60 days. This "float"—the lag time between when you pay your bills and when your customers pay—is a powerful tool, because it means more cash on hand for your business and less money tied up in inventory. Suppliers may also give you discounts for early payments. Many entrepreneurs attribute their success to building sound relationships and staying on good terms with suppliers.

GETTING PAID

Some of your customers will pay their bills on time, others will pay late, and some won't pay at all. Don't make the mistake of focusing so much attention on getting new business and making money that you neglect to collect overdue payments. When you send out an invoice (and be sure to use duplicates), make sure you follow up within a reasonable amount of time—15 to 30 days. Also, consider putting on the invoice that there's a service charge for any bill that is more than 30 days past due—the norm is 1 percent to 5 percent.

Monitor your accounts and separate them accordingly: new accounts, accounts 30 days past due, 45 days, 60 days, and so forth. Many accounting software packages have modules for invoicing and tracking accounts receivable, open balances, and partial payments. Also, implement procedures for each phase of the billing cycle. For instance, customers or clients with accounts that are 30 days past due might receive a phone call. Payments that are late after 60 days warrant a letter (either from your company or lawyer) notifying the customer that while his or her service is valued, you will be forced to turn over his or her past-due account to a collection agency. Any bill that has been outstanding for more than 90 days justifies bringing in a collection agency. Of course, the last resort is to take deadbeat customers or clients to small claims court.

But before you run out and hire a collection agency, note that it will take a percentage of the debt owed, anywhere between 10 percent and 40 percent, eating up some of your profit. The agency's efforts will be a combination of telephone calls and letters. You have a 33 percent chance of the agency ever recovering your money, according to the American Collectors Association, Inc.

Granted, you want to give valued repeat customers a chance to rectify their situation. Find out if they have some sort of problem paying the bill and if they would like you to arrange a payment schedule. A collection agency has the power to place the debtor on a bad credit list, jeopardizing his or her credit rating. Go to a collection agency when the customer or client has ignored requests to make payments or breaks his/her payment arrangement.

To check out a particular agency, contact the Chicago-based Commercial Law League of America (312-781-2000), which provides licensing information and detailed reports on collection agencies. Also, ask for a free copy of *Commercial Collection Guidelines for Credit Grantors* from the International Association of Commercial Collectors, Inc., in Minneapolis (800-859-9526; www.commercialcollector.com). Be sure to familiarize yourself with state laws about extending credit and collecting debts (check statutes under Collection of Debts or Consumer Protection).

CONTROLLING INVENTORY

Depending on the type of business, a large portion of a company's assets can get tied up in inventory, impacting cash flow and ultimately profitability. You need to put in systems for tracking your supplies and products—how quickly they are moving and what it is costing you.

If you are a service business, let's say you need to make a major presentation for a client but are out of printing paper, color ink cartridges, and transparencies. Normally, this could be easily rectified. But because you didn't plan properly, you have a choice between replenishing your supplies or paying all of this month's rent. Or, if you are a business that manufactures widgets, how do you handle the situation when a client cancels an order for 1,000 just because two pieces were damaged? And at some point, every business owner has to account for the theft of goods and the spoilage or damage of items.

Because they haven't had enough steady activity to establish sales history or patterns, it is hard for new businesses to get a fix on planning how much inventory they need. If sales are below expectations, you will have too much inventory on hand, which means your money is tied up and you are limited as to what purchases you can make. Too low an inventory can cause you to lose profits, because you are unable to supply the demand. Unsatisfied customers could mean the loss of customers to the competition. Also, it's imperative to know how to make allowances for fluctuating inventory that may be seasonal.

Controlling inventory involves two things: optimal inventory levels and inventory-related costs. To help determine whether you are carrying the right level of inventory, use the inventory turnover equation, which is net sales (or the cost of goods sold) divided by the average value of inventory on order and on hand. This formula tells you how many times in a year you are turning over, or selling inventory. For example, if the cost of goods sold is $200,000 and the average value of inventory is $30,000, the inventory turnover rate is 6.6.

Higher numbers are better because they mean you're moving merchandise quickly. But if your numbers are low, it could indicate you are carrying too much inventory. Of course, what's considered high or low varies from industry to industry. Consult your accountant or a trade group to learn the average rate in your market. For perishable items (where freshness is important), you will want to calculate the turnover rate for daily, weekly, and monthly periods instead of annually.

Another important procedure is the "just-in-time" inventory method, meaning that if you time your purchases and deliveries accurately, you will have goods or supplies when you need them for that month for your use or to accommodate sales, and you won't have to worry about overstocked inventory. The ideal is for you to be able to convert your materials or goods into dollars in the shortest amount of time. Again, working out arrangements with your suppliers is critical. You must plan all purchases in advance and monitor all factors that affect inventory. Be conservative with your inventory while you get to know your business.

A popular technique you can use to save costs up-front is to sell your products on consignment, whereby you promise to pay store owners after they sell your products. Usually, a store buys and pays for the items it sells and then waits to collect a profit when a customer buys those items. Store owners are willing to sell on consignment because they still make a profit every time a product is sold and they don't have to pay to have the merchandise displayed in their shops.

This is a big help to your business because you get to showcase your products in more than one store at little cost. Of course, you have to wait to collect your money. Any unsold merchandise of yours, the store owner can simply give back to you.

Obviously, you can't be an expert in every aspect of your business. This is why it's important that you find people with the strengths to complement your weaknesses. Make sure you hire the right people who can shore up areas where your business is lacking. The key to success is to surround yourself with qualified, capable people to help manage the business.

Alternative Financing: Factoring Accounts

A dilemma typical of young, rapidly growing companies is being short on cash flow but high in product demand. As sales increase, the cost to pay for the company's goods equally increases. If the business doesn't get paid until 45 to 90 days after a shipment, then there's a big gap in cash flow—money flowing in and out of the business. One remedy for this situation is factoring, where you sell your accounts receivable to companies that will buy your invoices and collect payment from your customers. This way, you don't have to wait more than 30 days to get paid on product already delivered.

Factoring offers a number of benefits to cash-starved companies, which can use the money to meet payroll, fund marketing efforts, or provide working capital. Just about any type of business has the potential to benefit from factoring, though it is traditionally associated with the textile and apparel industry.

A business that extends its customers and suppliers credit will have 10 percent to 20 percent of its annual sales tied up in accounts receivable at any given time. The owner can't pay the rent or this week's payroll with a customer's invoice. But a factor can pay the business cash now for the right to receive future payments on his or her invoices.

The amount factors are generally willing to fork over is generally 75 percent to 90 percent of the net face value of your receivables. In turn, you have to pay a finance charge (or discount fee) on the total amount of the receivables, usually anywhere from 1 percent to 5 percent. So, even though factoring is a ready source of cash, it eats into your profits. What happens if you withdraw money against the receiv-

ables before the factor gets paid? You will be hit with 1 percent to 3 percent interest above the prime rate of the
advance.

Unlike bank loans, which are largely dependent on the
borrower's ability to pay up, factors care more about
the financial soundness of the client's customers. The key
to landing a factoring deal is the age of the accounts
receivable. The older the account, the more difficult it is to
collect. Some factors don't like to see a single client representing more than 25 percent of total accounts receivable.

The factor will assess the creditworthiness of your
accounts. The best way to find a factor is to get referrals from
companies similar to yours. Or you can check *The Edwards
Directory of American Factors* (Edwards Research Group;
800-963-1993), which provides detailed information on over
200 companies in the United States.

TOM SCOTT AND TOM FIRST, FOUNDERS AND CO-PRESIDENTS OF NANTUCKET NECTARS

It was essentially on a whim that Tom Scott and Tom First
started Nantucket Nectars, a "New Age" bottled juice drinks
company that generated $60 million in sales revenues in 1998.
Tom and Tom (as they are referred to) first met as freshmen at
Brown University in the fall of 1985. Scott, who hailed from
Chevy Chase, Maryland, was studying American Civilization,
and First, a native of Boston, was earning a degree in history.

In 1988, before his last year of college, Scott created
Allserve, a boat business that serviced boats and visiting yachts
in the Nantucket harbor. The next summer, after the Toms'
senior year, First joined the business. The two friends knew that
the jacket-and-tie life of corporate America was not for them.
They were determined to make it on their own.

Nantucket Nectars

TOM SCOTT AND TOM FIRST

Out of the 22-ft. red powerboat, they delivered newspapers, ice, groceries, coffee, laundry, and a variety of items that were not easily accessible to the local boatmen.

Tom and Tom survived their first round of business relatively unscathed. But the following winter proved harsh, not only due to weather conditions but because of departing summer vacationers, who had been their biggest customers. The partners found themselves barely able to make ends meet. They began to come up with other income-producing ideas.

The one that paid off was a fruit drink. Driven by his passion for cooking, First recreated the taste of a peach nectar he had sampled during his travels in Spain. After a few tries of mixing some peaches, sugar, and water in a blender, the Toms had their dream concoction—named Nantucket Nectar. They experimented with other flavors, buying fruits from a local grocer. During the summer of 1990, the innovative partners started selling their fruit juice off their boat and out of the store. Scott admits that they were clueless and naïve about the juice business.

It was a very sophomoric and innocent type of thing. We had contacted some glass suppliers but they said they couldn't sell to us. We started out using cups, wine bottles, milk cartons, beer bottles, different things we could put the drink in. Putting the stuff in bottles was a hellish process. We didn't know about pasteurization, therefore, we didn't pasteurize. So, we had a lot of product go bad. We didn't know all of the pitfalls ahead of us. But [we] just had to learn each step of the way.

While Tom and Tom managed to sell around 2,000 cases of juice at $9 each, profits did not flow freely. Revenues were poured back into production and distribution. In fact, from April to September of 1991, Scott found himself living out of his '78 Chevy Suburban. Both Toms were forced to take odd jobs to keep money flowing in.

During those first two years, Scott and First had invested their personal savings into the business—a combined $20,000. They hired a professional bottler and microbiologist to help mass-produce and package their product, and they found distributors to help deliver their juice beyond the original island boundaries to retail stores throughout Cape Cod, Boston, and Washington, D.C.

Once we looked at the volume that was required for minimum production, we decided to branch out. At the time, the factory required 1,400 cases. We sell 30 times that in a day now. But back then, it would have taken us a summer to move that amount. When we first started out, we thought that if we sold one case a week that would be great. The store actually ended up selling 10 cases a week. Getting stores to buy our product wasn't easy. We were turned down several times. But we had to get up off our butts, go out, visit the stores, and meet the owners. We went from door to door at local delis, convenience stores, and chain restaurants.

As demand for their services grew, they opened the Allserve General Store in the summer of 1993 (which is still in operation today selling T-shirts, hats, newspapers, and juice), a converted icehouse on Straight Wharf in Nantucket, an island located 30 miles off the Massachusetts coast.

By 1993, Nantucket Nectars was in 120 stores and sales reached $1 million. But First and Scott were in serious need of expansion and working capital. An "angel" answered their prayers. Michael Egan, then former chairman of Alamo Rent A Car, invested around $500,000 in the business in exchange for a 50 percent ownership stake in the company. Egan met First and Scott during the summers on his yacht in Nantucket and became impressed with the young entrepreneurs' enthusiasm and hard-work ethic (they scrubbed his deck).

At the time, we were looking for ten different investors. We had spent three months at the library putting together a 30-page business plan with a lot of financial projections. It was a very thorough document. We also did a private placement memorandum. But he [Egan] wanted to invest in the whole thing himself.

But it wasn't all smooth sailing from then on. The Toms leased five warehouses and 18 trucks, hired a sales force, and began distributing Nantucket Nectar along with other beverages, including Arizona Iced Tea. The business lost more than $1 million, mostly from having to replace damaged goods and stolen merchandise (workers were pilfering bottles from the warehouse and selling them for some fast cash).

Distribution is a challenging business in terms of trucks, inventory, warehouses, and so on. On the surface, it seemed sim-

ple. But as we grew, we became overwhelmed. It seemed that the more cases we sold, the more money we lost. It was a classic case of not managing your systems properly. But you become a collection of your mistakes. You learn from them and then you move on. At that point we brought in a great CFO who got everything in line.

Most beverage companies manufacture the product and utilize outside distributors for deliveries; rarely does a company create, manufacture, and distribute its own product. The Toms were forced to scale back to their original operation, hiring independent distributors to deliver Nantucket Nectars.

In 1995, the business turned its first profit, $850,000, having sold $15 million worth of juice. And in 1996 the 100-employee company topped $30 million in sales. Sales reached $45 million in 1997.

Nantucket Nectars was placed as Number 13 on *Inc.* magazine's 1996 rankings of the fastest growing private companies in America. Still, the Toms realize they are doing battle in a fiercely competitive market dominated by established beverage giants. By comparison, Snapple had more than $600 million in sales in 1997; Arizona Iced Tea, $337 million; and, Veryfine, $125 million.

In spite of their lack of business experience and formal training, the Toms' lesson on the importance of establishing strong relationships with wholesalers and suppliers has contributed to their success. Nantucket Nectars is now available in more than 30 states and international markets, including Brazil, Korea, China, South and Central America, Canada, and France. It is most often found in small convenience stores, delis, some grocery markets, gourmet food shops, health food stores, gyms, and cafeterias.

Because of our experience in distribution, we are good at doing the mundane things that make a distributor happy — paying credit quickly, getting deliveries on time, and staying well organized. We have over 100 distributors and we are sold in some

70,000 stores. We sell direct, not through the warehouses [there are two primary methods of distribution, direct store delivery — where the manufacture sells to each individual store — and warehouse delivery — where the manufacturer delivers to a warehouse, which in turn supplies individual stores].

Tom and Tom's portfolio started with three flavors. Today, they have 36 varieties in six product lines: 100 percent juices, juice cocktails, teas, and lemonades. Nantucket Nectars (which uses pure cane sugar versus fructose corn syrup to sweeten its cocktails) includes traditional juices, such as apple, orange, and cranberry juice, and the more colorful flavors like papaya, guava, mango, and kiwi berry. The drinks are packaged in proprietary 12-, 17.5-, and 32-oz. molded glass bottles (standard sizes are 10 and 16 oz.). Their newest line of nutritional drinks are called Super Nectars, such as Green Angel, Ginkgo Mango, and Chi'i Green Tea.

Today, the Toms have bottling plants in California, Rhode Island, and Florida, and a headquarters in Cambridge. Playing on their early days, they continue to use the slogan: "We're The Juice Guys," which is pasted on their labels and bottle caps. This won a beverage packaging award in 1995.

Their brilliant purple bottle caps feature inside facts on the Toms, company employees, and Nantucket. Their label pictures a young Tom First and Tom Scott in their Allserve Boat, while their college buddy "The Naked Guy"(his real name is Paul Conti) is jumping from the roof of the Allserve General Store and a salesman sits fishing from the dock. Conti helped Tom and Tom start Allserve and worked in sales for years. Today, he heads the juice guys' bar mission.

Even though it was a major expense, we wanted to have a unique design and look. We wanted something that would speak to us beyond a generic item. We always wanted our own bottle design. But by our fourth year in business, we were able to afford to make our own 12-oz. and later a 17.5-oz. bottle. We mix our own formulas. A lot of companies tend to contract that job out to a flavor house. But by going to those places and paying attention to how they did it, we are able to come up with the ingredients for the flavors ourselves.

Sales and marketing continues to be a strong point for the Toms, who have teams of promoters from the East and West hit the road in purple Winnebagos and 25-ft. bottle-shaped trailers. The marketers scour college campuses, beaches, stores, malls, and anywhere else Tom and Tom's market can be found, to do tasting. Other marketing efforts include a newsletter, *Bottle Recap*; a Website (www.juiceguys.com); charitable giving; and speaking engagements.

The Toms, who are both 32, have divided much of the company's operations between marketing, which Scott is head of, and sales, which First oversees. Meaning, Scott is responsible for anything that has to do with promoting the brand, which includes in-store marketing, public relations, and advertising. First handles distributor relations, sales training, and contracts. Both Toms do their share of hiring employees.

Early in 1998, Ocean Spray Cranberries Inc. purchased a huge chunk of the company, but the two Toms still retain about half of the company's ownership and remain active in the day-to-day operations of the business. Ocean Spray offers Nantucket Nectar's production team more efficient ways to produce and distribute its product.

Ocean Spray offered us the opportunity to take Nantucket Nectars to the next level without sacrificing the company's independence or philosophy. With the infusion of capital, Nantucket Nectars can focus even more attention to maintaining and increasing quality, and increasing our marketing and consumer reach.

The Toms still have an office on Nantucket, refuse to wear suits and ties, and take their dogs to work. First is married. The Toms also have a juice bar, much like those that have popped up across the country.

We are good at what we do, because we are our target market.

We know what we like. We also listen to what our customers have to say. We pay close attention to e-mail, letters, and taste tests. You have to work at selling your product. You won't survive in business just sitting there. You have to keep pushing.

MARLEY MAJCHER, FOUNDER AND OWNER OF ABIENTO RESTAURANT & CATERING CO.

Each day patrons spend their hard-earned dollars at eating and drinking establishments from New York City to Los Angeles, making this business a flourishing $220 billion market. Still, restaurants have a reputation for being a high risk industry, with only a small percentage lasting in business after the first two years of opening their doors. These establishments have more than a 50 percent greater chance of failure than a general business.

Since 1993, Marley Majcher has had her plate full. The 28-year-old owner of Abiento Restaurant & Catering Co. is responsible for running three food businesses—a 185-seat restaurant and a catering service in Pasadena, California; and a banquet facility in Arcadia, California.

Majcher started her restaurant business at the tender age of 23, just two years after graduating in 1991 from the business school at Georgetown University, where she majored in marketing. The food aficionado had spent the summers of her sophomore and junior years at a cooking school in France.

She also got a year's worth of kitchen experience as a cook at 1789, a restaurant in Georgetown's upscale neighborhood, where she oversaw the dessert station, did a lot of prep work—chopping and cleaning food—and prepared appetizers. While her education and kitchen experience opened her eyes to the restaurant business, Majcher had no way of foreseeing what awaited her in running a restaurant.

Looking back, I didn't have anywhere close to the knowledge I should have had going into this business. I liked the idea of own-

ing a restaurant, but I underestimated what was involved. After college, I went to work for a food purveyor. I did inside sales, processing orders for supplies from different restaurants nationwide, including the one I used to work at. I did that until the end of February 1992, when I moved back home to Pasadena. But there were so many more things that I could have learned on someone else's payroll. Like, I wish I had apprenticed as a general manager at a restaurant.

It was during her last months at Georgetown that Majcher and her family began to seriously talk about the idea of owning a restaurant. On top of that, she became engaged to Richard Steffann, an executive chef at Georgetown's 1789 Restaurant. Steffann, a graduate of the Culinary Institute of America, had been working as a chef since 1976 and was an instructor of international and classical cuisine at the New York Institute of Technology.

For six months, Majcher's parents combed Pasadena for the ideal spot. Taking the advice of resident consultants, they decided to invest in purchasing some land rather than leasing a building. It was while attending church one Sunday morning that the Majchers learned—by way of the owner's niece—of an Irish pub that was up for sale. The zealous family bought the 26-year-old establishment.

Financed from family savings and bank loans, Majcher started construction in August 1992. Start-up costs, which included purchasing the land and renovating the pub, were in the neighborhood of $3 million. Abiento (derived from *a Bientôt!*, which means "see you soon" in French) was originally scheduled to open in October of 1992. But a series of delays stonewalled the restaurant's grand opening until May of 1993.

We didn't yet have a roof on, and in January of 1993 it started raining straight for more than 60 days. There were a lot of unforeseen problems that seemed to double our costs. As a result, we had very little operating capital in the beginning and that hurt us. It became very tough to catch up. That's why you really have to plan on spending one-third more than you think you will need. You have to plan for the unexpected, and know that you won't be out of business because of one bad month.

Majcher learned the hard way a valuable lesson in the business. Restaurants operate on extremely tight profit margins (the amount of profit you make on each sale). Meaning, an act of nature—such as a snowstorm—or a few slow nights a year can shut down for good an otherwise fine restaurant.

It wasn't until almost a year after we opened that a consultant came in and pointed out a couple of things to me, like that our labor costs were very, very high. The consultant, who my father found, had tons of restaurant experience. He informed me that I was sure to be out of business in six months. But he was very condescending toward me. I think he really wanted to be the general manager of the restaurant and to take it over. I ended up firing him.

After only a year in business, Majcher found herself in court. The consultant sued the restaurant on the grounds that Majcher's father had hired him and agreed to pay him, regardless of performance. He won, but only received a fraction of his asking price.

I was determined to succeed and train myself in all of the areas in which I was deficient. I decided to soak up as much information as possible and to take advantage of the resources around me. So, I took classes at a local hotel and restaurant management school. I read articles. I took seminars through the American Management Association. I adopted mentors in the industry. I participated in marketing seminars to improve sales. I did all of this while working six days a week in the restaurant. The consultant has since opened and closed his third restaurant, leaving all of his backers in the lurch. And we are still in business.

Today, the 70-employee enterprise is right on track. Abiento generated $1.6 million in sales revenues in 1997. The business has benefited tremendously from promotional events and its quarterly newsletter, which is mailed out to some 8,000 patrons.

Our market is saturated (in terms of the number of restaurants). So, we have to compete on a totally different level; it is not just about providing good food and service. We created a newsletter to set ourselves apart. It is an 8½-by-11 sheet that is printed on both sides and folded down the middle, so you open it like a book. Our sales have gone up, because we get more reservations and requests for parties from the newsletter. We also send out flyers each month to promote special events; we collect business cards; we hold recipe contests. All of this helps us build up our database. Also, we monitor our efforts to see what kind of turnout we get and to determine how much we are spending to get customers.

To contain the costs of sending out the bulk mailings, Majcher offers incentives—like giving customers a free dessert for correcting a zip code or address. Total cost to produce and distribute the newsletter is about $2,500. Majcher's promotional efforts were by no means whimsical. The idea and costs for the newsletter were included in her business plan.

I did a business plan from the very beginning. That was a big part of my learning experience at Georgetown. Writing business plans were part of the projects we had to do. It is real important to do a business plan, because it forces you to answer a lot of questions and to be realistic about financing. Of course, it is a work in progress, because you can't plan for everything. I continued to update it. By the second year of business, I really started tracking my expenses on a spreadsheet. By year three, I was reworking the marketing plan and strategizing about our management team.

Other changes Majcher made were to adapt the menu to her market by either adding or deleting items. Abiento's cuisine is described as California eclectic. Majcher married Steffann in 1993, though the couple has since separated, and Majcher bought out his ownership share in 1998.

Abiento's market is three-fold: ladies who dine while their husbands are at work, business people, and families who come in on the weekends. On the other hand, Majcher's secondary ventures, the catering business and banquet facility, draw a corporate clientele.

Back in the spring of 1997, a customer introduced Majcher to a couple who owned a local hotel, the Santa Ana Inn. Majcher assumed charge of their banquet facilities—two gazebos and a rose garden that traditionally had been used for wedding receptions. Now, Abiento uses spacious quarters for business clients' holiday parties, meetings, and retreats.

I had delegated 50 percent of my responsibilities to my general managers (I now have three), and I hired an assistant to help make me more efficient. I had to step back and look at the big picture. I couldn't spend all of my time making pies, hosting, or answering phones. I needed to concentrate on ways to bring in business and to make more money. Because I had streamlined a lot of my duties, I was in a position to take on the banquet business, which is all about servicing parties. I had done this kind of work before and I knew the market. So, it made perfect sense.

Like most business owners, Majcher found controlling her finances to be a formidable task. There were times when she had to call on her parents to bail her out of a cash crunch. But ultimately, she had to fend for herself. Even though Majcher had an accountant and a bookkeeper, her company was not properly managing its cash flow.

I prepared the invoices and signed off on all checks. Still, our bookkeeper was not managing our cash flow properly. One of our banks, unbeknownst to us, was not depositing our credit card receipts until a week later, whereas it normally takes 48 hours. We were counting on that money. Also, because we have so many catering clients, mostly corporations, we have a lot of house accounts—which means, they don't pay cash upfront. It's part of our accounts receivable (which the restaurant business is not normally set up to handle). It represents 15 percent of our business. Our bookkeeper was not following up and collecting the money owed on those accounts.

Most new business owners don't anticipate that they will have problems. That could end up being their downfall, Majcher warns. She advises business owners to have as many systems set up as possible to address their business's areas of operations, and to always have backup plans.

As Abiento approached its fourth year, the business began to show a profit. Statistically speaking, Majcher says her business is ahead of the game, since most new restaurants don't make it past their first anniversary.

The young restaurateur is quick to note the support she has received from such groups as the California Restaurant Association and the South Lake Business Association. She has especially benefited from her affiliation with the Young Entrepreneurs' Organization (YEO).

Founded in 1987, YEO (www.yeo.org) is a chapter-driven organization that targets business owners under age 40, whose companies gross annual sales exceeding $1 million. YEO has some 2,000 members in over 60 cities and 11 countries. In addition to hosting an annual national and international conference, YEO sponsors skills workshops, lectures, and social events.

Majcher says she had particularly benefited from YEO's "Forum" program, which is headed by each chapter. The Forum is a group of 10 to 12 YEOers from different industries who get together once a month to share their business war stories and seek advice from their peers. Each meeting, at least one member of the L.A. chapter gives a presentation at his/her office, allowing other members to see the company's operations and meet employees.

It's important to belong to a support group of other business owners. When you start a business, you feel like you are on a four-foot island. You are going to have all of these issues to deal with that other people—friends and family—aren't going to understand. Every six months I set new goals and I evaluate previous ones. You really have to be out there in the industry and you have to keep sharpening your skills, because the market is constantly changing.

14

FORMING STRATEGIC ALLIANCES OR PARTNERSHIPS FOR PROFIT

Coming together is a beginning; keeping together is a
process; working together is success.
—*Henry Ford, founding CEO, Ford Motor Co.*

In the business world, the 1980s is synonymous with mergers
and acquisitions, while the 1990s has been the decade of strategic alliances and joint ventures. In addition to faster growth and
shared economic risk, the benefits of forming such cooperative
partnerships include expansion into new domestic markets,
new product development, and acquisition of marketing or distribution expertise.

The six most common types of business-to-business partnerships or alliances are:

• *Merger/Acquisition.* A permanent arrangement involving the purchase of an entire company by another, or the legal
combination of two entities into one. Mergers/acquisitions are
often used by companies to eliminate competition or to cement
a previously existing alliance. Consider a merger or acquisition
if you're in a partnership that's really working and there is redundancy between the companies; meaning, you could combine
forces and then cut costs.

No longer relegated to corporate giants, many fast-growing companies are buying up the competition. For a growing number of companies, rapid expansion has been fueled through acquisition. Take Michael Rubin, the 26-year-old CEO of Global Sports, Inc. in King of Prussia, Pennsylvania. He built up the $130 million shoe company by acquiring Rykä, a woman's shoe company, and Apex One, athletic footwear and apparel, and merging the two with his closeout company, KPR Sports International. As in Rubin's case, buying another business can fulfill several company needs, including broadening a product line, increasing distribution, and providing access to international markets. Some companies merge or buy up their smaller competitors simply to expand geographically or to enhance technology.

Increasing market share is just a part of it. You have to think about whether the two company's products or distribution channels can be integrated. There are some calculated risks. For starters, as the company doing the buying, you would need to understand the value of the company being targeted for acquisition as a stand-alone entity. There also has to be a clear understanding of what added value is created by combining the two companies. You have to plan ahead as to how you will integrate the new entity into your company's day-to-day operations. Due diligence is required, otherwise, you might find that acquiring another company could actually compound existing management or operational problems. You have to give careful consideration to the fact that key employees could walk away from the business on both sides. Major clients or customers could also seek to do business elsewhere. Also, you have to take into account how the company is going to measure the success, or lack thereof, of the acquisition. Some firms go outside their field when they make an acquisition. In this case, it's important to have someone on your team with experience or a keen understanding of that new industry.

- *Joint Venture.* Two companies come together to form a third independent company, with its own set of employees and a separate board of directors. A joint venture involves a formal agreement. Solid candidates are companies that need to partner with someone else to pursue a specific market they can't penetrate because of cost or other barriers, or to produce a specific product, service, or technology.

- *Strategic Alliance.* Two companies band together to work on a project, sharing resources, risks, and rewards of the alliance, yet, each company remains independent. The idea is for each company to bring complementary specialties to the table. For instance, one may be strong in technology and the other in sales and distribution. Together, the companies can reel in more customers than they could separately without investing new capital.

- *Consortium.* Here, more than two companies in different geographic regions or specialties come together. This group of companies unites to engage in business to benefit each other, with the relationship entailing cooperation and sharing of resources. Generally, members refer business to one another or work on projects jointly as needed. A consortium may be formed on an ongoing basis or a one-shot deal for a particular venture. Consider joining a consortium if you want the benefits of appearing bigger without incurring fixed costs. All parties must be clear about two things: what they want to gain from this type of alliance, and what they are comfortably willing to exchange. Keep in mind that you will be managing several company relationships. All parties should sign a business-to-business agreement that includes a list of products or services each company is bringing to the alliance; time frame for rendering of services; payment of money; specific guarantees of quality of labor and materials, and remedies if services or products are defective; consequences for breach of the agreement; and conditions under which a party can terminate the contract.

- *Outsourcing/Subcontracting.* A number of major corporations are forming alliances in the way of outsourcing—where companies farm out certain job functions, such as accounting and human resources, allowing them to focus on their core business. Many companies are paying outside vendors to handle bookkeeping, mail services, customer services, telemarketing, and the like. In the wake of corporate restructuring, major corporations are scrutinizing every area of their operations to see which job functions can be performed more efficiently and economically by outside firms. You can contact a company directly to find out how you can get placed on its preferred vendor list. For an online list of companies in your industry, check out Companies Online (www.companiesonline.com), which is a joint product of Dun & Bradstreet and Lycos, and will give you a company's street and Web address and a description of your products/services. For about $20, you can get your hands on a full D&B report of an individual firm.

• *Virtual Corporation.* This kind of informal alliance is created when a company assembles a team of professionals for a specific project or client. These temporary partnerships are often used by companies looking to extend their market reach. Essentially, you are building a stable of colleagues and combining talents. What makes a virtual corporation appealing is that it broadens the capabilities of each member without increasing individual overhead and it creates the image that the virtual company is actually bigger than any one individual. The first step is to define the company's objectives and outside skills needed. You need some kind of blueprint; otherwise, you're not likely to identify the kinds of talents you need from your associates. Such relationships are not easily formed and managed. Since you won't be working side by side with members of your virtual company, you need to establish rules for communication. In other words, how frequently should associates check in, either via telephone calls, e-mail, or faxes? How often will the group meet and where (if some associates aren't local)? How will you track the progress of each member? Also, you'll need to devise a time-line and work schedule for each project.

FORMING A STRATEGIC ALLIANCE

Cooperative strategic alliances among small and large companies alike are taking place in every industry and every area of
the country, and throughout the world, as global partners cut
deals. According to studies by the national accounting firm of
Coopers and Lybrand, companies that use strategic alliances
are growing much more rapidly—by as much as 30 percent—
than those that do not. Productivity among such partnerships is
also higher—more than 50 percent.

At the same rate, more than 50 percent of all strategic
alliances fold within the first four years, at least when it comes
to businesses entering such partnerships for the first time.
Companies tend to do better the second go-round, having
upped the learning curve. Success depends on the managers'
abilities to coordinate and integrate the resources of the two
firms.

That said, before you enter any kind of agreement, do some
serious self-analysis. What are your company's strengths and weaknesses? If you don't know what you are lacking you won't know
what you need in a partner. Don't commit what you can't deliver
and the same goes for your partner. You have a better chance of
succeeding if you understand what you are getting into.

If you have the financial wherewithal and business resources
required to enter a new market by yourself, then do so. If you
find a potential partner who has a complementary resource, proprietary technology, or access to a market that you don't have
and can't get any other way, then a strategic alliance may be the
way to go, notes Gene Slowinski, a managing partner of Alliance
Management Group Inc. (www.strategicalliance.com). The
Gladstone, N.J.–based consulting firm assists companies in the
formation and management of strategic alliances, joint ventures,
outsourcing relationships, and mergers and acquisitions.

Slowinski, who is also director of strategic alliance studies at

Rutgers University's school of management in New Brunswick, N.J., offers five key issues to consider:

1. *Intent.* The alliance must provide a mutual benefit. To achieve this, both parties must share the same intent or objective. Make sure you are clear about both companies needs, expectations, agendas, and goals. As a software developer, your goal may be to bring a proprietary product to market within a year. Your strategic partner, a large technology company, may be interested in spending years in R&D and keeping anyone else from accessing the technology.

2. *Boundaries.* Where does this alliance begin and when does it end? In other words, what products or resources are accessible to both parties and which ones are not? You may decide to work for a year or on a discretionary basis.

3. *Exclusivity.* Can each party work with another company in the same field or industry? If there is an exclusive arrangement, then both parties can't work with the other's competitors.

4. *Intellectual Property.* There are essentially two kinds. One is background intellectual property, where you bring information to the relationship that is already yours. The second is jointly developed information or technology between both parties. In order for the two companies to work together, each will be privy to certain inside information, databases, resources, contacts, clients, business practices, marketing tools, proprietary technology, patents, trade secrets, and so on. The question becomes: What rights do you have to use the other company's intellectual property—be it knowledge or technology—inside and outside of the alliance? What happens once the alliance is dissolved? You can't erase from memory everything you discovered.

5. *Termination Conditions.* It is difficult to maintain long-term relationships. How can the two parties end the alliance

gracefully—without the help of hundreds of lawyers? It is crucial to discuss how and when you will end the relationship. You may choose to end it on 90 days notice in writing. Or there may be other more exacting stipulations or circumstances under which to end the alliance.

Each one of these issues is like a thread in a fabric, so you have to consider all of them together because they are intertwined. Slowinski adds another important element to the mix: "How will you link the decision-making structures of the two companies?" Most problems that occur are structural. Meaning that the management teams of both companies are not in sync. Each may have a different vision for growing the company. Meet with company managers upfront: Who's responsible for what? Put a contingency plan in place, in case key managers are demoted, transferred, or jump ship to another company. Alliances are not about relationships with companies but relationships between people. Discuss from the outset what levels the company will pass on certain deals or projects because it is either too small or too big for that company to handle.

For instance, a larger company may not enter licensing or merchandising deals that are below a certain monetary threshold, because their overheads are too high. On the other hand, the smaller company could live quite well on small licensing deals. Moreover, the larger company may have rules, regulations, and time frames that differ from those of its smaller partner.

Equally important, make sure the partnering firm is well managed and financially stable. You also need to measure each company's corporate culture, which is expressed in the values, beliefs, and goals of the people of the organization. Are the two cultures in sync? Cultural differences may be a bigger factor when dealing with international partners.

Just as you need a business plan to guide your business, you need a strategic alliance plan to manage the cooperative relationship. After a series of meetings and negotiations, get everything in writing in terms of what is expected of both parties, what are the shared goals, how you will address customers in a collaborative way, how you will address issues of quality, how you will determine what's unacceptable performance, how performance will be measured, and how disagreements will be handled. Also, figure out the financial pie equation—how will you divvy up earnings and profits.

Don't enter into any agreement until you have weighed the costs and benefits of the alliance. After thorough consideration, you may decide it's better to go it alone, to seek support elsewhere, or to form a third entity, which would be considered a strategic venture.

Strategic alliances don't apply to any one sort of business or type of industry. As long as you can find a prospective business partner with complementary skills and resources to those of your firm, you could well establish a long-lasting and prosperous relationship.

CHRISTY HAUBEGGER, PRESIDENT AND PUBLISHER OF <u>LATINA</u> MAGAZINE

Since she was ten years old, Christy Haubegger always wanted magazines with pictures of women who looked like her or had information that related to her experience as a Mexican-American. A native of Houston, Texas, Haubegger was adopted by white parents. She was reared in a middle-class neighborhood by the Haubeggers who always stressed the importance of her Mexican heritage, and emphasized a bilingual and bicultural lifestyle for her.

It was in this context that Haubegger's idea for *Latina* magazine was born. Today, 29-year-old Haubegger is the publisher and president of the glossy lifestyle publication that covers issues of interest to Hispanic women in the United States. It is distributed in the 35 cities where 95 percent of the Hispanic population lives, and has an initial distribution of 300,000 copies.

CHRISTY HAUBEGGER

I took some business courses at Stanford. I had a class on entrepreneurship. The professor told the class, if you are ever going to start a business, you have to start something you feel really passionate about. [In class] we talked about looking at a product or service that you feel consumers want but don't have. The thing that came to mind for me was a magazine for Hispanic women. I was a voracious magazine reader. I wanted a magazine that reflected who I was, what I looked like, and my experience. I remember looking at other magazines that represented beauty

*and thinking to myself, if we are not represented in here, then
what is that telling us about ourselves.*

Haubegger toyed around with the idea of publishing a magazine while attending Stanford Law School, after receiving a
degree in philosophy from the University of Texas at Austin in
1989. While at Stanford, Haubegger joined the editorial staff of
the *Stanford Law Review* and inevitably rose to the position of
senior editor. She also served as class president.

But it wasn't until the ripe old age of 25 and just out of law
school that Haubegger set out to create a bilingual publication
to address the needs and dreams of women like herself, women
who live between two cultures and two languages: Latinas. She
went to work on a business plan, putting in hours as a legal
researcher to pay the rent on her San Francisco apartment.

*I had a really wonderful mentor from the business school at
Stanford. She was so supportive of me. She knew that I was
unhappy after my experience working during the summers at different law firms. She encouraged me to launch my own magazine. She told me that if it didn't work, I could always still be a
lawyer. For about three years, I lived off of love and ice water.*

Haubegger raised about $250,000 from private investors and
formed her own company, Alegre (which means happy)
Enterprises, Inc. Armed with her business plan, she proceeded
to call upon the titans of magazine publishing. The 100-plus-
page comprehensive plan was full of Census Bureau statistics,
marketing surveys, analysis, and media studies that showed
there was a market out there for *Latina* magazine. She also
demonstrated that there was enough print advertising directed
at Hispanics in the United States to support her magazine.

Haubegger sought the guidance of mentors who themselves
had spearheaded major national magazines. She was introduced to Stephanie Stokes Oliver, who was then executive editor of *Essence* magazine (now editor-in-chief of *Heart and Soul*
magazine). In turn, Haubegger met with Ed Lewis, Essence
Communications, Inc., the publisher of *Essence* magazine, a

preeminent African-American women's publication. She convinced him that the Hispanic population was being underserved by the American media. More important, she was able to illuminate the financial potential of her venture.

Mr. Lewis came to San Francisco. We met over coffee, which turned into lunch and lunch turned into dinner. I took him for a walk through my neighborhood (the Mission district, a largely Latino community). I pointed to young Latinas stepping off the bus and coming out of the subway station. They were carrying McCall's, Glamour *and* Mademoiselle. *I told him these were the women who needed to be reading my magazine.*

Lewis invited Haubegger to speak to Essence's board of directors, who were overwhelmingly impressed with her pitch but wanted to see more proof. Haubegger began working on a prototype of the magazine using funds from Alegre. Essence footed the bill to hire an independent firm to conduct nationwide focus groups in cities with major Latino populations.

We needed to do some quantitative analysis. I had a small office at Essence, with a desk and a phone—almost like a little incubator project. With an editor, I put together a 32-page prototype, which we used to create a direct-mail package. Using a list broker to rent a dozen different lists—six in Spanish and six in English, we mailed about 80,000 pieces to see if the magazine was really a viable concept. We got a 4 percent response, which is good in terms of direct mail (the average rate is 1 percent). We used the focus groups to verify the editorial content we came up with. We gave them a questionnaire and a mock table of contents.

After two years of several prototypes and 21 focus groups, *Latina* magazine was launched in May of 1996 under the banner of Latina Publications LLC. It was a joint venture between Essence Communications and Alegre Enterprises.

It is very interesting when you are negotiating something with a long-term partner. It's not like negotiating a deal for a car, where the goal is to get the best price. I don't really care what the

*car dealer thinks about me after I buy the car. Once I get the keys
and drive off the lot, I won't see the dealer again. However, if you
have to work ongoing with someone, the relationship becomes
much more important. We had to look at things that would preserve a good relationship.* Essence *and* Latina *share key
resources—production, distribution, and accounting. Everything
that has to do with putting the magazine together and selling it
is my responsibility. It is not a passive investment. I contract services from* Essence*—I pay for their employees' time. I rent space
here in the building. No other company would have given me the
autonomy I have.* Essence *respected the fact that I knew more
about my market.*

In purely marketing terms, the combined demographics of
Latina and *Essence* working together offer advertisers 23 percent of the women in the country—proving there is strength in
numbers. Haubegger notes that compromises had to be made
on both sides.

*It has been an interesting learning experience. Someone once
told me that the first deal you make will be the worst deal you make,
because the second, third time around you will have more leverage
than you did the first time. You know how to approach a deal.*

After a year and four issues, *Latina* went from a bimonthly to
a monthly publication. The magazine commissioned an independent market research firm to compile its first subscriber
study: Readers are upwardly mobile, college-educated Latinas
in their 20s, 30s, and 40s. *Latina's* bilingual format scores major
points with readers.

*The biggest thing we are doing right now is direct mail, which
is the most efficient and economical way for us to build our circulation. We are mailing 1.5 million pieces at about 50 cents per
piece. We are still in a testing mode. We have advertised on radio
and cable. We also did outdoor advertising. Now we are looking
at network television.*

Haubegger handles much of the magazine's administrative
work. People line up outside her door each day with hosts of

questions. Her to-do list is divided by departments: "What does circulation, art, and editorial need today?" She also meets with advertisers, pitching the magazine.

I have a rapport with my staff (36 in all). I want to build an enduring institution as well a great place to work, which is not easy to do. As a guide, I follow Martha Stewart, who created a branded empire (television show, Website, book) that started as a magazine. I want to develop Latina into a major brand.

Haubegger believes that she is making a difference. Industry insiders seem to agree. She was chosen as one of the Most Inspirational Women of 1996 by *NBC Nightly News with Tom Brokaw.* She was lauded by *Crain's New York Business* as one of the youngest Latina businesswomen in the United States.

Very few people are able to quit their jobs and pursue their dreams. If you do what you are really passionate about, it can happen. If you are not passionate about it, you won't want to stay up all night revising your business plan or risk getting your phone turned off. You won't want to make the necessary sacrifices.

SKY D. DAYTON, FOUNDER AND CHAIRMAN OF EARTHLINK NETWORK, INC.

The Internet was practically alien territory to commercial enterprises and ordinary consumers nearly a decade ago. Despite its ability to connect thousands of sites across the world, it was a difficult place to access. Today, the Internet connects up to 70 million people and the sky's the limit for access providers like Sky D. Dayton, Chairman of EarthLink Network, Inc. in Pasadena, California.

EarthLink's 27-year-old founder has taken the upstart company from 30,000 subscribers at the end of 1995 to around 800,000 in 1998, with a staff of 1200, a 200,000-sq.-ft. facility, and estimated sales revenues of $200 million. Sales revenues in 1997 were $32.5 million, a tenfold jump from $3 million the previous year. The publicly-held Internet Service Provider

(ISP) (NASDAQ:ELNK) took its place as number one in the country (ranked by *PC Magazine*, September 1997), providing access to more than 1,000 U.S. cities.

Through its TotalAccess Internet Software, which includes the Netscape and Internet Explorer browsers, EarthLink provides an inexpensive, direct connection to the Net. The company has grown by forming strategic alliances or co-branding deals (a.k.a. Affinity marketing partnerships) with companies that have agreed to bundle TotalAccess disks with their owngoods or services—adding extra value to EarthLink members.

Affinity partnerships account for more than 40 percent of all EarthLink members. EarthLink has cut deals with over 500 companies. In 1998, partnerships included Simon & Schuster (sells TotalAccess disk with their Internet books), UUNET Technologies (a telecom that leases locations to access the Internet), Sony Music (includes TotalAccess with select music CDs), Hard Rock America, Sir Speedy print shops, United Airlines, and Apple Computer.

I realized early on that there were companies who could bene-fit from what we were doing and vice versa. By partnering with them we got to leverage all of their strength. The idea is to come up with a win-win situation—something that is equitable on both sides. If a strategic alliance doesn't work out in the long run it could do damage to your business.

Dayton established EarthLink in 1994 after experiencing difficulty (80 hours) and expense getting on the Internet. As soon as he was connected, he realized the Internet was the next mass communications medium on earth, but the only way it would be accepted in the mass-consumer market was if it were easier to get on and to use. A better link: EarthLink.

At first, I thought I could solve the problem by creating a soft-ware package that would allow people to use the Internet. But the problem to my approach was that you still had to have an access provider. It's like providing someone with a great phone that has a

*lot of functionality, but there's no telephone company to provide
the line. I did my research and determined that the point of failure
was not the software but that no one was providing reliable access
in a way that made it easy for the average person.*

At the time, the entrepreneurial wonderkid was running two
other businesses, Café Mocha on Melrose Avenue in West Los
Angeles, and Dayton Walker Design, a graphics design firm
specializing in the entertainment industry. Dayton had opened
the popular coffee house at the ripe old age of 18, just two years
after graduating in 1988 from Delphi Academy, a prep high
school, and managing the computer graphics department at
Mednick & Associates.

Dayton got a $10,000 loan from his grandmother and his
partner borrowed another $10,000 from a family friend—way
too little to start out, he acknowledges. The duo were clueless
about the restaurant business, still they managed to gross
$250,000 by their second year in business.

While running this operation, he went to work for Executive
Software only to leave in 1992 to launch his graphics design
firm. Dayton's love affair with computers and design is a natural
extension of his birthright; both his parents were artists and his
grandfather was an IBM Fellow—he was among Big Blue's top
40 engineers.

Dayton sold his shares in Dayton Walker Design to concentrate his efforts on EarthLink. He began with just one other
employee, a 600-sq.-ft. office, and used furniture. He did everything: sell the accounts, provide tech support, handle the
billing, and even clean the floors.

*I forgot to devise a billing system. I got off the phone after
someone placed our first order and said, oh my God, how am I
going to bill this person. I typed out my first invoice in Microsoft
Word and mailed it out to the guy. I immediately hired a consultant to put a billing system in place.*

Determined not to make the same mistake twice, Dayton set
out to raise $100,000 in investment capital. Armed with a 30-

page business plan, he made a list of everyone he knew. It was through friends that he found EarthLink's initial investors and board of directors, Kevin O'Donnell, a venture capitalist, and Reed Slatkin, a money manager. The two controlled 40 percent and Dayton maintained 60 percent of the company. Sidney Azeez became a private investor and board director a year later along with Chip Lacy, CEO of Ingram and Bob Kamer, former CFO of AT&T. Dayton's biggest challenge has been managing rapid growth.

The Internet access business has a very low barrier to entry. It's a modern day BBS industry—anybody with a computer and a few modems can be an ISP. But there is an extremely high barrier to growth in the business. It is a very capital intensive, people intensive, and technology intensive business.

EarthLink doesn't have the same problems as competitors, such as AOL, which provides both content and access. EarthLink doesn't do content, build browsers, or make hardware. Its strong point is member services.

For starters, EarthLink provides quick and reliable access—taking just 10 minutes from start to finish. It charges $19.95 for unlimited use. About $12 of every $19.95 subscriber fee is spent on member-maintenance costs. EarthLink's software makes it simple to customize a start-up page with links to whatever Website the user likes to browse. The company also offers member support and education. One service, called Guardian Angels, provides technical assistance for account installation and education.

The company's e-mail solutions deliver tens of millions of messages per week. Another nicety is a monthly newsletter for subscribers. This explains why Dayton views EarthLink as a company that resolves communications issues instead of one that provides technology solutions. EarthLink's Affinity partners are all banking on the company's customer service and technical support.

When EarthLink started running out of cash in the summer of 1997, Dayton snared international finance wizard George Soros to invest $15 million. EarthLink had net losses of $59.4 million, but is expected to show a profit in 1999. Dayton has put a great deal of financial and intellectual capital into the business, building a top-rate management team. He created an organizational structure based on seven divisions when there were just two people working at EarthLink.

As we started to grow, I was immediately able to identify where to put people and to fill in key positions as we went along. The structure has changed quite a bit since then, but the one thing I learned from my previous businesses was that it is better to have an idea of what your company's organization is going to be when you get big and operate within that framework from the beginning, instead of trying to make up one down the road.

The first person he hired was a human resources director. Over the next two years key positions were filled by experienced executives: vice president of operations, chief financial officer, vice president of sales and marketing, and vice president of strategic planning.

One of the toughest decisions Dayton had to make was to hand over the reins to president and CEO Garry Betty, a 39-year-old IBM veteran and vice president at Hayes Microcomputer Products. He handles the day-to-day operations and internal controls of the business. As chairman, Dayton works on strategy and long-term product direction. He's also the one brokering lucrative partnership deals and setting forth EarthLink's vision.

It's like playing chess. The ability to see three moves ahead gives you a lot of clarity on the move you are about to make. It takes time, but at some point it starts to click in your head and you begin to see when you make a change how it affects so many other things. My dream for EarthLink is much bigger than what we have created thus far.

KEITH T. CLINKSCALES, PRESIDENT AND CEO
OF VIBE VENTURES, INC.

Keith T. Clinkscales is well-versed in the toils of start-ups. For the past five years, the 34-year-old entrepreneur had been the driving force behind the urban magazine *VIBE*, which is published 10 times a year. The Harvard MBA has embarked on a brand-building strategy likened to Martha Stewart's. To date, the *VIBE* franchise includes a Website, music seminar, special events, a fashion and music trade show, books, television, film, and merchandising.

VIBE magazine was launched in September 1993 as a joint venture between Time Inc. Ventures and Quincy Jones-David Salzman Entertainment (QDE). Under Clinkscales's leadership, *VIBE*'s growth and receptivity in the market has been phenomenal as it relates to magazine start-ups. In general, magazines take three to seven years to break even (in the case of *Sports Illustrated*, ten years). *VIBE* debuted with a circulation of 100,000, soaring to 600,000 subscribers by 1998. In addition, *VIBE*'s ad pages have grown from 575 in 1994 to 1,047 in 1997. Advertising revenues climbed to $20 million that same year.

Today, the magazine is under VIBE Ventures, a partnership between QDE; Clinkscales, president and CEO; Miller Publishing Group (owned by Robert Miller, publishing magnate and former Time-Warner executive); and John Rollins, group publisher. After helping to get *VIBE* off the ground, Time sold its interest back to the partners in June 1996.

It was back in 1988 that the Trumball, Connecticut native and son of a Harlem Globetrotter first cut his teeth in publishing when he founded *Urban Profile*, a bimonthly magazine dedicated to issues affecting 18-to-34-year-old African-Americans. Clinkscales abandoned the world of finance to enter the media realm with three associates: Derrick Furgeson, Douglas Austin, and Leonard Burnett. At the time, Clinkscales was an account officer at Chemical Bank, where he had toiled for two years since graduating with honors in 1986 from Florida A&M University.

The partners kicked in $1,000 of their own money to finance the shoe-string start-up and raised another $11,000 from 11 personal investors (friends and colleagues). Clinkscales and Furgeson did a skeleton business plan for *Urban Profile*. But it wasn't until the two partners went to Harvard Business School that they were able to put some meat on it.

I worked on the editorial, advertising, marketing, and operations. Derrick covered the financial projections and circulation. What I learned from putting the business plan together was to be concise and to make sure that we had an operational plan and not a wish list. We were going to use this plan to raise capital. Another important thing we learned about was circulation. It costs on average $20 to obtain one person. It is very easy to lose a lot of money on circulation even though you have thousands of subscribers.

The magazine reached a circulation of 75,000 readers. Clinkscales continued to run *Urban Profile* while attending Harvard, graduating in 1990. It was a tough climate for magazines—a lot of well-funded publications had gone out of business.

Launching a magazine is very capital intensive. I projected that we needed $1.2 million to put together the kind of magazine we wanted and provide investors a favorable rate of return. We never came close to raising that amount. I realized we didn't have a lot of money. Whatever we did we had to make sure our revenues would exceed our expenses. We had to make sure that we were close to breaking even at all times. Looking back, we really needed $4 million.

Time executives were soon coveting Clinkscales's publishing expertise, and in 1993, they called on him to help launch a new music magazine founded by Quincy Jones, the Emmy- and multi-Grammy–winning arranger, composer, and record producer. At that point, *Urban Profile* had been sold to Career Communications Group.

Time did a test issue of the magazine in the fall of 1992. There were 54 ad pages in the test issue in 1992 and 67 in the September 1993 launch. The business plan called for a modest initial circulation of 100,000 for four issues scheduled for 1993 and 200,000 for ten issues in 1994. I came to VIBE in March of 1993 with an empty desk, business plan, and a note pad. We built the magazine from there.

To get the word out, *VIBE* sponsored a 200,000-piece direct mailing at the end of August 1993, broadcast commercials on MTV, and another 2-million direct mail drop in the beginning of 1994. Results from the reader response cards in the test issue indicated an audience that was mostly male and between 18 and 24 years old. After five years of covering a culture that has grown up with hip-hop and contemporary R&B—music, fashion, sports, and politics—*VIBE* has a broader demographic mix in terms of gender and race.

VIBE has had its share of controversy. First, founding partners and record moguls Andre Harrell and Russell Simmons backed out of the deal in 1993. *VIBE's* first editor Jonathan Van Metter resigned after clashing with Quincy Jones over the direction of the magazine in 1994. He was replaced by Allan Light, a former writer for *Rolling Stone.* One season after its television debut in the fall of 1997, the *VIBE* show was cancelled, despite the popularity of host and stand-up comedian Sinbad.

Now that *VIBE* has stepped out on its own, Clinkscales, and his 55-employee staff must leverage *VIBE* as a brand without losing its core audience. Citing the golden rule taught in every media course across the country, Clinkscales notes that "Content is king."

I always had in my mind a strategy for growing VIBE. Between 1993 and 1994, it was all about making the magazine strong in terms of the editorial content. Readers don't lie. They will let you know in a number of ways whether or not they like the magazine: how they respond to newsstand sales, insert cards, and direct mail. Also, how they pay up. Meaning, if they don't like it, they won't pay their bills on time or at all. So, we concentrated on getting the magazine right the first four issues in 1993 and over the next couple of years. At that point, I began to think about how I could build VIBE as a brand.

It has been through strategic partnerships that Clinkscales has been able to successfully build the VIBE brand. It was the backing of Time that propelled the launch of VIBE OnLine in 1994. VIBE inked a deal with Crown Publishers in 1997 to publish *Tupac Shakur*, an illustrated biography of the slain hip-hop star. VIBE's now defunct one-hour late-night syndicated talk show was produced by VIBE Productions and distributed and marketed through Columbia TriStar Television Distribution.

The key thing with ancillary projects is how much they are going to contribute to the company's bottom line. Are they going to make money or lose money? All the key people in the company must be involved in deciding what benefits these ancillary products offer and if it is truly worth spending money on them. We financed our projects from the cash flow from company operations and the revenue stream charged for those projects. For instance, revenues for the VIBE music seminar and Urbanworld Film Festival are generated from registration fees and corporate sponsorship dollars. For the Website, revenues come from advertisers.

VIBE's biggest coup came in June 1997 when it acquired *Spin* magazine. With the acquisition of *Spin*, Clinkscales emphasizes that sales reps can now go to advertisers and say the company fully represents the young adult market (age 18 to 34) in an area that they feel the most passionate about—music. And it covers two major branches—R&B/Hip-hop and rock and roll. *VIBE* recently unveiled two more magazines: *Blaze*, a monthly devoted to hip-hop, and *Vibe Biz*, a joint venture with *Variety* that covers all aspects of the urban music and entertainment industry.

In addition to strategic alliances and venture partnerships, Clinkscales stresses the importance of building strong relationships with suppliers and treating them as partners. Recalling his days at Harvard, he points to the fact that the American business philosophy treats suppliers like suppliers; the Japanese philosophy treats suppliers as partners.

As an entrepreneur there are going to be more times when you are low on funds than those when you are plush with cash. I learned that the more I could make my vendors feel like they were partners, no matter how small they were, the more they felt as if they benefited from my success. So, they would be willing to help me manage through difficult times.

15

MONEY BASICS: KEEPING MORE OF WHAT YOU EARN

Yesterday is a canceled check. Tomorrow is a promissory note. Today is cash in hand, so spend it wisely.

—Anonymous

It doesn't matter whether you own a one-person shop or a 100-employee operation, there are bound to be special concerns about managing money. You don't want to fall into the trap of spending all of your time planning for your business that you fail to create a personal savings plan.

Once the business becomes profitable and you start taking a real salary, it is going to be more imperative that you understand how to save and invest your hard-earned cash. Just as you have to learn how to manage the financial affairs of the business, you must have a strong grasp on your personal finances, which includes developing and following a budget.

Unfortunately, if you are like most Americans, you are a great consumer but a lousy saver. Many people in their 20s and 30s are indebted from their college days and early working years, when they accumulated thousands of dollars of debt on their credit cards, and spent more than they brought home in their paychecks.

While business debt may be unavoidable in terms of loans

and lines of credit, you don't want to spend the rest of your life straddled with student loans and other high-interest payments. Before going into business you need to tally your assets and debts to pinpoint where you stand (remember Chapter 2).

SAVINGS PLANS FOR THE SELF-EMPLOYED

In planning for the future, you may want to add company savings plans to your list. The hassles of IRS filings and the costs of setting up pensions are the traditional gripes companies cite for not offering such employee benefits. But offering stock options and retirement plans are big employee incentives. Besides, new federal laws are making it easier for business owners and their employees to accumulate personal wealth.

Many mutual fund companies and brokerage firms administer company savings and retirement plans, including Merrill Lynch (800-Merrill, ext. 2190), the Principal Financial Group (800-774-6267), Charles Schwab (800-345-3533), Fidelity Investments (800-544-5373), T. Rowe Price (800-638-3804), Vanguard (800-851-4999), American Century (800-345-3533), and American Express Financial Advisors (800-840-6935).

Don't fall for off-the-shelf plans. You want one that is tailored for your company's needs. Consult your accountant and include your staff in on the decision making. Find out if they already have any personal investments and what type of company plan they would be interested in.

Here are some retirement plans you'll want to consider:

• **_Individual Retirement Accounts (IRAs)_**—You can contribute $2,000 a year to an IRA, lowering your tax bill. Say you are in the 28 percent tax bracket, your $2,000 contribution is really only $1,440, saving you $560. The money you put in your IRA grows tax-deferred (meaning you don't have to pay taxes on it until you withdraw it—after age $59\frac{1}{2}$, otherwise you'll have to pay a 10% tax penalty). You can deduct your annual contributions on your taxes if your adjusted gross income (AGI) is

$30,000 or less ($50,000 for married couples). If your business earns below these levels, it probably makes sense to start out with an IRA account. You also have the option of contributing $2,000 a year to a Roth IRA if you earn less than $100,000. You can take out the money you put in a Roth IRA before you reach age 59½ free of penalty charges (this doesn't apply to capital gains, dividends, or interest earned on your savings). While your contributions aren't tax deductible, your money grows tax-free while in the account. Also, you have to wait five years from the day you open your Roth IRA before withdrawing your earnings.

- *401(k) Plans*—Employees make pretax salary deferrals into their accounts. Your company can match all, some, or none of their contributions—most companies match 50 cents on every dollar put in. Individuals can contribute $9,500. Combined employee and employer contributions to each account may not exceed 25 percent of salary or $30,000, whichever is less. Set-up fees for these plans run between $1,000 and $3,000, and annual administration costs range from $800 to $5,000. You'll have to offer employees five or more different investments and provide information to help them make prudent investment decisions. Some mutual fund companies let employees switch among their family of funds up to six times a year.

- *Simplified Employee Pension (SEP) Plans*—SEPs are offered by banks, credit unions, mutual fund companies, and brokerage firms. They offer some flexibility in that you can vary the amount you contribute each year, up to 13 percent of earned income—with a cap of $22,500 a year. Your money grows tax deductible and tax-deferred; you don't have to file annual tax returns. Make note that you'll have to make SEP contributions (a percentage of salary) on behalf of eligible employees, even part-timers. The percentage has to be the same for all, but you can vary it, or even skip it, from year to year. This plan is easy to set up and administer.

- **Keoghs** — Named after Eugene Keogh, the congressman who came up with the idea, this plan lets you put away as much as 20 percent of your net self-employment income. The money is tax deductible and the earnings grow tax-deferred. The idea is that by the time you retire, you would be in a lower tax bracket. You must file annual tax returns with the IRS. Defined contribution Keogh plans are the more popular kind and can be set up as:

1. **Profit-sharing Plans.** You can invest up to 13 percent of your income or a maximum of $22,500.

2. **Money Purchase Plans.** You can put away up to 20 percent of your income or $30,000, whichever is less. The catch: You have to choose a set percentage; that's the amount you are stuck with paying every year in good and bad times. You're penalized if you don't make your payments.

3. **Paired or Combination Plans.** You get the best of both worlds. You have a set percentage but you get to add more to the account as business grows, for a total of 25 percent of your income. Starting out, you might choose to put away 10 percent of your income every year and then build up to 15 percent or more in years to come when business is booming.

- **Profit Sharing Plans** — Companies usually contribute as much as 15 percent of each worker's pay, but no more than $30,000 per employee to an account. Typically, employers decide once a year how much of a contribution they will make to a master profit-sharing account, which is divvied up among all eligible employees. Many plans are set up like a 401(k) allowing employees to allocate the money among several different investments. Some plans allow employees to borrow against their funds and to take hardship withdrawals — severe financial situations, such as medical bills, tuition, expenses to prevent eviction, and the costs for a down payment on a home. These plans may run from $1,500 to $3,000 to set up, and up to $3,000 a year to administer.

BUILDING AN INVESTMENT PORTFOLIO

There are two concepts you need to understand and follow to minimize your risks and maximize your investment returns. The first is asset allocation, which means figuring out how much of your investment portfolio to divvy up among stocks, bonds, mutual funds, cash investments, such as CDs and money market accounts, and in some cases, hard assets, such as real estate. The principle of diversification is spreading your risk by investing in several different sectors or industries (i.e., health care, technology, and financial services).

Your best bet for reaching your goals is to create a broad portfolio of individual stocks and mutual funds. It's clear for the long run, stocks—equities as they are called in investing circles—are the best investment vehicle. Over a 10-year period, stocks almost always outperform bonds and cash investments like money market funds and bank CDs. In fact, since 1925, the Standard & Poor's 500 index of larger company stocks has produced an average total return of 10.5 percent, according to Ibbotson Associates, a Chicago investment research firm that has calculated the long-term results for various types of investments. Stocks are subject to price swings—gaining as much as 50 percent in one year and losing as much as 25 percent in another.

The good news is that time is on your side. Rule of thumb: Subtract your age from 100 and add a percent sign—at age 25 that's 75 percent. That figure is how much of your portfolio you should have invested in stocks and stock mutual funds. You should try to spread your investments across 10 different company stocks.

Your portfolio should include at least three to five different mutual funds. Mutual funds pool your money with the money of many other investors to buy a portfolio of securities. Thus, the job of selecting individual stocks and other securities is left up to a mutual fund manager.

Of the 8,090 funds compiled by Morningstar, the Chicago firm that tracks mutual fund performance, roughly 5,500 have an initial minimum outlay of $1,000 or more. However, many mutual funds waive their initial minimum requirements if you agree to an automatic investment plan, where you arrange to have as little as $50 or $100 deducted from your bank account each month and invest the money straight into the fund.

This falls in place with a key investment strategy referred to as dollar-cost averaging. The idea is that regardless if the market is in a boom, recession, depression, or recovery, you should invest a set sum every month. This minimizes risks, because when stock prices are higher, your monthly investment buys fewer shares. When prices are lower, your monthly purchase will garner more shares. Since share prices rise over time, in the long haul, you end up with shares that are worth more than the price you paid for them.

GO FOR WHAT YOU KNOW

There are various styles or strategies for picking individual stocks. The first thing many industry gurus agree on is to consider companies you already know. Start by taking a look around you—say, your bathroom, kitchen cupboards, refrigerator, and clothes racks. Wouldn't it be nice to own a part of the companies that make the clothes you wear and the food you eat? The products that fill your house, or even the corporations that provide services that you couldn't do without often yield investment ideas.

Looking to household brand names can lead to market leaders whose earnings-per-share are growing. Among the most consumer-driven stock sectors are soft drinks, fast food, specialty retail (like fashion), and entertainment.

Several financial top guns have made money the same way, simply by observing what's going on around them and following trends. Take for example, Peter Lynch, the former manager of the world's largest mutual fund, Fidelity Magellan. Lynch often bragged that he came across one of his best investments by noticing that his wife liked the quality of L'eggs hosiery and the fact that she could conveniently buy the egg-shaped package at the supermarket. Lynch scored big with his legendary investment in Sara Lee Corp., the product's manufacturer.

Hot industry trends can be another source of stock picks. A word of caution though. It may not be a safe bet to follow the herd after the latest "craze" sector, like health care or technology, unless you are familiar with those industries.

If you are techno-savvy, look at what new software is making your life easier, find out the manufacturer and if the company is publicly traded. Or if your teary-eyed, three-year-old niece is begging for a particular toy, chances are that plenty of parents will be shopping for that same product. Take a trip to retail stores and check to see how many people are buying the product. Stand in the aisles for a little while and just observe. Talk to the store manager and ask how well a particular product is selling.

The obvious downside to this type of homespun research is that you could come in late on the cycle, when the buying frenzy is ending. And of course, you risk a glitch cropping up in the product, causing sales to slow down.

Popularity alone doesn't make a company a good investment. Look for a good balance sheet, consistent sales, and strong earnings growth. Ideally, you want to buy a company with a price-to-earning (P/E) ratio that is lower than its earnings growth rate. You can find a company's P/E ratio by looking at the stock tables in the newspaper or online investment sites.

Call the company's investor relations department and ask for annual and quarterly reports. If the company is large and has a broad product line, a new product may not significantly impact the bottom line. But if the company is small, a new hot selling product could boost earnings.

Don't be afraid to ask questions. If the company is currently unprofitable, you're allowed to inquire about when the company expects to turn a profit, how fast it thinks sales will grow, and what sort of competition it faces.

When it comes to buying mutual funds, look at the different fund categories: aggressive growth (invests in high-risk companies with a significant potential for capital appreciation), growth and income (consists of stocks that pay dividends), growth (invest principally in common stock with a significant earnings potential), balanced (consists of bonds, preferred and common stocks), and so forth. Everything you want to know about a particular fund and its manager can be found in the prospectus—a legal document containing a mutual fund's investment objective, performance information, management background, fees, and shareholder services.

Total returns—dividends, interest, capital gains, and changes in share price—are the best indicators of a fund's performance. Study annualized returns for the various time periods, usually three and five years. Look for consistency; long-term performance is the most important consideration. Compare the fund you are interested in with other funds in the same category.

Another major consideration are sales charges. Since expenses can eat away at your returns, hefty sales charges can turn a winning fund into a mediocre one. You might want to consider low-load funds, which charge 3.5 percent or less, compared to 8.5 percent for load funds. Also, check out no-load funds that don't have any sales charges. Watch out for back-end loads; meaning, you'll be hit with a fee when you take your money out of the fund, usually 5 percent for the first year. Some funds also charge a marketing fee, which can cost as much as 2 percent.

Think big picture. If one of your mutual funds plunges 20 percent, look at what has happened to the value of your entire portfolio. If that fund was just 10 percent of your investments, your portfolio's overall value would be down only 2 percent.

CASTING THE WIDEST NET

The fundamental rule of investing is to investigate. You have to research potential stock picks before actually going out and buying shares. On the Net, there are literally mountains of statistics to be found—stock and mutual fund quotes, earnings per share information, price-to-earnings (P/E) ratio analysis, 52-week high and low stock prices, and industry information.

While many investment sites offer free access, others require a monthly fee much like a subscription to a magazine. It should be further noted that stock quotes online are delayed at least 15 minutes. To get real-time quotes, you'll have to pay an extra $10 to $20 a month. But you may want to think twice, given that on-the-spot quotes won't give you an edge worth paying for.

 • *What to look for:* You will want to examine market information—the ups and downs of the Dow Jones Industrial Average, for instance—as well as industry statistics, brokerage analysts' opinions, current news, and individual company data, such as financial statements and management decisions. Many sites let you input information on your portfolio of stocks and mutual funds, and then allow you to track their share prices over time. Most investors look at a stock's P/E—the ratio of price to the amount of earnings the stock generates. Financial analysts use P/E ratios to make projections of company revenues. However, a P/E reports past, not future earnings. The average P/E ratio is 13 or 14. Above that is high and below it is low. Generally, the higher the P/E the riskier the stock. Small emerging companies often have high P/Es, because analysts have high expectations for future earnings growth. Although every company is bound to have some down periods, look for an upward trail—an overall increase in sales, revenues, dividends, accounts receivable, and profits over the last three years.

- *Where to go:* DBC Financial's site (www.dbc.com) is a great place to begin. It offers stock quotes, statistical ratios to use in researching companies, and links to news sources and online trading companies. Daily Stocks (www.dailystocks.com) offers links to several dozen sites. You can access company and statistical information from Zacks Investment Research (www.zacks.com), Yahoo!, and Morningstar. Morningstar's site (www.morningstar.net) includes interviews with institutional investors. Perhaps the most comprehensive site is Stocksmart (www.stocksmart.com), where you can find hundreds of links to investment-related Websites offering company information and stock analysis. The Financial Data Finder (www.cob.ohio state.edu/dept/fin/osudata.htm) contains such sites as CNN Financial Network (www.cnnfn.com), so you can tap into late-breaking news affecting your stocks. Also worth checking out is the Stock Research Group (www.stockgroup.com/). A great place for getting company-specific information is the Securities and Exchange Commission (www.sec.gov/). While many companies release news on the Web, it's important that you get your information from brokerage firms or third-party sources. Company sites often offer information that is self-promoting. The key is to look for consistency in sales and earnings growth. Examine numerous resources and analysts' reports to see if they offer the same commentary and then formulate your own opinion.

Check out the jokers at the Motley Fool (www.fool.com), a free online personal finance forum, which aims to educate, amuse, and enrich individual investors. It was founded as a newsletter in 1993 by 26-year-old Tom Gardner and his brother David (they serve as co-CEOs of the Alexandria, Virginia–based company). The Motley Fool debuted on America Online in 1994 and is now a syndicated column in more than 115 newspapers. It's also available on Yahoo! and *USA Today* Online. The site provides updated stock quotes and a series of articles on such topics as how to buy blue-chip stocks. It also allows visitors to explore model stock portfolios.

- *Do you need a broker?* Brokers come in two flavors: full-service and discount brokerage services. Full-service brokers, such as Merrill Lynch and Fidelity Investments, provide advice on which stocks to buy and sell, and provide investment resources. Discount brokers, such as Charles Schwab, essentially offer do-it-yourself investing, meaning that they don't make stock recommendations or provide you with analysts' reports. Because you don't get any hand holding from a discount broker, they are a lot cheaper. Generally, they assess a fixed fee—often from $19 to $40—every time you purchase stock. Full-service brokers charge commissions ranging from 1.5 percent to 3 percent per trade—that's $30 off the top of a $1,000 investment. However, discounts on commissions don't become significant until you start investing in blocks or shares (unit of equity ownership) of 100. If you are on a limited budget and have the time to research stocks on your own, you can get by with a discount broker. Better still, you can avoid paying hefty brokerage fees by using dividend reinvestment plans (DRIPS). More than 1,000 companies allow you to buy single company shares through DRIPS. You may need a brokerage firm to make the initial buy. Instead of paying out dividends—distribution of earnings—DRIPS automatically reinvests them for you to purchase more company shares. And many companies offer discounted shares, taking 3 percent to 5 percent off a stock's trading price.

The bottom line is that no one understands your financial needs and situation better than you. So, you need to adopt a hands-on approach to managing your finances. Keep this in mind: if you were to put away $100 each month, in 25 years, you have a six-figure account waiting for you—if you know how to work it. When all is said and done, it's your money, and knowing an inside tip here and there can help you reach financial freedom for the rest of your life.

MATT SETO, GENERAL PARTNER OF THE MATT SETO FUND

Matt Seto is an investor's dream. In 1992, he set up a mutual fund that returned an average of 34 percent annually for the first two years, beating the Dow Jones Industrial Average by 31 percent and outperforming 99 percent of all mutual funds in 1994. He was all of 15 at the time. These days, the Troy, Michigan native capitalizes on his financial savvy by managing both a hedge fund and a retirement account.

Michael Britto

MATT SETO

That is unless he is analyzing the mathematical complexities of economic theories or researching a paper on the writings of Socrates. Despite his years of expertise, Seto is still just 20 years old and a graduate of the University of Michigan.

Before traveling the road to the world of stock prices and profitable portfolios, Seto showed much promise as a child and began as an enterprising fifth grader. His first business went beyond the typical lemonade stand, he created his own yo-yo enterprise.

Yo-yos were real popular back then. When the fad first started, there only a few stores that carried them, unlike today. Detroit is the motor city, so you needed a car to get anywhere. Most of my class-mates didn't have access to a car, so I took orders from them and gave them to my mom who would pick up the yo-yos at the store.

Setto sold yo-yos, which cost $3.50 each, to his classmates for a commission of 50 cents per item. After two weeks, he made over $20 and split the profits with his mother. It was the 1987 stock market crash—Black Monday—that first piqued a nine-year-old Seto's curiosity about stocks. An initial roadblock was his parents, who emigrated from China in the1960s.

Because of his Confucian-style beliefs, Seto's father tried to discourage his son's early desire "to make money." He wanted him to focus on getting an all-around education before his col-lege years. He urged him to be more patient and imposed restric-tions in hopes of dissuading the preteen from investing. Seto's father refused to give him money to buy financial books, forbade cable TV, so he couldn't watch CNBC, and prohibited him from using his computer to get financial data and business news.

But all of those obstacles did nothing to wane Seto's desire; instead it fueled his need to learn more about the workings of Wall Street. Soon he was devouring financial information from publications such as *Standard & Poor's*, *The Wall Street Journal*, and *Forbes*, with the appetite of a hungry wolf. And he could often be found hanging out around the local Charles Schwab office (the nationwide discount brokerage).

It wasn't until I was thirteen that I was able to convince my father otherwise. It was a four-year war. At the end, they got tired and gave in. That period represented my greatest growth spurt. By then I was able to hit my parents with more knowledge about investing.

Armed with a ton of information culled from his extensive reading, Seto was able to ease his parents' fears. He was allowed to make his first investment at age 13, taking $700 saved up over the years given by his grandparents on Chinese New Year. Seto bought stock in Cyberteck, a Dallas-based software insurance firm. He was too young to legally invest in stock, so his father placed the order for him. Seto watched Cyberteck's stock climb 114 percent over the next three months.

Two years later, in 1993, Seto formed a limited partnership hedge fund, modeling himself after billionaire portfolio manager Warren Buffett and legendary stock picker Peter Lynch. While his parents agreed to let him put together a private fund for the family, it wasn't easy needling money from one of his two older sisters, uncles, and cousins. In fact, one of Seto's cousins threatened that if he lost his money, Seto would have to mow his lawn for the rest of his life. Nonetheless, he put together a prospectus and managed to pull together $23,000. After its first year, the Matt Seto Fund gained 38 percent, outperforming 90 percent of all mutual funds in the aggressive growth category.

I always knew that I wanted to manage a fund. I was driven by the fact that I actually needed more money to invest than I actually had. I wanted to make money; you do that by acquiring more capital. I decided to manage a hedge fund instead of a mutual fund. There are a lot of restrictions with mutual funds. They are scrutinized by the SEC; no more than 15 percent of their assets can be in any one stock.

The meteoric rise and solid performance of the Matt Seto Fund portfolio led to a front page profile in 1994 in *The Wall Street Journal*. Soon, Seto was being hailed as "the whiz kid of

Wall Street." He started receiving a million dollars in pledges from investors around the world who wanted him to manage their money. But Seto's father felt that a sixteen-year-old was too young to have the responsibility of managing so much money and suggested his son turn down the offers to extend his financial reach.

A fairly long waiting list has developed of people who want me to invest their money. Once I graduate from college, I will have to make a decision about whether I want to expand the fund or work as an analyst for another investment company.

While many industry observers remained skeptical about Mr. Seto's success, he continued to charge forward and in 1995, released a book entitled *The Whiz Kid of Wall Street's Investment Guide* (William Morrow & Co.). Today, the Matt Seto fund has 14 limited partners, all of whom are friends and family members.

I haven't opened up to outside investors. This limits the amount of work I have to do. I divided the Matt Seto Fund into two different divisions. One is a hedge fund and the other is a retirement account. I am investing retirement money for family friends.

The young portfolio manager attributes his success to reading a lot of investment books and carefully studying the market. Starting out he had three stocks in his portfolio, right now he has five. He doesn't want to have more than nine stocks in his portfolio at any time.

My investment goal has been to find undervalued stocks. It is really a matter of how much I think a company is worth, future earnings. I look at a company's P/E [price-to-earnings] ratio. There are three major areas that I judge a company on. The first is product superiority. The second is a strong company balance sheet and income statement. The third is a good evaluation. I don't evaluate management a lot. If a company's product is positioned strongly and it has done quite well in the past, to me that speaks to management. I try to concentrate more on the bottom line.

Seto says that Peter Lynch has had the greatest impact on

him, since his book, *One Up On Wall Street* (Penguin) was one
of the first investing guides he read at a very young age. He particularly liked Lynch's commonsense approach to evaluating a
company. He acknowledges that today the Internet has made it
easier for individuals to locate information such as earnings estimates, stock quotes, company profiles, and annual reports. Seto
is also looking to the future, and is very bullish on technology
stocks, a vision that he does not believe his heroes Warren
Buffett and Peter Lynch share.

*For all my admiration of these men, you can't escape the fact
that they are products of an earlier generation. For them, the
technology revolution came a little too late. They may be somewhat afraid of it. But since technology is so prevalent today, it's a
lot easier to understand. Generation X practically eats computer
chips for breakfast.*

Seto's investment style demonstrates that stock picking is not
as difficult and intimidating as people think. He believes there
are enough resources out there to help people make their own
investment choices. According to Seto, it is not how much
money you have, but how you invest it. As he counsels individuals on how to make the right investment choices, Seto points
to the three principles he outlines in his book:

1. *Educate yourself thoroughly.* If you hope to earn any money
in the market, learn everything you can—not only about investing but also about current affairs, history, and economics. You
must also know what's going on at the shops in your local mall.
What stores are people talking about? Where are customers jam-
ming the doors?

2. *Think independently.* While you must be aware of all of the
latest developments, you need to study them with a discerning,
independent eye. If you ride the bandwagon on the way up,
you're just as likely to tumble with it on the way down. Seek your
own path and discover good solid companies that the crowd may
be ignoring in its rush for the latest fad.

3. *Be logical.* If you keep your wits, and think things through carefully, you're bound to avoid painful mistakes. Careful reflection and common sense will amply reward you.

I don't think that cognitively, young people have a tremendous advantage over older people. But one of the major things that they do have going for them is less fear of risk. The main point I want to stress is that investing is really important for our [Gen Xers'] financial well-being. But more importantly, investing is a lot of fun. The key is just to invest.

JEFFREY A. MILLER AND ERIC D. JACOBS, MANAGING PARTNERS OF MILLER & JACOBS CAPITAL LLC

Wall Street has never been for the faint-hearted. Stock prices can fall on a headline. Wealth can disappear in seconds. That, however, did not deter Eric D. Jacobs, 29, and Jeffrey A. Miller, 27, from entering an area where the best performers boast steely resolve and fund managers have a head full of gray hair. Jacob's and Miller's gray-haired days are more than a decade away, but their resolve is rooted deep in the entrepreneurial spirit.

In February 1997, the duo launched the Acadia Fund I hedge fund—a financial vehicle which invests in 10 to 25 stocks at any one time. The financial hedge fund posted a 65.5 percent gain in the first six months and 166 percent in its first year. Shortly after Jacobs and Miller started their fund, the stock market dropped and Wall Street veterans began whispering that the bull market—which had jettisoned many stocks into dizzying highs—was about to end. Experts also noted that the best bank stocks to invest in were the biggest ones. The young savvy portfolio managers decided that the best advice would be to follow their own. With $2.5 million in funds from family, friends, and former clients they began investing predominantly in small banks and savings and loans.

Miller stresses that investing boils down to being able to stomach the risks and making decisions without hesitation.

We don't trade on economics, interest rates, or what the daily market is doing. We do not time the market, nobody can. The trading history of stocks dates back to the 1100s. There have always been maniacs in the stock market. People have always thought they were geniuses before. We are very aware of what can happen on the downside. But we are good at managing risk for our investors.

Jacobs handles the trades, marketing, and administrative duties, which includes working with brokers. Miller manages the portfolio, works with analysts, and talks to bankers. Combined, Miller and Jacobs have 10 years of investing experience. An adept trader with a contagious smile and a Rolodex of clients, Jacobs did stints at Lehman Brothers, Inc. and Paine Webber, Inc. Miller was a wonderkid bank analyst who cut his teeth at Smith Barney and Harris Upham & Co. It was while he was vice president of equity research at Keefe, Bruyette & Woods, Inc., a prestigious New York brokerage house, that Miller got an itch to start his own business.

So far, the business synergy between the two and their innovative style has paid off. The fund has ballooned to $25 million under management and boasted 1997 returns of 54 percent. Strong returns also are the result of their approach to investing. The duo are value investors who look for strong companies whose stocks have been hammered as a result of market volatility. They also value companies using cash-flow earnings analysis as opposed to the popular price/earnings ratios. In addition to having to face the volatility of the market, Jacobs notes that they still must face challenges that come with running a business.

The challenge of being in business is being creative enough to handle the diversity, frequency, and severity of problems that are going to be tossed at you. You need to be able to be a problem solver without having anyone around to bail you out. We have to deal with administrative trading, and more industry-specific operational hazards. Once you understand the business you are in and what goes into that business, it really comes down to how much self-confidence you have and your comfort in living without a steady paycheck.

Miller and Jacobs note that a hedge fund is one of the most entrepreneurial investment vehicles and among the most risky. The managers invest their money as well as those of their clients in various securities and attempt to offset the risks by employing a variety of arbitrage techniques. If the performance of the fund is poor, the managers also feel the losses. In turn, if it does well the managers reap significant gains. Miller and Jacobs take a cool 20 percent of the profits from their fund.

This was not a venture that the two entered lightly. Miller and Jacobs heavily weighed the pros and cons of forming a partnership. But in the end, they felt they had complementary skills and a solid friendship to make the business a success. The two have been friends since 1995.

Eric lived in the apartment above mine. It was a walk-up building on the Upper East Side of Manhattan. One day it started to rain in my apartment, because Eric's pipes broke. It took a week for them to work on his bathroom. So, he was coming down to my apartment every day for a week to use my bathroom. We started hanging out after that. We started talking and I said wouldn't it be great if we could run our own fund one day. I would do the research and he would manage the fund.

In the fall of 1996, they began to act on their conversations. They educated themselves on the different legal structures and options available to them. Managing a hedge fund seemed like the optimal choice. It afforded them the greatest amount of flexibility and it was cheaper to set up than a mutual fund. The duo spent several months with lawyers creating their limited partnership, Miller & Jacobs Capital—an umbrella for the Acadia fund and for future funds. They also spent four to five hours a day for three months drawing up a prospectus.

The long hours are not over. Both spend 14 to 15 hours a day at their office crunching numbers and swaying clients. Initially they cut down on their overhead by subletting space from a New York broker. At a discounted rate, Miller and Jacobs had 200 sq. ft. of office space. The two firms shared the main conference room, fax machine, copy machine, and other office equipment. Miller and Jacobs enjoyed additional amenities such as access to the brokerage's research services. As a result, the young fund managers saved about $5,000 a month on data services. Still, they needed to curtail costs, so they moved their offices to Villanova, Pennsylvania in 1998.

Running a hedge fund actually encourages the best performance from the manager. If you manage a mutual fund, you take your fee off the top and whether or not you do well for your clients, you still get your fee. If you think that your returns to investors are going to be about average then it is more advantageous to manage a mutual fund.

Jacobs and Miller decided to infuse the fund with bank and financial stocks because the most successful managers invest in what they know. In fact, Miller has been interested in stocks ever since he was six, and has been investing in stocks since the age of 12.

My grandfather managed money for insurance companies and my father started his own investment bank. When I was six, I asked my father to show me how to read the stock page in the newspaper. Throughout elementary and grade school, I would pick stocks and follow how they were doing as if I had actually invested money in them. When I got older, I took $300 I had saved up and purchased shares in Campbell Soup, H&R Block, and Disney.

Miller, the oldest of three children, grew up in Philadelphia. He learned about the dynamics of starting a company from a high school program called the Free Enterprise Fellowship. He earned a bachelor's degree in history and an MBA from Cornell University.

Investing also is not new to Jacobs, whose father worked in corporate finance for Allied Signal. Jacobs began investing in junk bonds at age 19. Jacobs, who grew up in Detroit and attended high school in New York City, earned a bachelor's degree in political science at Allegheny College in Pennsylvania. After college and a short stint at a law firm, Jacobs went overseas, spending a little over a year in Switzerland. Upon his return in 1992 to the United States, he decided to attend Richmond Law School but left there after just one summer session. A friend and trader with Deutsche Bank took Jacobs under his wing. Ultimately Jacobs landed a job at Lehman Brothers (which was later acquired by Paine Webber).

Miller and Jacobs have words of wisdom to share with their peers about investing. For the basic investor, Miller recommends the fundamental principle of Peter Lynch: "Invest in what you know." Jacobs believes anyone can invest in the stock market and do a good job at it by just focusing on the basics.

Pick up a book and learn about the stock market. If you don't have the patience, time, or inclination to evaluate a company, then hire a professional to manage your money. People our age have to look out for themselves financially. I remember reading about a 55-year-old man who got fired two years before his retirement and had to live off a $10,000-a-year pension, because he didn't make it to retirement age. I remember thinking, This is not how I want to end up. I think a lot of us [Generation Xers] have heard those kinds of stories growing up and developed a mentality that we have to take care of ourselves.

Failure is the chance to begin again more intelligently.
—*Henry Ford, founding CEO, Ford Motor Co.*

If you made it this far in the book, you have a wealth of information to help you get going. With just about anything worthwhile, the first and hardest step is getting started. The second step is to keep going. Now is the time to learn as much as you can and to meet the right people who can help expand your knowledge and level of expertise in your area of interest.

The fact that you are contemplating running a business sets you apart mentally from the institutional mindset that permeates America's culture. Our generation has been described as the poorest, but yet most educated generation since the depression. If you take that to heart, then you have nothing to lose by venturing out on your own in the business arena.

Like many of your peers, you probably realize that the grass isn't so green in the caverns of corporate America. Many of us have seen what putting our future solely into the hands of the empty promise of the mega-merger and the colossal buyout has done to our parents or older siblings. This doesn't mean we are denigrating everyone over 40, but that we are ready to find a better path that incorporates our personal values and goals, and safeguards our future.

Now's the time to craft the lifestyle you feel you deserve. Stop sitting on the sidelines and get into the game, pick up the ball and start running with it, always aiming for the goal line. The key: Know what you want. Set your own agenda. Measure its progress. And you will be in control of your life. Don't let society interfere with your game plan. This is not a mission impossible.

With the right attitude, self-motivation, resources, contacts, and ongoing education, you can build a challenging, lucrative, and stable enterprise. As renowned comedian Bill Cosby once said: Decide that you want it more than you are afraid of it. So, don't let fear of failure prevent you from starting a business. Being your own boss won't be easy. It may even be painful at times. Perseverance is the key. Win or lose, it's all up to you.

TOP COLLEGES/UNIVERSITIES OFFERING ENTREPRENEURIAL PROGRAMS

The first U.S. University to offer a course in entrepreneurship was Harvard Business School, in Cambridge, Massachusetts, back in 1946. It wasn't until 1971 that students were allowed to major in entrepreneurship with the University of Southern California as the forerunner. Today, courses, programs, and business centers dedicated to entrepreneurship are popping up on campuses nationwide. The number of U.S. colleges and universities offering one or more courses in entrepreneurship has grown from 150 in 1979 to 400 in 1997. The explosion of student interest in entrepreneurship has ignited several colleges including MIT, Northwestern University, and Columbia to launch venture capital funds to help students start new business ventures. The following list is a fraction of colleges and universities with entrepreneurial programs.

1. Babson College Center for
Entrepreneurial Studies
Forest Street
Babson Park, MA 02457
781-239-6459

2. Boston University
Entrepreneurial Management

Institute
685 Commonwealth Ave.
Boston, MA 02215
617-353-9720

3. Carnegie Mellon University
Graduate School of Industrial
Administration

5000 Forbes Avenue
Pittsburgh, PA 15213
412-268-2272

4. Chicago State University
College of Business
9501 S. King Drive
Chicago, IL 60628
312-995-2269

5. Columbia University School of
Business
702 Uris Hall
New York, NY 10027
212-854-4403

6. Cornell University
Johnson Graduate School of
Management
315 Malot Hall
Ithaca, NY 14853
607-255-8748

7. Dartmouth College
Tuck School of Business
Tuck Drive
Hanover, NH 03755
603-646-1110

8. DePaul University
Entrepreneurship Program
1 E. Jackson Blvd., Suite 7014
Chicago, IL 60604
312-362-8471

9. Duke University Fuqua School
of Business
134 W. Towerview Drive
Durham, NC 27708-0104
919-660-7700

10. Florida A&M University
School of Business
1 SBI Plaza
Tallahassee, FL 32307
850-599-3000

11. Georgia State University
College of Business and
Administration
35 Broad St.
Atlanta, GA 30303
404-651-3550

12. Georgetown University School
of Business
37th & O St. NW
Washington, DC 20057
202-687-4200

13. Harvard University School of
Business
16 W. Bare Hill Rd.
Cambridge, MA 01451
617-495-6292

14. Hampton University School of
Business
East Queens St.
Hampton, VA 23668
757-727-5361

15. Loyola University
820 N. Michigan Ave.
Chicago, IL 60611
312-915-6780

16. Massachusetts Institute of
Technology School of Business
50 Memorial Dr.
Cambridge, MA 02139
617-253-7155

17. Morgan State University
Earl G. Graves School of Business
Management
1700 E. Coldspring Lane
Baltimore, MD 21251
410-319-3333

18. Northern Illinois University
College of Business
Wirtz Hall 118

De Kalb, IL 60115
815-753-5000

19. Northwestern University
J.L. Kellogg Graduate School of
Management
Leverone Hall
2001 Sheridan Road
Evanston, IL 60208
847-491-3741

20. Rensselaer Polytechnic
Institute Center for
Entrepreneurship
110-68th St.
Pittsburgh Bldg. 3100
Troy, NY 12180-3590
518-276-8398

21. Spelman College
Entrepreneurial Center
350 Spelman Lane
Atlanta, GA 30314-4329
404-223-1482

22. Stanford University Graduate
School of Business
518 Memorial Lane
Stanford, CA 94305-5015
650-723-2146

23. San Diego State University
College of Business Administration
5250 Campanile Dr.
San Diego, CA 92182-1915
619-594-2781

24. Tennessee State University
College of Business
3500 John A. Merit Blvd.
Nashville, TN 37209-1561
615-963-5000

25. Tuskegee University College of
Business
Tuskegee, AL 36088
334-727-8116

26. Thunderbird-American
Graduate School of International
Management
11249 N. 59th Ave.
Glendale, AZ 85306
602-978-7607

27. University of California,
Berkeley
Walter A. Haas School of Business
350 Barrows Hall
Berkeley, CA 94720
510-642-1405

28. University of California, Los
Angeles
John E. Anderson Graduate
School of Management
405 Hilgard Ave.
Los Angeles, CA 90024
310-825-6121

29.University of Southern
California
Graduate School of Business
Briage Hall 101 M 142
Los Angeles, CA 90089-1421
213-740-7846

30. University of Iowa
John Pappajohn Entrepreneurial
Center
108 PBAB, Suite S 160
Iowa City, IA 52242-1000
319-335-0260

31. University of Illinois Chicago
Institute of Entrepreneurial
Studies
601 S. Morgan
Chicago, IL 60607-7106
312-996-2670

32. University of Maryland
College of Business and
Management

Mowatt Lane Room 2368
Van Munchang Hall
College Park, MD 20742
301-405-2278

33. University of Michigan School
of Business Administration
701 Tappan
Ann Arbor, MI 48109-1234
734-763-5796

34. University of North Carolina-
Chapel Hill
Kenan-Flagler School of Business
Campus
Box 3490
Chapel Hill, NC 27599-3490
919-962-3179

35. University of Pennsylvania
The Wharton School of Business
Sol. C. Snider Entrepreneurial
Center
102 Vance Hall
Philadelphia, PA 19104
215-8980-3430

36. University of South Carolina
College of Business Administration
1705 College St.
Columbia, SC 29208
803-777-5980

37. University of St. Thomas
Center for Entrepreneurship
1000 LaSalle Ave.
Minneapolis, MN 55403
612-962-4403

38. University of Texas at Austin
Graduate School of Business
P.O. Box 7999
Austin, TX 78713
512-471-7612

39. University of Wisconsin-
Madison
The Enterprise Center School of
Business
975 University Ave.
Madison, WI 53706
608-263-1664

40. University of Washington
School of Business
Box 353200
Seattle, WA 98155
206-543-6737

ENTREPRENEURIAL RESOURCES

Governmental Organizations

Bureau of the Census
4700 Silver Hill Road
Suitland, MD 20746
301-457-4608

Copyright Office
101 Independence Ave. NW
Washington, DC 20559
202-707-3000

Internal Revenue Service (IRS)
Taxpayers Services/Department of
the Treasury
111 Constitution Ave. Room 2422
Washington, DC 20224
800-829-1040
www.irs.ustreas.gov.

Securities and Exchange
Commission (SEC)
450 5th St. NW
Washington, DC 20549
202-942-7040

National SCORE Office
(Service Core of Retired
Professionals)
409 3rd St. SW
Washington, DC 20024
800-634-0245
www.score.org

U.S. Chamber of Commerce
1615 H. St. NW
Washington, DC 20062
800-537-IBEX

U.S. Department of Commerce
14th St. and Constitution Ave. NW
Washington, DC 20230
202-377-3176

U.S. Department of Labor
200 Constitution Ave. NW
Washington, DC 20210
202-219-7316

U.S. Government Printing Office
North Capital and H Street
Washington, DC 20402
202-512-1803

U.S. Patent and Trademark Office
(PTO)
2021 South Clark Place
Crystal Plaza 3
Arlington, VA 22202
800-PTO-9199
703-308-4357

U.S. Small Business Administration
409 3rd St. SW
Washington, DC 20416
202-205-6600
www.sbaonline.com

U.S. Trade and Development
Agency
1621 N. Kent St.
Arlington, VA 22209
703-875-4357

Business Organizations

American Association of Home-
Based Businesses
P.O. Box 10023
Rockville, MD 20849
800-447-9710

Association of Small Business
Development Centers
1300 Chain Bridge Rd., Suite 201
McClean, VA 22101
703-448-6124

Center for Entrepreneurship
Management (CEM)
180 Varick St., Penthouse
New York, NY 10014
212-633-0060
www.ceoclubs.org

Home Office Association of
America
909 Third Ave., Suite 990
New York, NY 10022
212-809-4622
www.hoa.com

Independent Business Alliance
111 John St. Suite 1210
New York, NY 10038
800-559-2580
www.iba.com

International Directory of Young
Entrepreneurs (IDYE)
376 Boylston St., Suite 304
Boston, MA 02117
617-867-4690
www.idye.com

International Mass Retail
Association
1700 N. Moore St., Suite 2250
Arlington, VA 22209
703-841-2300

National Association of Home-
Based Businesses
10451 Mill Run Circle, Suite 400
Owings Mills, MD 21117
410-363-3698
http://usa.homebusinesses.com

National Association of the Self-
Employed
2121 Precinct Line Rd., Suite 201
Hurst, TX 76054
800-232-6273

National Business Association
P.O. Box 7007128
Dallas, TX 75370
800-456-0440
www.natlbiz.com

National Business Incubation
Association
20 E. Circle Dr., Suite 190
Athens, OH 45701
614-593-4331
www.NBIA.org

National Business Owners
Association
1200 Eighteenth St. NW,
Suite 500
Washington, DC 20036
202-737-6501

National Federation of
Independent Business (NFIB)
600 Maryland Ave. SW, Suite 700
Washington, DC 20024
202-554-9000
800-634-2669
www.nfibonline.com

National Restaurant Association
1200 17th St. NW
Washington, DC 20036
202-331-5900

Small Office Home Office
Association (SOHOA)
1765 Business Center Dr., Suite
302
Reston, VA 20190
888-SOHOA-11
www.sohoa.com.

U.S. Council For International
Business
1212 Ave. of the Americas, 21st
Floor
New York, NY 10036
212-354-4480

U.S. Junior Chambers of
Commerce (USJOC)
4 W. 21st St.
Tulsa, OK 74121
918-584-2481
www/sggc.org/

Young Entrepreneurs Organization
(YEO)
1010 N. Glebe Rd, Suite 625
Arlington, VA 22201
703-527-4500
www.yeo.org

**Women and Minority-Interest
Organizations**

American Indian Trade and
Development Council
1305 4th Ave., Room 307
Seattle, WA 98101
206-224-4338

American Woman's Economic
Development Corp.
71 Vanderbilt, Suite 320

New York, NY 10169
212-688-1900

Association of American Indian
Affairs
245 5th Avenue, Suite 1801
New York, NY 10016
212-689-8720

National Association of Female
Executives
30 Irving Place, 5th Floor
New York, NY 10003
212-477-2220

National Association of Women
Business Owners
200 N. Michigan St., 3rd Floor
Chicago, IL 60601
312-541-1212

National Black Chamber of
Commerce
2000 L St. NW, Suite 200
Washington, DC 20036
202-416-1622

National Federation of Black
Women Business Owners
1500 Massachusetts Ave. NW,
Suite 22
Washington, DC 20005
202-833-3450

National Minority Supplier
Development Council
15 W. 39th St., 9th Floor
New York, NY 10018
212-944-2430

Small Business Administration
Office of Women's Business
Ownership
409 Third St. SW
Washington, DC 20416
202-205-6673

800-ASK-SBA
www.sbaonline.sba.gov/womenin-
business

U.S. Department of Commerce
Minority Business Development
Agency
14th St. & Constitution Ave.,
Room 5096
Washington, DC 20230
202-482-2000

United National Indian Tribal
Youth Inc. (UNITY)
P.O. Box 25042
Oklahoma City, OK 73125
405-236-2800

U.S. Hispanic Chamber of
Commerce
1030 15th St. NW, Suite 206
Washington, DC 20005
202-842-1212

U.S. Pan Asian American
Chamber of Commerce
1329 18th St., NW
Washington, DC 20036
202-296-5221

Women's Business Development
Center
8 S. Michigan, Suite 400
Chicago, IL 60603
312-853-3477

Women's Collateral Worldwide
Inc.
1529 Walnut St., 4th Floor
Philadelphia, PA 19102
215-564-2800

**Nonprofit Assistance
Organizations**

American Association of
Fundraising Council

25 W. 43rd St., Suite 820
New York, NY 10036
212-354-5799

National Council of Nonprofit
Organizations
1001 Connecticut Ave. NW, Suite
900
Washington, DC 20036
202-833-5740

The Foundation Center
79 Fifth Ave.
New York, NY 10007
800-424-9836

The National Center for Nonprofit
Boards
2000 L. St. NW, Suite 411
Washington, DC 20036
202-452-6262

The Nonprofit Management
Association
310 Madison Ave., Suite 1630
New York, NY 10017
212-949-0990

Capital Resources

ACE-Net
www.ace-net.sr.unh

Blue Chip Venture Co.
201 E. Fifth St.
Cincinnati, OH 45202
513-723-2300

Capital Quest
www.usbusiness.com/capquest

Commercial Finance Association
(Factors)
212-594-3490
www.cfa.com

FinanceHub.Com
www.financehub.com

Inroads Capital Partners
1603 Orrington Ave., Suite 2050
Evanston, IL 60210
847-864-2000

Money Hunt
www.moneyhunt.com

National Association of Small
Business Investment Companies
1199 N. Fairfax St., Suite 200
Alexandria, VA 22314
703-683-1601

Small Business Capital Access
Association
www.sbcaa.org/

SCOR Report
P.O. Box 781992
Dallas, TX 75378
972-620-2489

The Capital Network
University of Texas at Austin
3925 W. Braker Lane, Suite 406
Austin, TX 78759
512-305-0826

The Technology Capital Network
Massachusetts Institute of
Technology
290 Main St.
Cambridge, MA 02142
617-253-7163

The Vine
www.thevine.com

VentureLink USA
13101 Washington Blvd., Suite
242
Los Angeles, CA 90066-5125
310-822-5628

Franchise Organizations

American Association of
Franchises and Dealers
1420 Kettner Blvd., Suite 415
San Diego, CA 92101
619-235-2556

American Franchise Association
53 W. Jackson Blvd.
Chicago, IL 60604
312-431-1467

International Franchise
Association
1350 New York Avenue NW, Suite
900
Washington, DC 20005
202-628-8000
www.franchise1.com

Marketing Resources

Event Seeker
www.eventseeker.com

Expo Guide
www.expoguide.com

Gallup Poll Organization
47 Hulfish St.
Princeton, NJ 08542-3400
609-924-9600
www.gallup.com

Guerrilla Marketing International
260 Cascade Drive, P.O. Box 1336
Mill Valley, CA 94902
800-748-6444
www.gmarketing.com

HSC (Home Shopping Channel)
P.O. Box 9090
Clearwater, FL 34618-9090
813-572-8585

ListCo Direct Marketing
620 Frelinghuysen Ave.
Newark, NJ 07114
973-802-1229

QVC
1365 Enterprise Drive
W. Chester, PA 19380
610-701-8282

Business Resources

American Business Information
www.abii.com/

Dun & Bradstreet Inc.
3 Sylvan Way
Parsippany, NJ 07054
800-526-0651

Gale Research Corp.
835 The Penobscot Building
Detroit, MI 48226
313-961-2242

Health Insurance Association of
America
1025 Connecticut Ave. NW
Washington, DC 20036
800-277-4486

Manufacturers' Agents National
Association
23016 Mills Creek Rd.
Laguna Hills, CA 92653
714-859-4040

National Restaurant Association
1200 11th St. NW
Washington, DC 20036
202-331-5900

National Small Business United
1156 15th St. NW, Suite 1100
Washington, DC 20005
202-293-8830

Small Business Service Bureau
(Insurance)
P.O. Box 15014
Worcester, MA 01615-0014
508-756-3513

Thomas Publishing Companies
One Penn Plaza
New York, NY
212-290-7200

World Association of Small
Business Electronic Commerce
www.wasbec.uca.edu/

**International Trade
Organizations**

Export-Import Bank of the United
States
811 Vernon Ave. NW
Washington, DC 20472
202-646-4600

International Commercial
Shipping Terms
ICC Publishing
156 Fifth Ave., Suite 308
New York, NY 10010
212-206-1150

Journal of Commerce
2 World Trade Center, 27th Floor
New York, NY 10048
800-221-3777

U.S. Department of Commerce
International Trade Administration
14th and Constitution Ave. NW
Washington, DC 20230
202-482-2000

BIBLIOGRAPHY AND RECOMMENDED READING

Alan Chai, *Cyber Stocks: An Investor's Guide To Internet Companies*.
  Austin, Texas: Hoover's Business Press, 1996.
Amazon.com, company archives.
William B. Davidson and Tonia L. Shakespeare, "10 Golden Rules to
  Apply When Buying a Franchise," *Black Enterprise* magazine,
  September 1996.
Don Debelak, *Marketing Magic*. Holbrook, MA: Adams Media Corp.,
  1994.
Iris Lorenz-Fife, *Financing Your Business*. Englewood Cliffs, NJ: Prentice
  Hall, 1997.
David Gladstone, *Venture Capital Handbook*. Englewood Cliffs, NJ:
  Prentice Hall, 1988.
Anthony and Diane Hallett, *Encyclopedia of Entrepreneurs*. New York:
  John Wiley & Sons, 1997.
Joan M. Hummel, *Starting and Running a Nonprofit Organization*.
  Minneapolis: University of Minnesota Press, 1996.
Jason Kaufman, "Air Supply: Looking for a Little Traveling Music? Amy
  Nye's Airport CD Stores Are Singing Your Song." *Swing* magazine,
  March 1998.
Kinko's, company archives.
Peter Lynch, *One Up On Wall Street*. New York: Penguin USA, 1990.
Daniel Lyons, "The Face of AI: pcOrder Hopes to Outflank Dell with
  Artificial Intelligence." *Forbes* magazine, November 30, 1998.
Joseph Mancuso, *How to Write a Winning Business Plan*. New York:
  Fireside, 1997.
—*How to Start and Finance Your Own Small Business*. New York:
  Fireside, 1997.
—*How to Start, Buy, or Franchise Your Business Success*. New York:
  Sourcebooks, 1997.

Mike Powers, *The 21st Century Entrepreneur: How to Open a Franchise Business*. New York: Avon Books, 1995.

Evan I. Schwartz, *Webonomics: Nine Essential Principles for Growing Your Business on the World Wide Web*. New York: Broadway Books, 1997.

Matt Seto, *The Whiz Kid of Wall Street's Investment Guide: How I Returned 34 Percent on My Portfolio and You Can, Too*. New York: William Morrow and Co., 1996.

Lawrence W. Tuller, *Exporting, Importing, and Beyond: How to "Go Global" with Your Small Business*. Holbrook, MA.: Adams Media Corp., 1994.